Toegye and Gobong Write Letters

Toegye and Gobong
Write Letters

by
Kim Young-doo

Translated
by
Louis Choi

JAIN PUBLISHING COMPANY
Fremont, California

jainpub.com

Jain Publishing Company, Inc. is a diversified publisher of college textbooks and supplements, as well as professional and scholarly references, and books for the general reader. A complete, up-to-date listing of all the books, with cover images, descriptions, review excerpts, specifications and prices is always available on-line at **jainpub.com**.

This book is published with the support of the Korea Literature Translation Institute in commemoration of Korea being the Guest of Honor at the Frankfurt Book Fair 2005.

Copyright © 2005 by Kim Young-doo. All rights reserved. No part of this book may be reproduced, stored in a retrieval system, or transmitted, in any form or by any means, electronic, mechanical, photocopying, recording or otherwise, without the written permission of the publisher except for brief passages quoted in a review.

Contents

Korean Translator's Notes xi
Translator's Note xxiii
Brief Introduction to Yi "Toegye" Hwang and
   Daeseung "Gobong" Gi xxvii
Timeline of Events xxxi

"The Everyday Letters"
1558–1561
The Beginning of Soulful Exchanges

#1	Raise Virtue, Think Profoundly	3
#2	Cherish Yourself for the Ages	3
#3	Longing for Virtue	5
#4	Inside the Tribulation of *Myeonsillye*	7
#5	Deeply Longing for My Teacher	9
#6	Between the Government Post and My Studies	12
#7	Hoping a Gentle Friend Completes His Studies	20
#8	Afraid of Becoming Spineless, Like a Bug without Bones	22
#9	If You Discover Your Illness and Want to Cure It	31
#10	Regarding the Rowing Songs about the Wuyi Nine Turning Streams	37
#11	After Receiving Various Letters and Words	43
#12	No Time to Read Your Letters	51
#13	After Receiving Word of Elderly Chuman's Passing	52
#14	Learning a Short Time Remains before You Come to Seoul	54
#15	On My Way to Seoul in the Spring	56

1562–1565
Sharing the Difficulties of Conduct

#16	Difficulties in Making Arguments about the *Four-Seven*	59

#17 Like a Caged Monkey and Bird 62
#18 The Three Obstacles to Truthful Studying 64
#19 Becoming the *Seungji* of the Royal Secretariat 66
#20 Regarding Appropriate Conduct 67
#21 The Difficulties in Offering My Resignation and
       Retiring 69
#22 Difference in Conduct 73
#23 Standing Face to Face Against a Steep Cliff,
       Straight as an Arrow 75
#24 My Second Son Has Died from Illness 79
#25 Worries until My Dying Days 80
#26 Apprehension and Worry Entangle My Body 81
#27 One Passage from Han Yu's Poem 82
#28 Like a Trapped Fish Caught on a Hook 84
#29 I Have Entered the Library 87
#30 While Submitting an Appeal, the Nation Mourns
       the Passing of Royalty 88
#31 During the National Mourning for the Passing
       of Royalty 90
#32 Asking About Several Suspicious Clauses 91

1566–1567
Between Seoul and Uiju

#33 Theory of the Human Mind and the *Dao* Mind 95
#34 Although I Have Left Two Government Offices 100
#35 Giving You the "General Summary" and "Postscript
       Explanation" of the *Four-Seven Thesis* 102
#36 While Moving from Many Government Posts 107
#37 Comprehensive Good View of the *Four-Seven Thesis*'
       "General Summary" and "Postscript Explanation" 108
#38 Arguments Regarding the Human Mind and the
       Dao Mind 111
#39 No Time for a Momentary Break 118
#40 Although Many People Claim to Study *The Way* 119
#41 Eliminate the Book in Circulation That Steals
       My Name 120
#42 Your Sickness Remains Unchanged 122
#43 Everybody Is Making an Effort Just to Win 123
#44 If You Come to Seoul after Recuperating 126

Contents

#45 According to Social Duty and Destiny 127
#46 I Burned the Xylographic Books in the Courtyard 129
#47 Resolving an Old Burden 130
#48 Some Parts upon Which I Could Not Agree 131
#49 After Hearing You Had Packed and Returned East 134
#50 Five Vexations and Two Concerns 136
#51 Replying in Detail Instead of Scolding 143
#52 Come and Comply with the King's Wishes 145

1568–1569
The Imbroglio of Sickness and Returning Home

#53 Two Agonies, Two Concerns 149
#54 I Have Not Made It to Gangneung Yet 151
#55 I Will Look into and Execute Your Request 152
#56 Sending You the *Ten Diagrams of Confucian Philosophy* 152
#57 As the *Ten Diagrams of Confucian Philosophy* is Very
       Precise and Accurate 152
#58 After Receiving Your Guidance 153
#59 Yesterday, After Greeting and Meeting You 154
#60 Enlightening Me on the Lacking Parts of the
       Historical Investigation 156
#61 Guard Correctly and Highly Regard Simplicity 158
#62 Extensively Refer to the Classical Books of
       Previous Times 158
#63 Sending the Abridged Transcript of What
       Jeongam Jo Had Informed the King 159
#64 Comparing the Present to Jeongam's Time 160
#65 I Presented the *Ten Diagrams of Confucian Philosophy*
       and the "Presentation Address" Yesterday Evening 161
#66 Discussing the Title of the King's Parents 162
#67 Revising "The Diagram of the Western Inscription" 1 163
#68 Revising "The Diagram of the Western Inscription" 2 163
#69 Revising "The Diagram of the Western Inscription" 3 164
#70 Do You Know Me! 165
#71 Truly Complicated Inside Story 166
#72 There is No Need to Come 166
#73 After Hearing News that the Respected Gwahoe's
       Father Had Passed Away 167
#74 I Want to Visit 167

#75 The Moral Principle for Leaving Government Service 1 168
#76 The Moral Principle for Leaving Government Service 2 168
#77 The Moral Principle for Leaving Government
       Service 3 169
#78 Afraid Like Stepping On Spring Ice 170
#79 Ijeong Did Not Understand My Intentions 170
#80 From Long Ago, the Difficulties that Exist Between
       Sovereign and Subject 171
#81 Yesterday, After Reading Your Letter 171
#82 Poems Do Not Mind Being Corrected 172
#83 My Colleagues Ask Me to Enter a Government Post 172
#84 Conduct Becomes Gradually Difficult 173
#85 After Hearing You Were Ill 174
#86 Facing Deep Waters and High Valleys 174
#87 Departure on the River, Remote as a Dream 175
#88 Reliving in Dreams the Tender Feelings of
       Departure 176
#89 Appointed to One More Position at the Office
       of the Censor General 177
#90 I Cannot Remain Calm as if Nothing Had
       Happened 178
#91 Carefully Transcribed in the Annex, the Outlines
       of the Arguments Regarding the Munso Shrine 179
#92 Clamorous Arguments inside the Imperial Court 179
#93 Requesting the Epitaph of My Deceased Father 180
#94 Sending Along Various Writings 182
#95 How Has the World Become This Chaotic? 186
#96 The Wood Engravings for the *Ten Diagrams* is
       Near Completion 191
#97 We Must Examine Ourselves 193
#98 Incurring the Wrath of the High-Ranking Official 196
#99 Unable to Avoid the Cold Sinking Through 199
#100 When Spring Arrives, I Will Discard my
       Government Post 200

1570
The Last Year of Letters

#101 Whether or Not One Will Be Exalted 205
#102 Savoring Words, Destitution Becoming
       More Enjoyable 207

Contents

#103	If You Cannot Control Your Drinking	209
#104	The Defects Incurred Because of Uneasiness at the Core of My Heart	212
#105	What Kind of *Dao* Says to Act Both Reverently and Impudently	213
#106	Honam and Yeongnam Are Far Apart	217
#107	Your Words, the Right Medication for My Disease	217
#108	Reading "Ganchunfu" During Leisure Hours	221
#109	Cleanse an Old Man's Dark and Intolerant Thoughts	222
#110	Arriving at the Principle of Inanimate Objects	225
#111	Life without a Government Post	230
#112	Responding to Gi Myeongeon's Discussion of the Revised "Diagram of 'The Mind Combines and Governs the Nature and the Feelings'"	233
#113	Long Time Since Giving Up the Thought of Saving Myself	237
#114	My Views Were Incorrect	239
INDEX		243

Korean Translator's Notes

The Letters of the Joseon Dynasty Era

It is difficult to find people who write letters these days. This makes sense considering to keep pace with the world, which moves at a blistering pace, we must budget our time efficiently—there is no reason to refrain from using modern conveniences to connect people living in two different spaces. Various high-tech communication devices such as the telephone and email have gradually replaced the letter. Letters are sent as greetings, in the form of New Year's cards and invitations or as an impassioned lover's secret weapon for expressing his or her deepest emotions.

During the era when the letters included in this book were exchanged, writing letters was the only way to connect people who could not meet face-to-face. Because there was no formal system for delivering personal letters, acquaintances traveling back and forth on official business or servants in charge of doing errands would deliver these letters. Unless you were wealthy with a plethora of servants at your beckoning call or a high government official who could easily access civil servants, sending letters was not an easy task. Letters were a good way to organize your thoughts in writing unlike spoken words which were hard to rein in once uttered. Accordingly, scholars of the time valued letters and saved them. In the anthologies of Joseon scholars, letters were considered as valuable as poems.

Not only did these letters relay everyday news or greetings, but also they were the grounds for scholarly debates and a vehicle for self growth. Therefore, from a modern point of view, these letters served not only as a way of relaying news, but also a way to present an academic thesis and a way to reflect on yourself and the world. Through these letters, we learn about their lives; in addition, we learn about various other matters such as the development of their ideologies, their values, and their political intentions. In short, we can consider letters the best kind of data for examining their overall lives, as well as a way to look at their lives from different perspectives.

Gobong Visits Toegye

This book is a translation of the letters exchanged between Yi "Toegye" Hwang (1501-1570) and Daeseung "Gobong" Gi (1527-1572) who were mid-Joseon Dynasty scholars and government officials. Starting from the 13th year of King Myeongjong's reign in 1588, these two people exchanged over a hundred letters for thirteen years until the third year of King Seonjo's reign in 1570, the year Toegye passed away. Furthermore, these letters were meticulously edited and passed on from generation to generation making them very accessible.

The occasion for Toegye and Gobong exchanging letters was special from the beginning. When they first met, Gobong was thirty-two, a young scholar filled with ambition and passion. He did not study merely to pass the civil service exam, to be considered a success in the world; he wanted to grasp the truth of a sincere life through the studies. That year, he headed for Seoul to take the civil service exam. On the way, he met famous scholars, Inhu "Haseo" Gim and Hang "Iljae" Yi in succession and argued with them about important subject matters in the *School of Principle* (or *Seongnihak*). His passion continued even after he arrived in Seoul. Gobong visited Toegye, who happened to be in Seoul at the time, and also debated with him. At the time, Toegye was already 58 years old and a prominent scholar who had moved back to the countryside; he had been exerting an effort only in the studies, but he was momentarily in Seoul because he could not continue to refuse the king's calling.

Toegye did not disregard or distance himself from Gobong but Toegye respected Gobong as a scholar. We know this because soon after they met, Toegye wrote a response to the points raised by Gobong. Gobong harbored complaints about Toegye's views about Jiun "Chuman" Jeong's "Diagram of the Heavenly Mandate." Toegye accepted his assertions and revised his thoughts; he inquired again through letter if his revised thoughts were correct. And so this was the beginning of their discussion regarding the famous *Four Beginnings-Seven Feelings Debates*, and as a result, these two people formed a relationship where they exchanged letters for the rest of their lives.

The Significance of Their Letters

Not only did the exchanges of Toegye and Gobong attract the attention of the people at the time, but also present day scholars have recognized these letters to be very important data. What has made their letters so important? There is a need to consider the importance of these letters from several viewpoints.

First, they wrote these letters at the time the *Sarim* faction gained power and at the beginning of party politics. As a result, these letters are remarkable data in depicting their views regarding politics. The protagonists of this book, Toegye and Gobong, were members of the *Sarim* faction, which was at the center of politics after the mid-Joseon Dynasty era. While enduring through several purges of the literati, the (members of the *Sarim* faction) gradually rose to become the mainstream, and they seized power when King Seonjo took the throne. Toegye and Gobong were well aware of these circumstances.

Furthermore, Toegye and Gobong discussed and grappled for a long time with the role of scholars participating in politics and the manner in which scholars should act once in politics. Would proper conduct entail discarding their government posts and living as retired scholars in order to observe the truth of their studies? Or should they walk the path as faithful vassals devoting everything they have to the king albeit it might be lacking? They repeatedly exchanged views regarding the righteousness of entering and leaving government service. When they exchanged letters—the tragic incident of the purge of the literati still fresh in the minds of people—underlying their words was a tension, an uncertainty of whether they would have to lay down their lives for the sake of righteousness.

Second, their letters are good data for depicting the mid-Joseon Dynasty era, a time when the *School of Principle* (moral and natural law) type system was just becoming internalized in the deepest part of the social order. Although one could say the Joseon Dynasty was established based on *School of Principle* views, it did not reach and affect the deepest parts of society from the onset. In reality, the customs of the *yangban* (Korean nobility) of the time were closer to resembling Buddhist attributes rather than the *School of Principle* philosophy. However, this began to change as generations passed. The noble men of the Joseon who had accepted the

School of Principle with more profoundness matched every part of their daily customs to a *School of Principle* based social order.

We can discover numerous discussions regarding this topic in the exchanges between Toegye and Gobong. They wanted to realize the foundational order outlined in *Zhu Xi's Family Rituals*, which was written with the paternal line as the central figure for the constitution and administration of one's family; they made an unceasing effort to shed the light of their ideology on the various royal household funeral rites and sacrificial rituals to reform established practices. Other examples of this can be when they criticized the *Chongbuje* (when the eldest son's wife administered the memorial service) and when they asserted that the *checheon* (moving of the ancestral tablets) should be done according to the standards of the paternal line. This Joseon Confucian order based on the *School of Principle*, which appears to us like a rigid fossil, became a fixed historical product after this period of adaptation.

Third, ideologically, we can discover enormous significance in the fact these letters contained the *Four-Seven Thesis*, which people judge to have realized a uniquely Korean study of Zhu Xi. The *Four-Seven Debates* which came into form in the course of Toegye and Gobong's exchanges transcended the level of Korean Confucianism simply accepting the studies of Zhu Xi, and regarding growing to the level that voiced an independent and original voice, people consider (the *Four-Seven*) as being the representative case.

As mentioned before, the *Four-Seven Debates* was the reason they started to exchange letters. Accordingly, at the time they started to exchange letters, they concentrated on the *Four-Seven*. This debate continued for four years, starting from Toegye and Gobong's first exchange in the 14th year of King Myeongjong's reign in 1559 up until the 17th year of his reign in 1562. That year, Toegye sends one poem revealing his desire to end the debate, and Gobong does not send any more letters regarding the *Four-Seven*. Merely four years after their debate had finished, in the 21st year of King Myeongjong's reign in 1566, Gobong reflects on their debate and organizes two pieces of writing, "General Summary" and "Postscript Explanation," and sends them to Toegye. He announces that they both have agreed with the opinions in these writings. Toegye acknowledges the mentioned points. This is how the famous *Four-Seven Debates* ends.

Their Debate

Although somewhat cumbersome, it might be a good idea to explain the *Four-Seven Thesis* to appease in advance some of the confusion people who are seeing the *Four-Seven Debates* for the first time might encounter while reading the book.

In the *School of Principle*, the placid state before emotions arise in the mind is referred to as *nature*, and the state after emotions have arisen is referred to as *feelings*. And since the nature which exists before the rising of emotions preserves perfectly the original natures of heaven and man, they considered it perfectly good. However, since human emotions arise in response to external inanimate objects, unable to be moderated, the original nature can be "chipped" or "covered"; hence, feelings can be good or evil.

Let us look at the *Four-Seven* with this fundamental understanding. You must not forget the *Four Beginnings* and the *Seven Feelings* are the conditions of feelings that transpire after there is some kind of movement in the mind. In the *Four Beginnings*, the natures of benevolence, righteousness, etiquette, and wisdom are not affected by the outside world and as intact, manifested feelings, they are always good. However, as the *Seven Feelings* arise by being affected by the outside world, they can be good or evil. This is the explanation of the mind according to the *School of Principle*.

In addition, the *School of Principle* explains creation by *principle* and *material force*. Principle is the fundamental of the world, and material force is the material substance of principle materialized. Principle and material force are two while being one; hence, they are contradictory. Dialectically, the fundamental principle and the materialized material force are distinguishable; however, this distinction does not transcend the logical and metaphysical. This is the case because in the real world, principle and material force exist together inside one inanimate object, never breaking apart for even a moment. Furthermore, the (*School of Principle*) considered the fundamental of the world, principle, to be good, and the materialized material force to be either good or evil.

Both Toegye and Gobong based their assertions on the before mentioned *School of Principle's* view of the world and man. However, their opinions differed when explaining the relationship between the *Four-Seven* and principle/material force. Toegye's assertion is clearly manifested in his revision of Jiun "Chuman"

Jeong's "Diagram of the Heavenly Mandate": "Principle reveals the *Four Beginnings*, and material force reveals the *Seven Feelings*." This remark by Toegye was the spark that ignited the debate regarding the *Four-Seven*. As the *Four Beginnings* is nature's exact manifestation of feelings, it is interconnected to principle, which is the foundation of the world and man. The *Seven Feelings* are the emotions that arise inside the mind when inanimate objects of the outside world come into contact with humans; hence, the *Seven Feelings* are interconnected to the material force which is the materialization of inanimate objects of the outside world. In this manner, Toegye places the *Four Beginnings* and *Seven Feelings* face to face and separates and connects principle and material force in this manner. According to the origin of human emotions, he separates what arises from principle and material force. Among these ideas, people have judged as an important part that clearly depicts the uniqueness of Toegye's philosophy his assertion that principle, which is the fundamental of inanimate objects, incites good emotions by its movement.

Gobong opposed the view that the *Four Beginnings* and *Seven Feelings* could separate and attach to principle and material force. According to him, the *Seven Feelings* is the concept which can be merged into all the feelings in that principle and material force join together and the possibility of good and evil coexists. On the other hand, by revealing nature perfectly, the *Four Beginnings* defines what is perfectly good and separates what is perfectly good in the *Seven Feelings*. Accordingly, if one places the *Four Beginnings* and the *Seven Feelings* face to face, the *Seven Feelings*, which unites all feelings including the *Four Beginnings*, will appear to be equal in stature to the *Four Beginnings*; if one separates and attaches the *Seven Feelings* to material force, the balanced viewpoints that principle and material force join together and that good and evil coexist would shatter, creating a danger of bias towards material force. Consequently, instead of separating human emotion according to their origins, he thought emphasizing the point that human emotion was one substance in which two possibilities coexist was more accurate and important.

The debate between these two scholars reached a relative resolution when Gobong wrote on a later date the "General Summary" and "Postscript Explanation," in which he accepted a large proportion of Toegye's assertions. However, their debate did not end here. Later, their dispute grew as future scholars once again confronted the issue, escalating into a confrontation of opposing ideologies regarding the *Juriron* (or the theory of principle) and the *Jugiron* (or the theory of material force). Not only that, but also some scholars judge that the seeds of the central *School of Principle* debates in the late Joseon Dynasty era—the *Dao and Human Mind Debates*, the *Inmulseongdongi Debates* (or debates regarding human nature and the nature of inanimate objects), and the *Seongsimuyeol Debates* (or the debates regarding nature and mind)—were planted and included inside the *Four-Seven Debates*. Truly, it would not be an exaggeration to say their letters provided a vital ideological foundation for the development of the Joseon *School of Principle*.

Regarding the Editing of Letters

The letters of Toegye and Gobong are well organized in Daeseung Gi's collection, *Gobong's Collections*. It was customary for scholars to include in their anthologies only personal writings; however, in *Gobong's Collections*, in what seems an exceptional case, all the letters exchanged between Toegye and Gobong are organized and printed. On the other hand, in Yi Hwang's collection, *Toegye's Collections*, the letters sent to Daeseung Gi are arranged in a separate section. Therefore, rather than *Toegye's Collections*, we can observe with more accuracy the exchanges between these two people in *Gobong's Collections*.

Consequently, this translation used *Gobong's Collections* as its original text. Although I used *Gobong's Collections* because it was easy to reference as it contained all the letters written by both people, more importantly, the letters in *Gobong's Collections* were remarkably close to the originals. Unlike *Toegye's Collections* where many parts, which may seem trivial, have been omitted, *Gobong's Collections* printed without omission the greetings at the beginning and end of the letters, dates the letters were written, and postscripts. Furthermore, *Gobong's Collections* included several letters written by Toegye that were not included in *Toegye's Collections*. For these reasons, I concluded the letters in *Gobong's Collections* were closer to their original forms and for that reason, I selected it as the original text for the translation.

However, while Toegye was concluding his famous *Four-Seven Debates* with Gobong, Toegye wrote his final letter to Gobong revealing his thoughts but did not send the letter. Therefore, this letter was not included in *Gobong's Collections*; it was only included in *Toegye's Collections*. I had no choice but to find it in *Toegye's Collections* and include the letter.

When looking at *Gobong's Collections*, it classifies the exchanges between Toegye and Gobong into two basic categories. The exchanges regarding the famous *Four-Seven Debates* are separated into one section titled "The Exchanged Letters of Both Teachers Regarding the Four-Seven and Principle/Material Force," and the rest of the letters are assembled into one section titled, "The Exchanged Letters of Both Teachers." When looking at this kind of organization, we can guess scholars from following generations who edited these letters regarded as extremely important among them, the debates regarding the *Four-Seven*. However, this kind of organization presented a few problems. For example: although a letter was sent on a certain day, that letter was separated and printed in two parts because of its content, and in some cases, a certain section was quoted and printed again in another part. So by organizing the letters into these two sections, it was difficult to get a sense of the entire relationship between these two people, including their *Four-Seven Debates*.

Therefore, I tried to make up for this. I looked at the dates appearing at the end of the letters and arranged them according to the dates they had written on them. I had difficulty deciding when one letter started and ended because in the process of delivering letters, many letters written on other dates which could not be delivered for difficulty in finding a courier were delivered all at once and sometimes they added writings of totally different subject matters in letters written on the same day. So I set as a standard the date from the standpoint of the person writing the letter, and for attachments to letters I considered them to be a part of the letter and then distinguished these letters. Of course, although all the letters do not have dates attached, I was able to organize them enough to avoid readers losing touch with the general flow.

However, including the *Four-Seven Debates* in the attachments, other various thesis' covered a wide range of topics—not only were they lengthy, but also they addressed difficult subject matters. Leaving them in place, I thought it would be difficult to follow the contents of the two people's exchanges. Finally, I thought it would be a good idea to organize separately in the back of the book the numerous exchanges written regarding the other subject matters of their ongoing debate. Merely, I noted in detail where these writings were originally and made it clear enough so that readers could understand from where this discussion was connected.

The Reason for a New Translation

A complete translation of Toegye and Gobong's exchanges has already been published. In the Korean Classics Research Institute's *Korean Version of Gobong's Collections* (1989), the translations of "The Exchanged Letters of Both Teachers" and "The Exchanged Letters of Both Teachers Regarding the Four-Seven and Principle/Material Force" are included, and the fifth book of the *Complete Works of Toegye* (1990) published by the *Toegye Studies Institute*, includes most of the letters Toegye sent to Gobong. Furthermore, their exchanges regarding the *Four-Seven Debates* have been covered in many books and dissertations at home and abroad. All this considered I had several aims in translating these letters again.

Foremost, I wanted to translate this into beautiful language easy enough for modern readers unfamiliar with Chinese characters or old idiomatic language to understand. Therefore, I was not modest in my effort to change into our language even those words that people familiar with Chinese characters could easily understand. As I did this, instead of a literal translation that tried to revive the atmosphere of the original text, I leaned towards a liberal translation that placed more importance on the meaning.

Next, even regarding those words that a majority of scholars commonly use in modern day academic circles, I made an effort to change these words into our language. For example: although I knew there could be some confusion regarding the "sim" character, I changed them all to "maeum" (or mind). In our everyday lives we use "mind" freely in various situations; that is because we are aware of its numerous connotations. There would have been no need to translate this book again for those people who use the word, "sim," as freely as the word, "mind"; however, very few people can do this. Translations that leave the Chinese character concepts intact require some effort to read. However, there were times when I added the original Chinese character to avoid misunderstandings. Of course, there was a limit to these efforts and I had no choice but to use the original Chinese characters for words like "i-gi" or "seong-jeong."

Finally, I tried to avoid ambiguity, although I did hesitate in cases when there were several possible interpretations or in cases where the meaning was unclear. As much as it was possible, I tried to express my thoughts clearly. I thought it would be worthwhile to provide a new translation for later generations to examine clearly even if my interpretations and choices as a translator might have been incorrect. However, because my skills as a translator are still lacking and clumsy, I might have been unable to grasp the more profound meanings or there might have been occasions where I completely misunderstood.

Although my original intention for starting this translation was an academic interest, I thought the value of these letters would attract more than just the attention of scholars. The way of thinking based on the *School of Principle*, which starting from the Joseon era, has gradually become the core of our society. It would be proper to say this trend has continued all the way up to recent generations. Accordingly, this is not some relic of the past; these teachings still survive and define us. Although its packaging remains hidden, we can say it has strengthened itself in a new mode. Although it appears as if efforts have dissipated lately, attempts to attribute the economic development of our country and other East Asian countries to a kind of "Confucian capitalism" may be because they have noticed these attributes. Whether you feel it or not, our lives and thought processes still lean on a past system based on the thinking of the *School of Principle*.

Because of this, while reading these letters, Toegye and Gobong's worries and their behavior seemed very familiar. Toegye and Gobong tried their best for the world in which they lived and they saw the crux of the problem in the issues they confronted. When reading their exchanges, we can empathize with many parts, although we live in another time. While reading and translating these letters, I could not help but to think about the dialectical origin of all the words and acts that we do unconsciously; I could not help but to think of the variety of strong and weak points this kind of dialectical origin possesses. Our task will be to resolve the problems of our times by discriminating between the strong and weak points of a system of thought based on the *School of Principle*, which continues to exert a strong influence over us.

Finishing the Translation

There was a personal reason I started this translation. Seven years ago, in 1996, Seogang University's History Department introduced a course titled "The Study of Korean Confucian Culture" during its second semester. Including this translator, nine students who took this course under the tutelage of Professor Duhui Jeong collected the exchanged letters between Toegye and Gobong; we entered the original letters into the computer, translated them, and added explanatory notes. The results of that effort became the basis for this translation. The results of that effort permeate throughout this book. I would like to take this opportunity to thank those eight people: Daejung Gim, Miyajaki Yoshinobu, Gyeongok Min, Yeongeun Yi, Hoyeong Yi, Seongbin Im, Gyeongran Jo, and Geon Han.

Several years later, feeling it was a waste to leave such material alone, I began organizing the data but I did not imagine it would be published as a book. When I started the project, I was confident it would take one or two months to complete; however, I kept encountering incorrect words and translations. In no time, I had spent two years correcting and refining these incorrect parts one by one. Professor Duhui Jeong who occasionally waited for me patiently and occasionally pushed me was instrumental in fixing this material, which had been stored away, and giving me the courage to have it published as a book. I would like to take this opportunity to thank him for all his help. I would also like to thank teacher, Inchan "Hoecheon" Choe, who always showered me with words of encouragement and love after I had visited him during the year I had turned twenty, asking him to teach me Chinese writings. Without him, I would not have possessed the courage to approach these writings.

In conclusion, I would like to thank Mr. Beom Gim of the National Institute of Korean History who meticulously read these long writings and I would like to thank Mr. Wonsik Jo of Sonamoo Publishing who spent more than a year polishing these unrefined writings making it possible to become a book. Meeting these people was one of the great benefits I received in the process of making this book.

Yeongdu Kim
The eleventh month of the lunar calendar in the year 2002

Translator's Note

The translation of these letters aims foremost at accuracy; however, a strictly literal translation would have been unreadable. Ignoring style would have done a great disservice to these poignant letters. Therefore, I tried to maintain the integrity of the text—expressing the voice of the authors and imagining they had written these letters in English—while attempting to make the letters more readable, even poetic, without simplifying the ideas or sacrificing the author's original intentions. This process led to bold decisions regarding certain sentence components and the vernacular spoken between two scholars.

Creating a readable style while maintaining the integrity of the text meant finding the delicate balance between a creative interpretation and a literal translation. I occasionally omitted certain extraneous phrases and clauses like "generally speaking" or "moreover" among others and expressions of degree such as "utmost" or "extreme" among others when they impeded with the flow and style of the letters. Furthermore, I did not strictly adhere to a formal map of linking a particular English word to a certain Korean word; according to the text and style, I occasionally varied the words to make the text less rigid and more readable. As Korean culture was (and is) extremely sensitive to the nuances of hierarchical human relationships, the proper use of polite language was very complex; finding the appropriate balance for a readable translation was, once again, a challenge. Those looking for a literal translation will find words omitted and added but will discover the overall ideas and emotions accurately conveyed. It is important to note that such decisions were made in order to present a clearer, more accurate translation of the psyche of the letter writers.

It was possible to be bold with this translation because this edition of *Toegye and Gobong Write Letters* omits the second part, which contains the philosophical debates between Toegye and Gobong. Although this collection of letters is titled the "Everyday Letters," there are some philosophical references and brief debates. While the East Asian Studies Professor or the Confucian scholar looking to brush up on the *Four-Seven Debates* may quickly understand and recognize the references and allusions, the laymen, for which this book was primarily intended, may have some difficulty understanding. I offer this quote from Professor Allan Bloom: "The translator of a great work should revere his text and recognize that there is much in it he cannot understand. His translation should try to make others able to understand what he cannot understand, which means he often must prefer a dull ambiguity to a brilliant resolution." Explaining all these references and allusions would have amounted to another book. I have kept the endnotes to a minimum to avoid distractions from the text. The original Korean endnotes are translated and numbered. The English translation endnotes are designated with a (*).

Regarding names, I used the *Revised Romanization of Korean* system instead of the *McCune-Reischauer* system because the former is more accurate. I used the pinyin system of Romanization of Chinese instead of the *Wade-Giles* Romanization System for the same reason. I used the Revised Romanization of Korean system for every Korean name except for the last name "Yi," which would be "I" under the revised system, to avoid the obvious confusion. I used the western order of name placements when possible for Korean names except for Yi Hwang because of his historic name recognition. Although I acknowledge Korean last names are written differently today, I adhered to the revised system not only because of its phonetic accuracy, but also because I hope and feel these names will be unified under the revised system in the future. Furthermore, I left the Chinese names intact because they were established philosophers.

I want to thank God for giving me this wonderful opportunity to discover myself. Every time I wrote of Toegye or Gobong struggling with their illnesses, I thought of my father bedridden but always full of hope. I would like to thank my family. I also want to thank my translation team at Kalbawe Press. I also want to thank Theodore Oberman for his helpful edits. I am grateful to Yeongdu Gim who translated the original text into Korean for all his helpful explanations regarding the letters. I would also like to thank Professor Bongrang Choe for her help with the romanization of Chinese names and places.

Translator's Note

I would like to extend a special thanks to the people at the *LTI Korea* who selected this book for the Frankfurt Book Fair and worked so hard to ensure the quality of this book.

Louis Choi
Daegu, Korea/Brooklyn, New York   February 2005

Brief Introduction to Yi *"Toegye" Hwang* and Daeseung *"Gobong" Gi*

People consider Yi "Toegye" Hwang (1501-1570) to be the top superstar produced by the Joseon *School of Principle*. So much so that the Joseon *School of Principle* can be divided into a pre and post Toegye era. Although Joseon adopted the *School of Principle* as its national ideology upon its inception, this ideology was not fully assimilated before the arrival of Yi Hwang. Although people talked about creating an ideal society based on the learning of the sages, politically, those in power toyed with the realism of Machiavellianism, and Buddhism and Shamanism still governed the minds of the people.

The reform politics of the *Sarim* faction headed by Gwangjo Jo attempted to overcome the disparity between their ideology and its real life application. However, Confucian idealism suffered a terrible blow when Gwangjo Jo and his followers were either massacred or purged in the *Gimyosahwa* (purge of the *Sarim* literati) when Yi Hwang was nineteen years old (1519). At the time, those who followed the *School of Principle* were left with little choices. They could either accept the oppressive realities or they could fortify and elaborate upon their theories. It was under these dire circumstances that Yi Hwang emerged as the hero of the Joseon *School of Principle*.

Although he was self-educated regarding the *School of Principle*, he was recognized as the greatest *School of Principle* scholar of the time. This can be considered something of a miracle like the neighborhood boxer becoming the world champion! However, he had his own secrets to reaching that level—he was unceasingly open in his approach to learning. He was far from being embarrassed from learning from Gobong or Yulgok, pupils who were young enough to be his grandson, going so far as to call them "classmates." He was overjoyed with discussing moral philosophy with them. He was a true Confucian scholar who knew the pleasure of learning from even a three old baby.

While his plan was simple, Yi Hwang was very fervent about his goals. On one hand, using the studies of Zhu Xi as his base, he eradicated all the heretical theories; on the other hand, he objectively authenticated the universal truth of the *School of Principle*. He attempted to establish a unified and unique truth in the world of Confucianism by denouncing Buddhism, Daoism, and the *School of Mind*, as well as sorting out the heretical scholars inside of Confucianism, people like Gyeongdeok Seo, Luo Qinshun, and Wu Cheng among others. In order to do this, he needed to systematize and establish a theory without a single fault and at the same time, he also needed to practice and apply this to his own life. Through the *Four-Seven Debates* among others he established himself as a superiorly intelligent theorist; however, his greatness did not end as an investigator of things in theory—he was fervent in his desire to reach the perfection of knowledge.

This was the reason he was the hero not only of his time and generations after, but also the hero of a universal Asian Confucianism that transcended merely the Joseon era. By modern Chinese thinker Liang Qichao referring to Yi Hwang as "Master Yi," a title on the same level as Confucius, he expressed his utmost courtesy by placing him in the realm of the sages. Furthermore, through Toegye's influence, Yamajaki, who was responsible for initiating modern Japanese Confucianism, revered Toegye calling him "Joseon's greatest" which was no different than saying Toegye was "Zhu Xi's direct disciple."

Daeseung "Gobong" Gi (1527-1572) was born in Gwangju in the Southern Jeolla Province in the 22nd year of King Jungjong's reign. He was born into a *School of Principle* world and while struggling to realize the ideals of this school, he died young at the age of forty-six while adhering to the ways of the *School of Principle*. Before he died at Gobu, away from his home, he lamented that he could not continue his studies because of illnesses.

This kind of disposition was a part of his family history. Members of his household for generations remained faithful to the *Sarim* faction. Although his great-great-grandfather, Geon, held the post of *Daesaheon*, he discarded his post and confined himself to his home after Danjong was dethroned; he remained loyal to his will without wavering. Although King Sejo called him to service on five separate occasions, he did not betray his loyalties. And his uncle,

Jun, was a prominent figure of the *Sarim* faction dying along with Gwangjo Jo during the purge of the literati. His father, Jin, upon his younger brother's death, moved his home to Gwangju and concentrated on his studies while refusing public office. From an early age, Daeseung Gi devoted himself to the studies and by the time he was twenty, people judged him to be an authoritative voice in the *School of Principle*. From early on, while arduously rebelling against the tyranny of powerful vassals, he was clear in his *Sarim* posture that was faithful to ideals.

In 1558, when Daeseung Gi was thirty-two years old, he passed the *singnyeon* civil service exam (exam given every three years) ranking first among test takers in the *eul* group and entered a government post. Starting as the temporary vice-*Jeongja* of the Office of Diplomatic Documentation, he served in important positions such as the *Jwarang* of the Board of War and the *Jeongnang* of the Board of Personnel before becoming the dean of the Royal College and the *Daesagan*; he also served as the *Chamui* of the Board of War. However, he suffered through continuous hardships in his government service career. He was pointed out as being the head of the *Sinjinsaryu* (group of new officials) and was evicted by the *Hungu* faction, and he was dismissed from office because of his dispute with Prime Minister Jungyeong Yi. This was the result of his staunch disposition and his mentality as a scholar which prohibited him from compromising with injustice.

He was also bold in front of the king. Through his royal lectures among others, while emphasizing the reform of the national discipline and protecting the livelihood of the people, he criticized the tyranny of political cronies. Asking the king to spearhead the promotion of a righteous government, Gobong spoke without reserve about widening freedom of speech and following the will of the people. In order to set straight the national moral fiber, he also asserted emphatically the restoration of scholars such as Gwangjo Jo and Eonjeok Yi among others who were sacrificed during the purge of the literati and bringing to light the crimes of people like Gon Nam, Wonhyeong Yun who persecuted scholars.

As propriety was something that arose from a heavenly mandate, he stressed that only upright propriety could effectively lead the people. Considering the people the foundation of the country, through taxing lightly and evenly he said the nation could be stabilized if the livelihoods of the people were abundant. In a concrete manner, he presented a people oriented political policy that protected the livelihood of the people and eliminated the evil practices inflicted on the people.

When Toegye left government service for the final time, he recommended that King Seonjo use Gobong effectively as a scholar of the studies. However, Gobong's pride was unyielding and his assertions were sharp. Enmeshed in the political imbroglio of the time, he was in frequent opposition to those cabinet members in power. Ultimately, he did not realize his dreams of political reform. However, after Gobong passed away, King Seonjo immediately gathered Gobong's royal lectures and made the book, *Nonsarok*, and took into consideration its political polices. We can see through this that King Seonjo was deeply impressed with the political principles presented by Gobong in his royal lectures.

The Events that Took Place During Toegye and Gobong's Thirteen Years of Correspondence (1558–1570)

YEAR	MONTH	TOEGYE	GOBONG
1558 Year of the Horse Year 13 of King Myeongjong's reign Year 37 of Jiajing Toegye, 58 years old Gobong, 32 years old	July		Meets Hang "Iljae" Yi and discusses an *Explanation of the Diagram of the Supreme Ultimate* on his way to Seoul to take the civil service examination
	September	Summoned by the king and comes to Seoul	Passes the civil service exam
	October	Becomes the dean of the Royal College Becomes the *Sanghogun*	Becomes the temporary vice-*Jeongja* of the Office of Diplomatic Documentation Meets Toegye in Seoul On his return home,
	November		meets Hang "Iljae" Yi again and discusses the Supreme Ultimate
	December	Becomes the *Gaseondaebu*, the *Champan* of the Board of Public Works	
1559 Year of the Sheep Year 14 of King Myeongjong's reign Year 38 of Jiajing Toegye, 59 years old Gobong, 33 years old	January	Sends a letter to Gobong and asks his opinions about the *Diagram of the Mandate of Heaven Explained* which he corrected	
	March	Returns home for vacation	
	July	Becomes the *Dongjijung-chubusa*	Writes his first *Four-Seven Thesis*
	October	Writes his first *Four-Seven Thesis*	Sends Toegye a letter and asks about the moral principle for entering government posts

YEAR	MONTH	TOEGYE	GOBONG
1560 Year of the Monkey Year 15 of King Myeongjong's reign Year 39 of Jiajing Toegye, 60 years old Gobong, 34 years old	August		Sends notice of Inhu "Haseo" Gim's death Writes his second *Four-Seven Thesis* Shows the discourse on the Supreme Ultimate which he exchanges with Hang "Iljae" Yi and Inhu "Haseo" Gim
	November	Writes his second *Four-Seven Thesis*	
1561 Year of the Chicken Year 16 of King Myeongjong's reign Year 40 of Jiajing Toegye, 61 years old Gobong, 35 years old	January		Writes his third *Four-Seven Thesis*
	July		Sends notice of Jiun "Chuman" Jeong's death
1562 Year of the Dog Year 17 of King Myeongjong's reign Year 41 of Jiajing	May		Comes to Seoul, becomes the historiographer of the Office of the Recorders of the Royal Command and the official writer of the Office of the Recorders of Political Affairs
	October	Writes his third *Four-Seven Thesis* and saves it without sending Sends a letter asking to stop the *Four-Seven Debates*	Returns home for vacation

Timeline of Events   xxxiii

YEAR	MONTH	TOEGYE	GOBONG
1562, cont. Toegye, 62 years old Gobong, 36 years old	December		Summoned by the king and comes to Seoul Becomes the *Daegyo* of the Office of the Recorders of the Royal Command Becomes the *Bonggyo* of the Office of the Recorders of the Royal Command
1563 Year of the Pig Year 18 of King Myeongjong's reign Year 42 of Jiajing Toegye, 63 years old Gobong, 37 years old	March		Becomes the *Juseo* of the Royal Secretariat
	April		Becomes the *Bonggyo* of the Office of the Recorders of the Royal Command
	May		Scores average on the evaluation of merits Becomes the *Busajeong*
	August		Returns home after getting attacked, reinstated with the help of his elder cousin, Daehang, after being dismissed because of Rhang Yi's envy Comes to Seoul and repays the king's kindness
	October		Enters the Library Becomes the *Seonmurang*, vice-*Suchan* and the *Gyeongyeomgeomtogwan* of the Office of Royal
	November		Lecturers, the official writer of the Office of the Recorders of Political Affairs
1564 Year of the Rat Year 19 of King Myeongjong's reign Year 43 of Jiajing	March		Replaced from his *Suchan* position, becomes the *Jeonjeok* and *Jijegyo*
	June		Becomes the *vice-Suchan* and the *Gyeongyeomgeomtogwan* of the Office of Royal Lecturers
	July		Elder cousin Daehang Gi dies
	October		Discusses mourning decorums with Toegye

YEAR	MONTH	TOEGYE	GOBONG
1564, cont. Toegye, 64 years old Gobong, 38 years old	October		Becomes the *Jwarang* of the Board of War and the *Jijegyo*
	December		Becomes the *Jeonjeok* of the Royal College and the *Jwarang* of the Board of War
1565 Year of the Cow Year 20 of King Myeongjong's reign Year 44 of Jiajing Toegye, 65 years old Gobong, 39 years old	April	Replaced as the *Dongjijung-chubusa*	
	June		Becomes the *Sunguirang, Seonggyunjikgang* and the *Jigegyo*, becomes the *Jeongnang* of the Board of Personnel and the *Jigegyo*
	August	Becomes the *Dongjijung-chubusa*	
	October		Becomes the *Gyori* of the Office of Printing and Seals
	November		Returns home for a vacation
	December		Meets Susin No and discusses the Human mind and the Dao mind
1566 Year of the Tiger Year 21 of King Myeongjong's reign Year 45 of Jiajing	February	Becomes the *Jaheondaebu*, the Minister of Public Works and the *Yemunjehak* and *Daejehak* of the Office of the Royal Lecturers, becomes the *Daejehak* of the Office of the Recorders of the Royal Command, the *Jiseonggyungwansa*, and the *Dongjigyeongyeonchun-chugwansa* Becomes the *Jaheondaebu*	
	April	and the *Jijungchubusa*	Becomes the *Tongdeong nang*, the *Jeongnang* of the Board of Rites and the *Jigegyo*
	July		Writes the "General Summary" and "Postscript Explanation" of the *Four-Seven Thesis*

Timeline of Events

YEAR	MONTH	TOEGYE	GOBONG
1566, cont. Toegye, 66 years old Gobong, 40 years old	October		Becomes the *Tongseollang*, the *Gyori* of the Office of Royal Lecturers, becomes the *Heonnap* of the Office of the Censor General and the *Jijegyo* Comes to Seoul and repays the king's kindness Becomes the *Sain* of the State Council
1567 Year of the Rabbit Year 22 of King Myeongjong's reign First Year of Longqing Toegye, 67 years old Gobong, 41 years old	February	Asks to eliminate the xylographic books–*Yonghakseogui* and *Eorokseok*	Becomes the *Jangnyeong* of the Office of the Inspector General and the *Jijegyo*
	May		Becomes the *Eunggyo* of the Office of Royal Lecturers Goes to Uiju, taking on the job as the *Wonjeopsa*
	June	Comes to Seoul after being selected as the *Jesulgwan* who was responsible for receiving envoys from the Ming Dynasty King Myeongjong passes away	
	July	Writes the biography of King Myeongjong Becomes the Minister of the Board of Rites and the *Dongjigyeongyeonchunchugwansa* Returns home before the departure of King Myeongjong's coffin	Returns to Seoul Argues that it is wrong for the former Queen, Gongui, not to wear mourning attire.
	August	Explains the reason he left the royal court hastily	Visits Uiju again as the *Jeonwisa*
	September	Sends Gobong a letter and discusses the traditional system of mourning attire Becomes the *Yongyangwidaehogun* and the *Dongjigyeongyeonchunchugwansa*	
	October		Becomes the *Josandaebu*, the *Jibui* of the Office of the Inspector General
	November		Argues that the memorial service held for the king's real parents was improper

YEAR	MONTH	TOEGYE	GOBONG
1568 Year of the Dragon	January	Becomes the *Sungjeongdaebu* and the *Uchanseong* of the State Council	Becomes the *Bongjeongdaebu*, the *Jikjehak* of the Office of the Royal Lecturers and the *Pangyo* of the Office of Printing and Seals
First year of King Seonjo's reign Year 2 of Longqing	February	Becomes the *Panjungchubusa*	Becomes the *Tongjeongdaebu*, the D*ongbuseungji* of the Office of Diplomatic Documentation, the *Jijegyo*, the *Gyeongyeoncham changwan*, and the *Ubuseungji*
	April		Withdraws as the *Seungji* because of illness Becomes the dean of the Royal college
Toegye, 68 years old Gobong, 42 years old	July	Comes to Seoul unable to deny the king's repeated calling	
	August	Becomes the *Jehak* of the Office of the Royal Lecturers, the *Daejehak* of the Office of the Royal Lecturers, the *Daejehak* of the Office of the Recorders of the Royal Command, the *Jigyeongyeonchunchugwan-seonggyungwansa*, and the *Panjungchubusa* Replaced as the *Daejehak* Presents the *Ten Diagrams of Confucian Philosophy*	Becomes the *Useungji*
	December		Comments on the *Ten Diagrams of Confucian Philosophy* Asserts that Seonjo should treat Toegye well enough to make him his teacher during the *Yadae*.
1569 Year of the Snake	January	Becomes the Minister of Personnel and the *Panjungchubusa* Arguments regarding the Munso Shrine arise	
Year 2 of King Seonjo's reign	February	Out of the city gates, presents an appeal for resignation	
	March	Bids farewell to the king and returns home	Sees Toegye off in the Dongho part of the Han River

Timeline of Events xxxvii

YEAR	MONTH	TOEGYE	GOBONG
1569, *cont.* Year 3 of Longqing Toegye, 69 years old Gobong, 43 years old	March, *cont.*	Recommends Gobong when he withdraws	
	April		Presents an appeal of the arguments regarding the Munso Shrine
	June	Requests that Gobong write the epitaph of his deceased father	Decides to return home after the king turns down Gae Gim's impeachment
	July		Replaced from the *Seungji* position due to illness Becomes the dean of the Royal College
	August		Replaced from the dean position due to illness
	September		
1570 Year of the Horse Year 3 of King Seonjo's reign Year 4 of Longqing Toegye, 70 years old Gobong, 44 years old	February		Discards his government post and rusticates
	June		Declines a royal summon for the *Bugyeongsa* position by sending a memorial to the Throne
	October	Sends a letter in which he amends his explanation of "zhizhi gewu" Sends a reply to Gobong's discussion of the "Diagram of 'The Mind Combines and Governs the Nature and the Feelings'"	
	December	Makes his nephew write down his will Ends his days	Sets an ancestral tablet and laments after receiving notice of Toegye's death

"The Everyday Letters"

1558-1561

THE BEGINNING OF SOULFUL EXCHANGES

[Letter #1 Toegye Writes Gobong]

Raise Virtue, Think Profoundly

Seondal[1] Gi, I write this letter to you as a token of my gratitude. I have been too invalid to step outside my door, but yesterday, how fortunate I was to fulfill my wish of meeting you! I was grateful in addition to feeling enormously humbled. You mentioned traveling south tomorrow; place health as the highest priority as you confront the cold and embark on this long journey. I sincerely hope you will raise virtue and think profoundly as you pursue your studies.

I humbly end this letter.

Respectfully, Yi Hwang

---

1. *Seondal* refers to somebody who has passed the military and civil service exams but has not taken office. Daeseung Gi (Gobong) passed the civil service exam during the Year of the Horse (1558, year 13 of King Myeongjong's reign) when he was thirty-two years old and ranked number one among test takers in the *Eul* group. The above letter was sent during the winter of that year.

[Letter #2 Toegye Writes Gobong]

Cherish Yourself for the Ages

I inquire about your well-being, *Jeongja*[1] Gi.

The year changed without warning and I failed to hear from you since our last meeting. Fortunately, I met Hwasuk Bak[2] yesterday and received the letter you asked him to deliver. My anxious and yearning heart was consoled considerably. After your triumphant return home from passing the exam, I am guessing your conduct and posture grow more venerable and generous with each passing day.[3] With every changing situation you encounter on the *outside*, become more introspective and conserved on the *inside*, advancing towards virtue and reaching the state of intimacy with perfect virtue. Could there be anything more joyful?

> *I am at a loss.*
> *Every situation I confront yields poor results.*

My sickness has deteriorated to the point of becoming an inveterate illness. However, the king continues to shed his grace in greater proportions. I fervently desired to leave my government post but to no avail. Although many people claim that the Board of Public Works has a light workload, how can I expect to work while being so ill?[4] I had no alternative and endeavored to resign, but I have been unsuccessful. Not only did I fail to depart, but also people around me advised that staying was the right course of action. What can I do, as choosing a course of action has become this difficult!

Although I fulfilled my wish of meeting you, our last meeting was like a transient dream—brief—and I did not have the opportunity to question your opinions. Although our encounter was curt, I was pleased that there were some points upon which we agreed. I heard through scholars your thoughts regarding the *Four Beginnings–Seven Feelings*. I was worried that what I had said about this topic was unjust. After hearing your rebuttal argument, I realized with further clarity that I was incorrect. Consequently, I offer the following revision:

> Because the manifestations of the Four Beginnings are due to principle, there is nothing that is *not* good; good and evil exist because the manifestations of the Seven Feelings coalesce with material force.

I am not sure if this is correct. From "The Letter Sent to Wang Guiling,"[5] you mentioned the "go" character was incorrectly combined with the "in" character to produce the "geuk" character, which resolved my previous doubts.

From the beginning, short in knowledge, I have received much help from you, as you were so erudite. If we were to grow close, could words describe how beneficial that would be! What makes things unpredictable is the fact that one of us lives in the north and the other lives in the south; like a swallow and a goose flying back and forth, it will be easy to miss paths.

I send you a calendar. If neighbors need a calendar, this might come in handy. There are many things I want to say, but as this letter has far to travel, I will stop here.
Solely cherish yourself for the ages.
I respectfully inquire about your well-being.
January 5, 1559 (the Year of the Sheep)
Hwang bows his head.

---

1. *Jeongja* refers to someone who works for the Office of Printing and Seals, the Office of the Royal Lecturers, and the Office of Diplomatic Documentation, affiliated with these senior groups with a ninth class ranking. Daeseung Gi (Gobong) passed the civil service exam and became a temporary vice-*Jeongja*.
2. Hwasuk Bak refers to Sun Bak. His pen name was Saam, his posthumous name was Munchung, and Hwasuk was his pseudonym.
3. Refers to someone who meets his parents after passing the civil service exam.
4. Toegye became the *Champan* of the Board of Public Works in December, 1558 (the Year of the Horse).
5. See *The Complete Works of Zhu Xi* 37.

[Letter #3 Gobong Writes Toegye]

Longing for Virtue

Dear teacher, Toegye,

I respectfully inquire about your well-being. How is your health? My respect for you is endless. Although presumptuous of me to say, I have been able to endure and preserve myself because of your warm sentiments. On February 16, I received the calendar and letter dated January 5. I read and reread your letter, savoring it. It was moving and comforting.

Unwise and knowing nothing, I have it in my heart to follow your teachings from afar, as I dwell by the sea. Fortunately, I had the opportunity to meet you last year. Able to learn from a closer proximity, I was enthralled because I was able to gain so much knowledge. I wanted to stay longer and keep you company.

However, my sick body could not withstand the cold and the realities of my situation obstructed my wishes. I planned to leave and turned my horse south. Although I appeased worries about my native village, my longing for virtue grew everyday. My every thought had me dashing to you but such remorse filled me when I was unable to act on those thoughts.

Being so far away from you, everything seemed so distant. What could I do? If this was not enough, the receptions I held after I passed the civil service examination were very vexing and cumbersome. Making me feel more miserable, I became ill: mentally, I was thrown into a stupor. Physically, I became very weak. What I learned in the past grew hazy and what I learn now is coarse. I fear I may desist from my lifelong ambition of advancing in my *Learning of the Way*, and I sigh at the difficulty of not being able to measure up to the ancient ones. My disposition grows faint. Swept away by the waves of the secular world, I can hardly stand firm. I cannot find my way out.

I deeply lament that my heart, which once yearned for the old and sought to act according to the *dao*, chases after the secular world and personal gains. However, the last time we met, I benefited from your open heart compelling me to realize I needed to make an effort. Did you regard me a suitable interlocutor early on in our relationship? I am humbled beyond expression!

My greatest doubts for the longest time have centered on the *Four-Seven Thesis*; however, as my opinions remain nebulous, how can I publish what might be false assertions? Moreover, I cleared all my doubts once I studied your revised theory. However, in my opinion, once principle and material force are understood, the meanings of the *mind, nature,* and *feelings* fall naturally into place. Then, we can easily classify the *Four Beginnings-Seven Feelings*. Although the theories of scholars from following generations are articulated and clarified, I think some discrepancies exist between their theories and the teachings of Zi Si, Mencius, Master Cheng, and Zhu Xi. This stems from the scholars of following generations inadequately understanding principle and material force.

I wanted to put forth my foolish opinions and wanted your critical review. However, as I was busy for a long time, I did not have the chance to peruse this again. In addition, I was afraid of putting my thoughts into writing in case my opinions were misrepresented. I have decided to visit Seoul sometime during the spring or summer.

I desperately want to meet and learn under your tutelage.[1] Exhausted and flustered, the penmanship was not as neat nor was the writing as smooth as I would have liked.

I am graciously apologetic. I ask for your understanding.
I respectfully bow and write this reply.
March 5, 1559 (the Year of the Sheep)
Yours truly,
Junior scholar, Daeseung "Gobong" Gi.

---

1. We know from following letters that Gobong did not travel to Seoul as planned to meet Toegye. In March of 1559 (the Year of the Sheep) Toegye also left Seoul for a vacation. Gobong did finalize and send his theory regarding the *Four Beginnings-Seven Feelings*.

[Letter #4 Gobong Writes Toegye]

Inside the Tribulation of Myeonsillye[1]

I inquire about your health and miss you unceasingly. I have been getting along fine thanks to your concerns. Having said that, I feel that I have fallen into a bottomless pit—my will has been anything but firm. Although I struggle to crawl out, I see no end in sight.

I was endlessly comforted and inspired to act by the letter you sent last spring. A day does not pass that I do not plan to travel to Seoul quickly and hold your words in high esteem. However, I am delayed by destitution, wasting my time sitting idly. As a means of delivery emerged, I wrote a reply, but you had already left for a trip down south. I lamented when I touched the futilely returned letter.

Finally, in early April, I mustered the strength to embark on the journey, but solemnly, the joy I was expecting at the beginning gradually subsided; my vast heart grew more remote. I was incessantly ill after my arrival in Seoul and failed to attend the *myeonsillye* at the Office of Diplomatic Documentation in the beginning. Only after being bedridden and recuperating for a long time was I barely able to venture out, and near the end of last month, I could finally attend the *myeonsillye*. With the temperament of a deer roaming the forest, the net of the world tragically fell on top of me without warning. I was chased from here to there. I fell and stumbled, eventually, being chased everywhere. Bewildered, I thought I was going insane and did not know when it would stop. Words can hardly justify the extent of that tribulation. Although my astonishment has slightly subsided, more than ever, my thoughts turn to the vast forest. I miss the abundant blades of grass. I do not know what it is about my innate disposition that makes me so odd and eccentric. I eagerly yearn for royal permission from the king to return to my native village and rediscover my previous scholarly endeavors. However, I do not know if such a request will come into fruition.

I am guessing you have left your government post and are recuperating. Even if you forbid yourself from becoming lax regarding your affections for the king, you must be experiencing more leisure time, quietly living in the forest.

I truly envy you.

Enmeshed in my own assertions, I can do nothing but review old writings. What is worse, because I lived in the country until I was old, my obstinate temperament has hardened, making it difficult for me to change, to become amiable. At last, I prepare to enter the world, but I am thwarted at every place because of my eccentricities and laziness. I can only sigh as I look at my worthless self.

Although I attempt to reacquaint myself with my old studies, making the effort not to abandon my original aim, trivial work entangles me continuously, never releasing me for the entire day. What can I do, as I lack a suitable interlocutor?

Gazing at the clouds covering the mountaintops, my head keeps turning unconsciously to the place where you reside.

When can we meet again?
I am filled with grief and longing.
I cannot fully describe the situation here through writing. I have not written about it in detail because I have been suffering from a cold for the past several days. I apologize.

Between the spring and summer, I could not write a single letter because I was bedridden due to illness and could not find a suitable courier. Deplorably, the words I spoke to you as we departed last winter became empty words. Along with this letter, I send the unsent letter I wrote during the spring. In addition, I wrote the

theory of nature and feelings on the annex. Please take into consideration that Jajung Jeong[2] knows in detail the remaining news. Would it be possible for you to send a reply through Jajung? I know this is terribly rude of me to ask. I apologize.
    Teacher, please excuse me.
    I respectfully bow and offer this letter.
    Junior scholar, Daeseung, respectfully bows his head and sends this letter.
    August 14, 1559 (the Year of the Sheep)
    Daeseung reiterates that he is sorry and embarrassed; I have haphazardly written this letter near the end of my illness.

---

    1. This was a custom called *myeonsillye*. Elders teased and insulted an official taking office for the first time. An official would begin working after passing through this initiation.
    2. Jajung Jeong refers to Yuil Jeong (1533-1576). His pen name was Munbong and his pseudonym was Jajung. He was Toegye's pupil and excelled in poems and improvisational poetic writing.

[Letter #5 Gobong Writes Toegye]

Deeply Longing for My Teacher

    Although I have finished writing my letter, I risk troubling you again because I needed to add something. I do not know the studies genuinely nor do I have any ambitions regarding the studies. Merely, when I was young, with my shallow skills, I read a wide range of ancient and modern books with a certain degree of proficiency; however, I wanted to be skilled in reading and writing solely because I wanted to enter government service. Afterwards, dissatisfied with the studies I did in preparation for the civil service exam, I probed the words of the sages and wise men. However, I did that for personal pleasure only, never daring to adopt those words sincerely, to accept them as obligations, and to act accordingly with all my strength. That being the case, you would be justified in accusing me of failing to know myself when I boldly comment regarding the theory of man's nature and feelings.

When I calmly ponder the matter, a person receives the various temperaments from the heavens indiscriminately. Although temperaments can wither in the clutches of worldly desire, they never disappear entirely—remnants always remain. How can a person solely blame lack of effort in the past and then never make the effort again? Without taking into consideration that what I had read and heard was so stubborn and contemptible, informing you of my theories, I boldly ask you to set straight my views. I beseech you to guide me.

In addition, my foundation is flimsy; I lack strength; and, I fail to concentrate on the things I need to study at great lengths. I started my studies late, hence, I am riddled with numerous weaknesses. I regret that my mind splinters or scatters every time I study; and, I do not know how to study the origin of nature and feelings. I know I must study this on my own, without the aid of teachers and friends. I have been indiscreet in asking you to enlighten me.

Intrinsically ignorant in the ways of the world, I have difficulty fitting in. On one side, it would be difficult to cover my tracks should I relinquish my government office and hide somewhere. On the other side, my mind and body would grow gaunt should I work hard. Both circumstances being equal, I would forego manners and do as I please. Although I have already made this decision (to leave my government office) and have kept it to myself, people have advised me differently. It appeared as if the elder, Chuman,[1] would respond forthrightly, but what he said did not transcend secular common sense. Either he did not explain because he thought I lacked character or his opinions had parts that were less than complete: what other explanation could there be for such a response? Perhaps he disregarded the saying, "When transacting business for others, I must be faithful."[2]

I knew going to the *myeonsillye* was not the right thing to do. I should have taken care of myself because I had not fully recovered from my illness; however, I rashly completed the ceremony because I could not avoid the pressure many people applied. What else can I say except that this was the result of faulty shortsightedness? In cases like this, a person who is slightly different from the world cannot avoid the ridicule and rejection from others; eventually, he will either jeopardize his life or suppress his will.

This is deplorable, truly deplorable.

I exhort you to guide me to the right path.

Letter #5

I have always said:

When conduct becomes difficult, I worry only that my studies have been incomplete. If my learning had been complete, acting would not be difficult.

What do you think about this remark? In addition, I ask you to examine one by one and comment on the things I have mentioned.

I have always revered and missed you, even though we have only met twice, and the times we did meet, we had to say our farewells hastily. What else could we do, as we were like swallow and goose, flying back and forth! I surmised we could not frequently visit because of the vast distance between the north and south; however, while apart, difficult to explain, delicate theories and worldly events that unfold chaotically, have piled themselves high like the mountains and clouds without warning and without effort. I am not worried nor do I profoundly miss you simply because you are far away.

Looking at this piece of paper, feeling remote, I have no idea what to write.

Please understand. Once again, I respectfully offer this letter.

Middle of August

Junior scholar, Daeseung, respectfully bows his head.

I write this letter with much difficulty as I lack strength. I am in awe and ashamed.

---

1. Chuman refers to Jiun Jeong (1509-1561). His pen name was Chuman and his pseudonym was Jeongi. He met Toegye in Seoul and received corrections regarding his *Diagram of the Mandate of Heaven Explained*, which prompted a dispute between Toegye and Gobong.

2. "The philosopher Tsang says, 'I daily examine myself on three points;—whether, in transacting business for others, I may have been not faithful;—whether, in intercourse with friends, I may have been not sincere;—whether, I may have not mastered and practiced the instructions of my teacher.'" See the *Confucian Analects*, Book I: "Hsio R," Chapter IV.

[Letter #6 Toegye Writes Gobong]

Between the Government Post and My Studies

My response to *Jeongja* Myeongeon Gi's remarks:
After I sent my letter to a courier in the far south in the spring, I immediately returned to the east. Confined to my home, I could not hear news from Seoul often. Considering Honam is even farther away, need I say more! After an inquiry regarding your whereabouts, I learned that you were in Seoul; although I mulled writing you a letter expressing my thoughts, I reconsidered when surmising the hardship you must be enduring as a newly appointed government official. I did not have the time to greet you personally because I was ill. My only recourse was to ask Jajung of your news every time he visited, but this time, he was late visiting. Finally, Jajung's assistant visited around the eleventh of the previous month and I received the two letters you sent in the middle of August, your March 5 response letter, and one part of your literary work. I was comforted beyond words and liberated from my worries. As I reviewed and examined the meaning of your three letters, I sensed how much your heart inclined towards me and how much you missed me. They filled me with boundless sorrow and lament.

I regarded as insightful words to live by, Hu Kanghou's[1] saying:

> Generally speaking, man must decide his course of action regarding whether he enters or departs a government post. It is not something upon which I can plan for others nor is it something that somebody else can plan together with me.

If you are not precise regarding reason and your will is weak, the decision you make on your own will be driven by personal wishes and yearnings, ignorant of the moral principle of the time; you will become unjust which is my worry.

I carefully read your letters especially where you mentioned: "I am concerned I will lose touch with my original intentions because of government service, as I have rashly entered this post while my studies have been inadequate. I want to return and complete my studies." However, even the ancient ones had difficulty possessing such a desire. I have yet to see someone pursuing this today. This is the reason I respect you and on the other hand, this is the reason I am concerned and afraid.

I will briefly talk about a personal experience. When I was young, I had the desire to study; however, I did not make any gains because I lacked the teachers and companions who could guide me, and I grew physically ill. I should have planned to enter and live the rest of my days in the mountains.

I should have built a small hut in a quiet place.
I should have read words and learned their meanings.
I should have replenished those insufficient parts of my studies.

If I had studied like that for thirty years, I would have cured my illness, completed my studies, and everything in the world would have happened according to my wishes. However, what happened instead?

Reflecting on the past, I took the civil service exam and pursued a government post saying to myself, "I will take the civil service exam and I will leave if it is not right for me or if I want to leave. Who can hold me down?"

In the beginning, I did not know the present world was so different from the world of the past and that we were different from the Chinese. I did not know scholars would forget the proper moral principle for entering and leaving government posts, that no cases existed of scholars voluntarily leaving their government posts, and that scholars would add increasingly to the superficiality of their names. I did not know that finding a way to leave government service would be this perilous. Today, as it becomes evident that I cannot freely enter or leave government service, criticism runs as rampant and as numerous as the mountains. My fearful thoughts reach extremes.

From early on, thinking I had a temperament suited for the mountains and fields, I did not desire any government office or stipend. My studies were naïve in light of reason and ignorant regarding my obligations to the times. I made a mistake and when I realized this mistake, I could not undo it, which has led me to these circumstances. However, the reason I could pursue old loyalties was that my illness was not an excuse: everybody in the country knew my condition. The entire world knew of my condition. The ghosts looking down upon us knew of my condition. In this regard, it might be more difficult for you to conduct yourself. Since you asked me about this problem, I will relay an outline of my thoughts.

Before entering your government post, people near and far recognized your excellent temperament and potential for becoming a future leader. The attention of the nation turned to you as soon as you entered your government post.

The wagon has just started moving for a long journey.

Unlike me, you are free from illness. If you discard your government post, enter into hiding—do you think people will willingly let you go? If you try, and the more you try to discard the world when it has not expelled you, the harder discarding it will be. In addition, compared to an invalid like me, it will be more difficult for you to repeatedly plea to leave government service. Have you thought about the reproach and how much fiercer it will be than those levied at me, someone who is ill? This is why I am worried and afraid for you!

Naturally, the best plan for you would have been to study with this as a fixed purpose of life before entering a government post. If you had done this, you could have concentrated on your studies and achieved the *dao*. You could have raised a red banner for a generation, becoming a pioneer for our stunted scholarly learning.

However, you did not follow this path.

Instead, having passed the civil service exam, you have already entered a government post.

You have finished the *myeonsillye* humbly bowing while enduring scorn.

Now, after traversing all this, you are asking people for advice on how to leave office and how to realize your wishes! You are very slow in grasping your present situation, right? When mentioning you had always harbored in your heart the desire to forsake the secular world and embark on your own path, it is unclear as to whether you had always harbored such thoughts in your heart.

You wrote in your letter, "When conduct becomes difficult, I worry only that my studies are incomplete. If my learning had been complete, acting would not be difficult absolutely." These words are truly sincere and earnest.

It is fair to say that your view of the *Four Beginnings-Seven Feelings Thesis* reached a high level of understanding. However, when someone as foolish as me looks at this, your elevated studies are worth considering on a wide and broad scale, but it fails to pierce through an elaborate and profound essence; regarding making up one's mind and governing one's actions, a person can gain much in that freedom bursts everywhere. However, it lacks in the study of gathering and solidifying a person's mind and body. Although your words and writings are exceptional, they cannot escape the occasional vice of scabrous contradictions.

The ordinary person would never have to think of the plans you have made for yourself. However, you have not been able to break free from deciding whether you want to place your heart *here* or *there*, *stay* or *leave*. You have been entrusted with a big task and have staked your name on it: *how could you think there would be no hardship while conducting yourself amidst gusting winds and crashing waves!*

While living, scholars enter and leave service, opportunities come and go; however, the only task remains to cleanse yourself and act righteously. There is no time to argue about fortune and misfortune. I have always considered it peculiar when most of our ancestral scholars, who possessed even the slightest intention of pursuing moral principle, would become ensnared in the troubles of the world. Although one could attribute this to our land being small and the hearts of the people being cold, they became trapped by hardships because after all, the plans they had made for themselves were incomplete. When I say *incomplete*, I mean they did not complete their studies but still elevated themselves; while being unable to surmise the times, they tried brazenly to reform the world. They failed for these reasons. Anybody entrusted with a big task who stakes his name on it must be wary of this. Therefore, how should you proceed?

> *Refrain from elevating yourself.*
> *Refrain from being too brave in reforming the world.*
> *Refrain from overly asserting your opinions in all matters.*

You have embarked on the path of public service and have agreed to sacrifice yourself for the good of the country: how can you hold steadfastly to your will of leaving public office! Since you have set your mind on adhering to moral principle, how is it that you know *how* to enter a government post but fail to know how to leave? An old teacher once admonished us saying, "Study if you have any strength remaining while working at your post; work at your post if you have any strength remaining while studying!"[2] Set this as a standard of conduct and examine if your conduct is correct in light of righteousness.

While serving at your post—outside of being worried about the affairs of the state—always take a step back, lower your head one notch, focus on your studies and ask: "How can I be held responsible for governing the country when my studies are incomplete?" When you do not agree with the times, do not be concerned in the slightest with the affairs of the world; plead to be moved to an easier post or plan to leave. While doing this, focus on your studies and think, "Since my learning is incomplete, this is a time to solemnly discipline myself and cultivate my studies." Pledge to live like this for a long time and when entering or leaving, act according to the standards dictated by your studies.

Furthermore, do not be content with yourself because pursuing righteousness has no end. Be delighted in hearing about your faults and enjoy becoming good. Then, if truth accumulates and if you exert an effort for a long time, you will achieve the *dao*; virtue will stand; your service will become more distinguished; and, the scope of your government work will naturally expand. Only then can you speak of the responsibility of spreading the *dao* and governing the world, as I have mentioned above.

After reading your letter, it seemed as if you were leaning towards leaving government service. When I said I wanted you to deliberate on both entering and leaving government posts, this seems like something anybody in the world would say. You might reject my advice, as it was similar to the advice given by Jiun Jeong. There are occasions when his theories are incomplete, and I am not sure what he says. Fly high, go away, never come back, and adhere to the principles, as the ancient ones did when they sought the meaning of the studies covertly: I am aware this advice is very tidy, transcending the thoughts of average people. I have heard about the conversation Teacher Zhu Xi had with one of his disciples regarding Master Cheng's refusal to be paid wages.[3] The gist of the conversation was as follows:

> These days, those who pass the civil service exam and enter a government post must conduct themselves like ordinary citizens.

You have already lost focus of your original aim of covertly studying in retirement, and while free from sickness, you passed the civil service exam and entered a government post. Of course, those people who earnestly exert an effort on your behalf would recommend that you launch yourself into the world. Is it possible that Jiun Jeong's suggestion arose from this line of thinking?

If what I say is even slightly amiss, you will become bogged down in an uneventful life, continuing with old ways and acquiescing to the customs of the world. Therefore, you must possess an undying will, an unbreakable spirit, and an insight that cannot be deceived.

By tempering yourself daily through the strength of your studies—planting your feet firmly in the ground—you can avoid falling in the face of secular glory, benefits, and power.

If you do not do this, you will gain nothing. The more you season something, the more it will lack flavor. The more you bore through something, the harder it becomes, making it impossible to pierce. Then, you will not be able to avoid your heart growing lazy. You will not be able to avoid your thoughts being obstructed and your will being compromised. In addition, the ensuing assertions regarding secular profit and loss, fortune and misfortune will lure you out and intimidate you. They will progressively melt down your original aims, enticing you to supplant your original intentions—eventually, you will want to compromise with the world.

You hope the world accepts you.

At this stage, very few people will consider it a bad thing to turn their backs on the *dao* and seek profits! This is something about which to be deeply worried, though I am not sure what your thoughts are regarding this matter.

Although I continue my study of the *origins*, I still do not know whether I have mastered them. I have dared to discuss the matter in response to your question; please set me straight regarding this matter. I have heard that the mind is the origin of all things, and nature is the source of everything good. When previous Confucian scholars discussed learning, they mentioned as the first things to repair, reeling in a lackadaisical heart and nurturing moral character. By completing the study of the origins, they believed a person would have laid the groundwork for gathering the *dao* and expanding his studies. Where else could he expect to start his studies?

Concentrate on one thing without departing[4] while being cautious and apprehensive.[5] Study on concentrating on one thing without departing has a relationship with the movements of emotions; caution and apprehension exist inside the boundaries where emotions have yet to arise. You must not forget to do either one of these two things. However, it is more urgent to control your *exterior* and cultivate your *interior*. Therefore, the "three examinations,"[6] the "three principles of conduct,"[7] and the "four inhibitions"[8] are all equivalent in cultivating your original studies. If people fail to do this and continue with a study centered only on the mind, very few will be able to escape becoming mired in the views of Buddha. What do you think?

Regarding your arguments about the *Four-Seven*, I have received your teachings—they will stir some commotion.[9] I have written my opinions separately. Although I am embarrassed as I may have been imprudent, overstepping my bounds, I ask that you carefully compare. Furthermore, regarding the phrases, "A void and formless mind is separated into principle and material force" and "Principle is completely void without any counterpart," you mentioned you were uneasy about these phrases but offered no reason for your uneasiness. Unclear as to how I should respond, I did not attach another clause with a written response. I ask you to reveal your thoughts and to expunge my foolishness.

Jajung received orders to escort. Because he abruptly returned to Seoul, I could not give him my letter to deliver. I wrote this letter and wanted to send it to Jajung through a courier. However, I am not sure if you are still in Seoul or if you have returned to Honam. Perhaps this letter will float around before getting to you. Placing this paper before me, words did not come easily, as I felt anxious. The cold will soon reach its climax, and it will be the season of frost. Cherish yourself for the ages. I respectfully bow and inform.

Jiajing (The era of Shizong of the Ming Dynasty)[10]
October 24, 1559 (the Year of the Sheep)
Bowing,
The invalid, Hwang.

Although it appears as if my letter frequently mentions concerns about hardships without reason, worries naturally fill me, as I am old and have experienced many things. Please do not consider it peculiar. In my view, man can barely reach completion regarding this matter if man studies while embracing a lifetime of adversity; however, whether in the past or the present, man's futile fame spreading from the very first step causes this kind of hardship, which merits it as being something of which to be afraid.

While not fully realizing the level of learning wanted, you might be surprised at the people's reception, as they begin to raise you to the level and entrust you with the work of the sages and wise men. However, if you do not know how to fear this and accept it and you assume yourself a sage or a wise man, you have no choice but to fool yourself and others by covering up, embellishing your name and the facts. Circumstances will always dictate that this happen; how can we consider it odd when all this ends in failure!

> *Therefore, fame and admiration are not always good news, and suddenly entering a government post is not something about which to rejoice nor is it something to be coveted.*

You cannot live the rest of your life without risking your life if you are in an important position, revered by many people. Although you may not feel the urgency of my message, later in life, when you confront such a predicament, my words will come to mind. I implore you to write these words indelibly in your heart and place being prudent and methodical as the highest priority.

I can write this in my letter now, but later, when you grow and rise in power, it will be difficult for me, someone who has retired from office, to correspond with you in this leisurely fashion. Therefore, I have spoken without hesitation everything that is on my mind.

---

1. Hu Kanghou refers to the Confucian scholar, Hu Anguo, who lived in the Song period. In his biography, he mentions that the remark about launching and withdrawing from office were said in response to Zhu Zhen. See the *History of Song* 435, "Biographies" 194, "Confucian Scholars" 5.

2. "Tsze-hsia said, 'The officer, *having discharged all his duties*, should devote his leisure to learning. The student, having completed his learning, should apply himself to be an officer.'" See the *Confucian Analects*, Book XIX: "Tsze-chang," Chapter XIII.

3. Master Cheng refers to the Song philosopher, Cheng Yi. A custom existed where an officer submitted a document requesting payment of his salary, but it was never submitted. See the *Reflections on Things at Hand*, Chapter VII: "On Serving or Not Serving in the Government, Advancing or Withdrawing, and Accepting or Declining Office." Refer to Clause 31.

4. "Reverence refers to focusing on one thing but not leaving." This is mentioned in Zhu Xi's commentary on the *Confucian Analects*, Book I: "Hsio R," Chapter V.

5. This is a phrase mentioned in chapter I of *The Doctrine of the Mean*.

6. "The philosopher Tsang said, 'I daily examine myself on three points:—whether, in transacting business for others, I may have been not faithful;—whether in intercourse with friends, I may have been not sincere;—whether I may have not mastered and practiced the instructions of my teacher.'" See the *Confucian Analects*, Book I: "Hsio R," Chapter IV.

7. "There are three principles of conduct which the man of high rank should consider specially important:—that in his deportment and manner he keep from violence and heedlessness; that in regulating his countenance he keep near to sincerity; and that in his words and tones he keep far from lowness and impropriety. As to such matters as attending to the sacrificial vessels, there are the proper officers for them." See the *Confucian Analects*, Book VIII: "Tai-po," Chapter IV.

8. "The Master replied, 'Look not at what is contrary to propriety; listen not to what is contrary to propriety; speak not what is contrary to propriety; make no movement which is contrary to propriety.' Yen Yuan then said, 'Though I am deficient in intelligence and vigour, I will make it my business to practise this lesson.'" See the *Confucian Analects*, Book XII: "Yen Yuan," Chapter I.

9. "The Master said, 'I do not open up the truth to one who is not eager *to get knowledge*, nor help out any one who is not anxious to explain himself. When I have presented one corner of a subject to any one, and he cannot from it learn the other three, I do not repeat my lesson.'" See the *Confucian Analects*, Book VII: "Shu R," Chapter VIII.

10. The era of Shizong of the Ming Dynasty.

[Letter #7 Toegye Writes Gobong]

Hoping a Gentle Friend Completes His Studies

I greet you, Myeongeon, and inquire about your well-being.

The year has changed. After such an auspicious time, may I assume that your accomplishments grow more profound and noble? Words cannot convey the extent to which I miss you.

I planned to write and send you a letter during the beginning of winter last year. I wanted Jajung to deliver the letter, but I reconsidered when realizing Jajung would come south on orders as an envoy. If he had already departed from Seoul, we would have missed each other—he could not have delivered the letter.

Time lingered on.

Winter passed.

Jajung left for the south and did not return for a long time. Finally, today, I asked him to deliver this letter, but I am not sure when it will reach you.

The official gazette for the Royal Secretariat[1] never makes it here. Therefore, I am not sure how they graded you in the yearend *jeonchoe*.[2] How many years of vacation did you receive? Upon returning home, I assume you reacquainted yourself with and put in order your old studies. Undoubtedly, your studying was more coherent. I am sure you could understand the more profound meaning. I lament being unable to visit freely.

Frequently catching the cold in the winter, I am resting and taking care of myself; however, I have all but abandoned my studies because my mind and eyes grow dim. As the prospects for any progress in my studies grow faint, I have nothing of worth to say.

I hope a gentle friend like you completes his studies.

I hope to hear floating in my ears, praise that you have made the hearts of the people kind and that you have helped the king in his rule.

I sent you this letter without sealing it because Jeongi Jeong[3] wanted to see my foolish assertions regarding the *Four-Seven*. After Jeongi reads it, I have arranged for Jajung to return it. He will give it to you along with a letter. If you send your brief response to Jajung's place, it will most assuredly be delivered to me.

In conclusion, please cherish yourself for the ages.

I end my letter here.

February 5, 1560 (the Year of the Monkey)

---

1. Or *jeobo*; refers to the official gazette written about the matters conducted at the Royal Secretariat; it was recorded and distributed every morning.

2. *Jeonchoe* refers to the examining and grading of an official's service record. The results were classified into grade—the best being "Choe" and the worst being "Jeon." This was performed twice a year on June 15 and December 15.

3. Refers to Jiun "Chuman" Jeong.

[Letter #8 Gobong Writes Toegye]

Afraid of Becoming Spineless, Like a Bug without Bones

I respectfully reply to you teacher, Toegye.
Daeseung deeply lowers his head, bows twice, and speaks.
When I was in Seoul last autumn, I sent a letter through my colleague, Jajung Jeong, inquiring about your well-being. By telling you pettily of all my shallow thoughts, I asked for your guidance, and I wanted you to correct my writings. By receiving your guidance, I did not want to stray in times of hardship.

Like a blind man, I wanted to see.
Like a deaf man, I wanted to hear.

My health progressively deteriorated and I feared staying far away from home for a long time. Without waiting for a response, I put into action my plans for an expedient return; but that does not mean I do not miss you earnestly or think about you.

I received a bad score on the *jeonchoe*[1] because I had not recuperated from my illness. Although I could not avoid people pointing fingers and turning against me, it is fair to say I have found my proper place when surveying my original intentions. When I imagine you savoring the *dao* in leisure, I want to visit and keep you company; however, I cannot go, as I am here in Honam, a long distance away. Regarding the letter I asked about the last time, I have not received it yet because I was in some remote, far away place. Could you blame me for sighing when seeing the fallen leaves!

However, finally, half way through April, a friend of mine traveling from Seoul, delivered your letter dated October 24, as well as Jajung's letter, one document of the *Four-Seven Thesis*, and the shorter letters you sent this February. I read and reread your letters and learned that you were doing well. You guided me and opened my eyes by warning me about the most important points. It felt as if I was with you and we were chatting—needless to say, I was unexpectedly overjoyed. I am ecstatic and grateful that someone so uneducated and foolish could have reached this level through the help and encouragement of a man of such virtue.

As August rolls around, the weather has turned slightly chilly. I hope you will find profit in raising the *dao*. I hope your life is filled with blessings.

Letter #8

I am preserving my worthless self because I know you are thinking about me from afar. However, as I have suffered through several major illnesses, I have lost incredible amounts of energy. My illness has finally regressed into consumption. Catching an illness is easy but managing the illness and recovering has been difficult. After frantically scurrying about, taking care of various matters, I was bedridden for several days because of fatigue.

I am in nothing but agony.

Furthermore, I left my government post and moved back to the country primarily to stop my activities and to cure my illness; I wanted to reacquaint myself with the ways of the old studies.

However, the stains marked on my disposition were hard to erase. The entanglements of the world were ponderous.

I feel anguished trying to comply with human relationships. My illness grows more acute, my studies thwarted with each passing day. It is not that I am incognizant of this: I lack the courage to conquer and discipline myself. Engrossed in my daily routine, I am helplessly anxious and afraid. What is the best thing for me to do?

I carefully read the letters you sent. You lucidly discuss in detail the way to contend with the world and the way to study the *dao*.

You have taught a blind man to see.
You have taught a deaf man to hear.

This is what is meant in the saying the benefits received from those who make me are equal to the benefits received from those who gave birth to me. What else can I do but to feel this in the depth of my bones and follow your words to the day I die! I feel very fortunate.

Concerning some of the things you wrote, I dare to trouble you by disclosing all my thoughts. I respectfully ask and it would be a relief if you would consider my thoughts. Whenever reciting Hu Kanghou's words—"A man must decide for himself whether he will enter or leave his government post"—while thinking he is correct, at the same time, I have always been skeptical. A long time ago, the teacher, Huian,[2] always consulted various fellow teachers including Nanxuan[3] and Donglai[4] through letters regarding entering government service. As I am a junior scholar, need I say more!

You say in so many words, "If one is not precise regarding reason and one's will is weak, the decision one makes will be unjust." You are truly correct; this was precisely the point upon which I harbored doubts. Since I have now learned this in detail, I have come to understand this point as well as others. Instead of acting only transiently, I will be able to conform to your words by devoting myself until exhausted of life. I had contemplated making the decision on my own; if I had done that, I might have missed many things, right?

Regarding what you wrote in your letters about your personal experiences and the reason why the worries of the world entangle the scholars of our country, I thought the same way from an early age, perhaps not as thoroughly; however, I was not entirely sure if I was right. Not only were your teachings precise and earnest like counting under the light of a burning candle, but also what you wrote on the annex was like a divination sign,[5] detailed and exact. Reading this prompted profound self-examination. You discuss in detail about the circumstances when I should speak, when I should decide the path to travel, when to make up my mind, and when to control my actions. You were like a ghost, the way you pinpointed everything as if you could see everything. It reminds me of the saying, "Mr. Yu knows me better than I know myself."[6] I have heard, "A doctor can prescribe medication and cure a patient once he knows the origin of the disease." You know the origin of my disease. I respectfully ask that you show me the cure in detail. Please stop me from becoming a worthless human being.

During the course of our exchanges, I feel compelled to mention something about which I feel uneasy. In my last letter, I wrote, "When conduct becomes difficult, I worry only that my studies have been incomplete. If my learning had been complete, acting would not be difficult absolutely." I have spoken these words during ordinary times but likened this to a starving, thirsty man talking about food: I am not saying I have become that person. However, while carefully reading your words, I got the impression that you thought I considered myself as someone who had completed my studies and was consequently free of hardship regarding conduct. I am ashamed and speechless. I know that you directed your words to someone in the learning position, to set him straight; but as a junior scholar, how can I feel at ease after receiving such admonishment?

A Confucian scholar does not do things like "fly high" or "go far." How can I make a decision on my own when I have not made any preparations throughout my life to make such a decision! Your

Letter #8

advice to consider entering and leaving office is truly something I had planned to do. I was able to lower my head, withstand the personal insults during the *myeonsillye* because I embraced this frame of mind. Now, since one illness after another strikes me, making (work) extremely hard to bear, I thought about leaving office temporarily: by departing, it was not that I never contemplated returning. However, as your letter warns, it was a concern:

I might walk down the wrong path.
I might grow comfortable with mediocrity.
I might nod my head to the customs of the secular world and sink into filthiness.

It is frightening to think of the possibility that I will harmonize with the secular world, that I will ask it to accept me and turn my back on the *dao* and pursue personal gain.

In the past, early one day when in Seoul, Hwasuk Bak and I invited teacher Chuman, and we discussed this very matter. I said at the time, "In the end, I am worried I will become spineless like a bug without bones." In response, teacher Chuman laughed heartily in seeming agreement. In most cases, people fall easily for visible profits and eye-catching splendors. The assertions of profit and loss, fortune and misfortune, that entice and intimidate people cut the flesh and pierce the bones. It looks as if these people have become bugs without bones and ultimately that is what they become. What is so odd about this! Fortunately, I will have several years of relaxation since I have left my government post. However, I worry about the time after, well aware I will confront indescribable hardships; I do not know what plan will be effective in coping with the situation.

Although my foundation is feeble, my spirit is strong and vigorous. My fame has spread before my actions have been perfected. If a feeble foundation lacks honest execution, a person becomes negligent in preserving himself. If he clings to a futile name through a strong and vigorous spirit, he will be deficient in responding to others. As I have a strong character, despise evil, and am outspoken, even someone like Ji Shuye[7] would have difficulty coping with me. How can I be useful to the world!

In today's world, when seeking out people, the realties of a person are not discriminated: people simply gather around hallow names. Therefore, people recognize and revere me. They want to place me in a post where I will be exposed, appear pristine, and look better than I really am. Although I try to graciously decline, I have no viable excuse. I want to escape but I have no plan. I am truly worried.

If people had ostracized me from the onset, considering me odd and offensive, I would have left for the country, dying an old man without regrets. However, I worry people will not readily ostracize me, time will linger on, and the number of people who dislike me will grow; disaster will strike at every opportunity, misfortune will hit at every possible occasion; and, I will end up walking down a dangerous path where previous wagons have tumbled. I tremble in fear, lose sleep, and worry about such an erroneous scheme. I do not know what to do.

However, since you have reiterated your teachings in such a meticulous manner, naturally, I will try to adhere to your guidance without losing hold of them. Merely, I have been going through this kind of turmoil. For this reason, I have been stammering and back peddling pressing to resign obstinately and hoping people of the world will forget about me. If this plan does not come into fruition, unquestionably, I will make a strong effort: I will leave my fate to the heavens. Need I say more about the questions of life and death, fortune and misfortune? Merely, since my learning has been deficient, I do not trust myself; therefore, I am worried that what I have learned will gradually wither away. How can I not exert more of an effort in reeling in a lackadaisical heart and nurturing moral character? I humbly hope that you will teach me to the end.

Teacher Haseo or otherwise known as Mr. Gim[8] lived in Jangseong, which is only about ten kilometers from my home. After leaving my government post and returning home, I immediately leaned on this teacher hoping to learn the old teachings from him. However, the teacher suddenly fell ill and passed away on January 16. The *dao* could not have suffered a greater misfortune, and my personal misfortune could not have been greater. When questions arise while meditating, there is nobody to ask. I realize I will never be able to meet that teacher again. Silently, I try to quell the sadness but to no avail. I know you were also acquainted with him for a long time. You must have been hurt as well when you heard the news.

I ask in detail about the respective clauses of the *Four-Seven Thesis,* and I have written the questions down separately in the book. There are many pestiferous words, as I was trying to explain my thoughts. I am guilty of speaking straightforwardly, absurdly,

and even arrogantly. Would it be possible for you to respond pertinently?
Cherish yourself for the ages and the *dao*.
I respectfully offer this unpolished letter.
Year 39 of Jiajing (The era of Shizong of the Ming Dynasty)
August 8, 1560 (the Year of the Monkey)
Junior scholar, Gobong respectfully bows deeply, once then twice, and sends this letter to teacher, Toegye.

Attachment [Letter #8]

I might have to trouble you again as I have a personal wish. I have always lamented my inability to work prudently because of my shabby character and lethargy. I was unable to rid myself of this habit whenever things happened. Most likely, this stems from my shortcoming of being unable to fix a purpose.

Last year, I wrote several letters to you. I wrote the letters carefully but failed to keep a copy of them. Thinking about it later, I realized it was an impolite thing to do because when I received your responses, what I had previously written grew remote—I could not remember the meaning of my previous words. The significance of exchanging letters has diminished as a result. I apologize. If you have not discarded my letters, I ask you to return them to me or I hope your private secretary[9] can copy and send the letters back to me. There is no hidden agenda in requesting this. I simply want to view our discussions from beginning to end.

As soon as I received your teachings, I immediately wanted to write a thank you letter, but I could not muster an outline, as I kept getting ill. After some time had elapsed, I finally arrived at a rough draft but coincidently left for the countryside and apathetically could not make revisions immediately and procrastinated until today. Inflicted with a light illness, I was barely able to hold the brush; I apologize to no end as my handwriting is less than proper and my arguments anything but detailed.

I want to use the "jon" character in naming my library. Would it be possible to write in big letters "Jon Jae"? Furthermore, I have included two bundles of blank sheets of paper. Would it be possible to write some words in square style or cursive whenever you have spare time? I want to make a folding screen and look at it during leisurely interludes. I would appreciate it if you wrote something from the "Wuyi Rowing Songs"[10] or some good aphorisms from Zhu Xi's poetry. Please consider this.

I did not know the head Gwangju official, Mr. Ryu,[11] but I had the opportunity to meet him several times after coming here; he seemed like a decent man. I heard he was from Andong, not far from your hometown. He said, "I want to meet Yi Hwang when I visit my ancestral graves in autumn." When I told him I wanted to send a letter to you, he had already agreed to deliver it. He will most likely visit his ancestral graves in early winter. If you meet him, would you consider asking him to deliver your letters to me? Since there will be couriers traveling back and forth on holidays, it will be easier to frequently exchange letters if we are both aware of this.

I do not have many servants because my family is poor; I have difficulty delivering letters. This time, I asked the magistrate of Jangseong, Yuseong Jo, to deliver my letters. Mr. Jo is a gifted scholar and he also has a fixed purpose in the *Learning of the Way*; he did not turn down my request. Please be advised.

Daeseung respectfully prostrates himself and bows.

Added note: I am sending you two rolls of Chinese paper. I ask you to write inscriptions for my two libraries, one that reads "Control a Lost Mind" and the other that reads "Be Virtuous." How about writing something like, "Words to be impressed in Jonjae's* heart," and enlightening a younger scholar? I bow once again.

Although I have poured out every tiny thought I possess and virtually nothing remains, I have another personal request. These days, because of greeting people, I had been meandering about and on one occasion, I regretted drinking too much and losing consciousness. By chance, I read a poem written by Zhu Xi, which was carried in the "Helinyuluji": he talks about guarding over himself. They said it was written about Mr. Hu[12] or "Zhanan." I was stupefied for quite some time after reading it, unable to understand it. Shortly after, I perused *The Complete Works of Zhu Xi* and I came across a title that read, "Two Passages of a Poem Advising Self Caution Written after Seeing the Theme on the Wall of Mr. Hu of Meixi's Tavern." The first verse from the top reads:

> *Lust to live, not embarrassed to eat cattle feed and beans*
> *Brazenly returns and plays with the noble man*

Letter #8

Do not wash sleeves in the pure water
I worry your dirty sleeves will spoil the pure water

Another verse reads:

Floating adrift for ten years, regarding yourself lightly
Returning, affections rise when looking at Ligian's dimples
Nothing more sinister in the world than a man's desire
How many have led a lifetime of wrong

Having affections for Ligian's dimples refers to Zhanan's saying:

Thanks to the king's grace, I have come home, enjoying leisure
Sitting next to me, dimples form in Ligian's cheek

    This refers to the *gisaeng* (song and dance girl), Ligian. Zhu Xi sighed and mocked Zhanan for his failed life.

    I am not sure what "Lust to live . . . to eat cattle feed and beans" means. There are no books here to help and I am dying of curiosity. I would appreciate a detailed explanation. These two passages urgently warn those who learn to control desire and to put themselves in order. Would it be possible to transcribe these two passages? I want to hang them on my wall in the room and reflect as I walk in and out of my room.

    I have thought about this repeatedly, as the ancient ones said this was a hard habit to break. The roots being so deep and firm, it is difficult to talk about this. If man cannot detect the signs, spot them early, and block them, he will most assuredly drown in a pit. How many will be able to escape and avoid leading failed lives? I do not know how to study to erase these thoughts and avoid drowning in a pit. I hope you can guide me regarding this matter; I will keep your words engraved in my heart.

    I truly committed a rash act by troubling you with such trivial requests impertinently. Since I can be very narrow-minded, I have no choice but to depend on and gain strength from someone who is already so enlightened. I have dared to speak repeatedly about this matter. It would be an enormous relief if you consider this.

    Junior scholar, Daeseung "Gobong" Gi, lowers his head, respectfully bows, and writes this.

    Jiajing (The era of Shizong of the Ming Dynasty)
    August 6, 1560 (the Year of the Monkey)

1. This was said in response to Toegye who asked about the results of the *jeonchoe* (evaluation of merits for officials).
2. Refers to Zhu Xi (1130-1200), the Confucian scholar of the Southern Song Dynasty in China.
3. Refers to the Confucian scholar, Zhang Shi, in the China Southern Song Dynasty period. His pseudonym was Jingfu and to other people he went by the alias of Teacher Nanxuan. He was very good friends with Zhu Xi.
4. Refers to the Confucian scholar, Lu Zuquan, in the China Southern Song Dynasty period. His pseudonym was Bogong and he was called by his alias, Teacher Donglai, in public. He along with Zhu Xi and Zhang Shi were called the "Three Worthy Men in Southeast China." The *Reflections on Things at Hand*, which he wrote with Zhu Xi, was especially well-known.
5. Or *sigwi*. Refers to the yarrow and the back skin of a turtle, which was used to predict one's fortune. It was considered as accurate as a divination sign.
6. See the *Comprehensive Mirror for Aid in Government* 95.
7. Refers to Xi Kang from the Jin Dynasty. Shuye was his pseudonym. He was a member of the Seven Sages of the Bamboo Grove and wrote "Nourishing Life" in his fondness for Lao-Zhuang's philosophy. He was famous for his open mind and poker face.
8. Refers to Inhu Gim. His pseudonym was Huji or Haseo and his pen name was Damjae.
9. Or *sisa*. Refers to a person in charge of handling a superior's documents at close quarters.
10. Wuyi was the name of a mountain that was located in the southern Chongan County in the Fujian Province. This mountain was famous for its nine valleys. Zhu Xi established the Wuyi Jingshe Academy on the fifth valley and wrote "The Rowing Songs about the Wuyi Nine Turning Streams" in 1184.
11. Refers to Gyeongsim Ryu. His pen name was Guchon and his pseudonym was Taeho.
  * This was another pen name for Gobong.
12. Refers to Hu Qian of the China Song Dynasty Period.

[Letter #9 Toegye Writes Gobong]

If You Discover Your Illness and Want to Cure It

I reply to you, Jonjae,

I respectfully bow my head twice. Although my visit to Seoul two years ago during the Year of the Horse was an utter failure, I felt fortunate because I was able to meet you. After that, I went south and since I ceased all travels and contact, we did not have the opportunity to meet again. While missing you unceasingly, you can imagine the joy I felt when I received your letter and the dissertation regarding the *Four-Seven* from Jajung. I immediately wrote a response and jotted down all my diminutive thoughts.

In addition, there were some questionable points regarding the *Four-Seven Thesis* and I could not hastily agree with your opinions. I roughly wrote my opinions and asked Jajung to set things straight on my behalf. Although I had no choice—as I sought the help of an upright, sincere friend realize my foolishness—I fear I might have been somewhat thoughtless. When I reconsidered after some time had elapsed, I realized I was uncomfortable with several points I had made in my view, but I did not have time to make revisions.

Jajung came down from Seoul this autumn and showed me the letter you had sent to Chuman Jeong. In several parts of your letter, you argue against my views, and regarding some of those parts, I have already reached an understanding. Near the end of your letter, you mentioned you would include in your reply an analysis of each clause. Since then, I have been eagerly anticipating your response. You have sent someone long distance to deliver a book that includes lessons about my writings, as well as revisions to incorrect parts. The arguments and proofs are plentiful and detailed; it reveals in detail your worries about guiding those who have lost their way. As the hot summer passes and the cool autumn approaches, I was unspeakably thrilled to learn that you were refreshed and blessed, as the heavens had helped to make your life very peaceful.

Lacking talent, void of any decent merits and never free from illness, when I entered a government post, people criticized me for being selfish. They criticized me for not being able to do the work properly. When I left my government post, people chastised me for betraying the king's grace by stammering and hiding in shame. These days, I grow decrepit; my mind grows befuddled; my eyes grow dim; and, my body withers like an emaciated wisteria. Soon it will be hard to classify me as human. I cannot turn back the time.

> *If I understood the dao in the morning, nothing would be better than dying in the evening.*

However, I lack the help and urgings of splendid teachers and diligent friends. Reading tattered books, I had reached some level of understanding, but what I had gained was incomplete and what little I have learned is beginning to crumble. Discussing moral duty and righteousness is futile, like trying to catch the wind or catch a shadow, and when I try to make a standard of consciousness, it seems as if I am doing it by force; therefore, many contradictions arise. Although I try to gain strength through the advice and guidance of good friends like you, ultimately I lack the admirable sincerity and the posture to open my heart and accept such advice and guidance; I believe I will fall short to a great degree in matching your sincerity.

Since I am the benefactor of your warm kindness, I hope you will teach me until the end, responding to each clause. However, dimwitted as I am, I can understand neither the sentences nor their meanings without many days of careful deliberation. I have quickly skimmed through your arguments and they are very extensive and subtle; except realizing my faults regarding the clause that good and evil are not defined, my thoughts have been remote, and I have not been able to grasp even the major points. On top of that, I did not have the time to study it as guests visited me for several days in succession. Because I could not keep the courier waiting, I wrote cursorily in my reply. I will save discussion on the debated clauses and send them on a later date through Taeho Ryu's courier. Generously forgive my lack of nimbleness. Will this be possible?

My good friend, you have learned extensively and achieved much. You have started a long journey riding a good wagon. Any other ordinary person would have undoubtedly proclaimed their work to be finished, professed greatness, and would have been satisfied unceasingly. On the contrary, you are not satisfied with the worldly successes you have achieved but make an effort to seek the truth. Regarding receiving the worst grade in the evaluation of merits[1]—how fortunate that the heavens have given you trials to make you complete! You had already grasped everything I mentioned in my letters sent last year, but my incomplete thoughts could not keep up with your understanding. In your letter, you did not regard my opinions to be wrong, but continuously reiterated explanations. I sense in your posture great generosity which enables you to embrace almost anything even those things that are presumably worthless.

I felt enormous relief.

Regarding the debate on entering and leaving government posts, you mentioned being skeptical about Kanghou's advice to make such a decision on your own. You were right when saying Huian consulted his friends. However, you should be aware that when Huian establishes a view, it soars like a towering cliff, and he does not waver or change because of what others say.

Furthermore, I mentioned I had no choice when confronting the times and the circumstances because of the hardship I endured; these are the words of a weak, dispirited, and cowering old man. However, you are in your prime, full of energy, but you do not reject me for being so lowly. You seek the profound meaning! Most assuredly, this is possible because you are loyal and you know how to conduct yourself properly!

A foolish doctor cannot give the proper diagnosis for a disease. How can he dare prescribe any medication? I heard Zhu Xi say early on:

> If you know and want to cure your disease, the will to cure that disease is the medication.

My good friend, please do not seek cures from others. If you find the answer in this phrase and place its acupuncture needle in the place where you hurt, you will discover a wondrous effect, which you would not be possible through eating bitter medicine.

Regarding the clause, "If my learning had been complete, acting would not be difficult," when I read this, I suspected you regarded yourself as a man who behaved in this manner. However, after reading your letter, I realized I misunderstood what you meant.

Regarding what you wrote after the passage "consider entering and leaving office," your demeanor and words were all good. In your letter you say, "It was like counting under candlelight, accurate as if divinely forecasted." If you said this referring to yourself, you might have been correct, but these words do not apply to me. Your words, "bug without bones," are worthy of a hearty laugh. This bug must not crawl down the wrong path of its predecessors; it must be heedful of the path it travels. This matter cannot be treated lightly, but must be treated delicately as if Cook Ding skillfully wields his knife.[2]

As the staunchest of vassals, Master Cheng and Zhu Xi witnessed all forms of misdeeds but did not let them slide nor did they become entangled in hardship because, if they were uncomfortable with something, they doggedly declined and adamantly pushed their wills. However, today the road for a vassal to discard and leave his government post has become forever impassable. If there is someone who wants to retire from his post, not only will the king deny his request, but also he will garner the anger and jealousy of many people. He will never again be able to leave or escape; he will be swirled up with other people.

> *If a scholar enters the royal court, he becomes a fish caught on a hook.*

The majority of those who are upright and despise wickedness will not be able to escape calamity. The sycophants and the feeble-minded will mix and exude a false sense of power and become grovelers.

Both scenarios are lamentable.

Even before the wagon leaves, its rumbling noise reverberates everywhere, and before closing the lid of his coffin, nobody will tolerate somebody who regrets before dying. Rushing to engage in politics before reaching a certain level of virtue is like turning over a pot of rice (before it is ready). With a sincerity that is unreliable, creating a fuss without giving up your post is the way to bring shame to yourself. You can trace the failure of the people who came before us to this point. Therefore, if you want to concentrate on the studies only, the best course of action would be to leave your post and hide. I mentioned this in my last letter because it came up by chance.

You must not imitate the moth that flies into a flame.

It is not reasonable to incur death by being pummeled while standing next to a wall made of rocks and dirt.

When somebody is not as ill as I am and has no choice but to enter the world, it is proper for him to keep his place and uphold all his responsibilities. There is a definitive law about discarding the fish and choosing the bear's paw.[3] That is what we mean when we say:

> Do not concern yourself with dying young or old but wait for death while cultivating virtue.

So, what is the difference between entering and not entering the world? In your letter, you mention, "I will do my best to follow the heavenly mandate." Those words are sincere and precise. In short, by embracing the heart to be dismissed from government service, adhere to these words, and if you do not change in the end, you will not betray what you have learned. It would be an enormous relief if you, my friend, made an effort to fulfill both of our hopes.

Haseo Gim and I had the opportunity to spend some time together while working at the Royal College and the Office of the Royal Lecturers. He liked traveling around, especially enjoying the outdoors. In his prime—because the majority of the places where he started his studies followed the Lao-Zhuang philosophy—pitifully, his conduct had become slovenly because of an excessive lifestyle of drinking and poems in the prime of his life. However, I have heard that during the twilight years of his life, he embraced the studies, and recently I had the chance to read his discussion about the studies; he had become quite insightful, which impressed me, as I imagine he had gained all this during leisurely times. However, upon hearing news of his sudden passing, I was filled with matchless sorrow. I have sent a consolatory letter to his son; I hope you will convey my deepest condolences.

Regarding the request written in your annex, I have asked the children to copy three of your letters. Concerning your request to write "Jon Jae" in big letters and writing something on the white sheets of paper and Chinese paper, how can I refuse? I will comply with your request; however, I must confess that I usually grow tired after writing on several pieces of paper and it gets worse with each passing day. Will I get the results I want by forcing the issue? If I make myself write, I worry the work will be sloppy and unworthy of appreciation. Need I say more about writing something like "Words impressed in the heart"? I plan to do this and send these things in the winter by coordinating schedules with Taeho Ryu's household courier, but I am not sure if things will go as planned.

Taeho Ryu's native home is somewhat far away from here. Furthermore, do you think it will be easy for him to visit me after traveling long distances to get home? Since meeting him will be onerous, I want to send my letters through his courier. This will be better than asking favors of a friend who has traveled all the way from Seoul. The possibility exists that rumors will spread rampantly if I send this letter through a friend but such fears are absolved if sent in this manner.

In conclusion, I respectfully end this letter, imploring you to cherish yourself for the studies. I respectfully bow and offer these words for my good friend, Jonjae.

Year 39 of Jiajing (The era of Shizong of the Ming Dynasty)
September 1, 1560 (the Year of the Monkey)
The old and invalid, Yi Hwang of Jinseong, apologizes for writing so haphazardly, as his vision dims.

It has been a long time since I have heard the name Iljae Yi, and I do not know what his studies are like. I received "The Exchanges While Discussing the Supreme Ultimate." I did not have time to look at it carefully but I captured the general essence of the work. I feel very relieved.

Although there is nothing much for me to say regarding the merits and demerits of his words, I will tell you the points about which I had suspicion on a later day. However, I will say one thing: I realized he had a festering disease when considering the warnings mentioned by the ancient ones, "You think you are only right and fail to consider anybody else." What can we do when considering this is not a minor ailment? Although there are one or two dubious points, they are not worth considering. We can discuss the studies with him only after he has cured this disease.

I know I am being impudent and rash by saying this. However, it may seem reasonable for you to scold briskly IlJae's faults, but you might not be able to break free from those same faults yourself. Or is it possible that I have been unable to liberate myself from those same faults and consequently misunderstood your explanation? I will meditate profoundly on this issue again and reflect.

On a later date, please tell me who Wang Yuanze is, in which books his words appear and explain their meanings. I have often heard senior scholars lament that Zhanan had lost his integrity. I felt uneasy, as I could not discover the origin of the verse, "Lust to live, not embarrassed to eat cattle feed and beans." However, I can guess Zhu Xi said this because Zhanan followed the steps of others,

unable to escape losing his integrity, considering (Zhu Xi's) usage of the "seop" character in the phrase, "Brazenly, he returns to play with the noble man."
I save the rest for later.
Hwang speaks again.

---

1. Or *jeongo*. In that year, Gobong received the worst grade in the Office of Diplomatic Documentation's evaluation of merits.
2. Refers to the essential portion where tendons attach to the bones. Cook Ding refers to the man whose skills for butchering an ox transcended human power after training for 19 years. See the *Chuang Tzu*, Chapter III: "Nourishment of the Soul."
3. "Mencius said, 'I like fish, and I also like bear's paws. If I cannot have the two together, I will let the fish go, and take the bear's paws. So, I like life, and I also like righteousness. If I cannot keep the two together, I will let life go, and choose righteousness.'" See *The Works of Mencius*, Book VI: "Kao Tsze" Part I, Chapter X.

[Letter #10 Toegye Writes Gobong]

Regarding the Rowing Songs about the Wuyi Nine Turning Streams

For *Jeongja* Gi:
Since the last time I sent a letter, autumn has passed and winter is nearly half over. How do you like your present situation of savoring the *dao* in relative leisure? Undoubtedly, you are reacquainting yourself with your old studies and discovering new things; I am guessing you are making daily progress. Fortunately, antiquated as I am, I have been able to avoid the discussions of a chaotic world and have been taking care of my diseased body, barely. The other parts of my life are not even worth discussing.

After receiving your response, I could not dare forsake your earnestness; I write in and send this book, which contains all my trivial views. However, my ideas are shallow and my discussion drawn out. I am ashamed you might find it cumbersome to read.

Being somewhat far away, I had difficulty guessing when Taeho Ryu's courier would be available. I gave my letters to the house servant and asked him to send it when a courier was available. I am not sure when those letters will be delivered. I have sent various scrapbooks and letters written on a tablet, as well. Although I have many things I want to say, I dare not trouble you further and end my letter. I sincerely hope you will send a response letter that will ride the winds to me.

I worry as I look at this paper before me.
I respectfully bow and write this letter,
From Hwang.
November 5, 1560 (the Year of the Monkey)
Please look at the "Ten Poems Which Were Composed by Using the Rhymes in the Nine Turning Streams."

As you requested, I have written and sent Huian's "Poem Advising Self Caution Written after Seeing the Theme on the Wall of Mr. Hu of Meixi's Tavern." After reading your letter, I noticed you learned to guard against, to be very cautious of, and to eradicate in advance the two harms, and thus avoided the shame of falling into a pit. You showed good intentions.

When reflecting on my life, I had fallen into a pit about ten years ago, only able to climb out of that pit after I had been dispirited by old age and disease—reaching a certain level of ruin. However, occasionally, I feel like the man walking home at night who has a weakness for observing hunters[1]: I am always afraid and cautious not to fall into that pit again. As this is the case, when will I find the time to help you?

I must be well endowed to be able to teach people so that when I speak, my words will be forceful; I will be able to affect people. However, how can I expect to affect people with my words if I am not that much different! However, since we have a relationship that depends on moral principle, I could not remain silent when you asked me to set you on the right path: I have answered boldly and with sincerity. I do not think we need to discuss this matter again, but I think you will find sufficient adhering to the motto poems* I send you.

If you know how to raise your moral character, you will not disregard the lucidity of the heavens and your obligation as a human being by acting like a cunning and sly person. If you know how to garner a frazzled mind, you will absolutely possess a respectful mind; you will preserve an earnest mind; you will block before seeing hints of plotting; and, you will exert an effort to be cautious when alone. If you accomplish these things, you will be able to suppress desire and guard over yourself. However, this is the danger of human desire:

> You might possess a temperament and integrity lofty enough to pierce the sun and stars, which bolster the heavens and earth, but in an instant, succumb to the craftiness of a dimpled cheek.

You will shame yourself and like Mr. Hu, you will be ridiculed by the world. Because this is such a frightening thing, even men like Zhu Xi behaved cautiously, as if walking on a tiger's tale or walking on melting ice with the onset of spring; he was cautious as if a blade of grass sprouting before the snow melts. If Zhu Xi was this cautious, what does this say about the way we should act!

Dissatisfied with my explanation given above, I will explain using a war analogy. I liken my attempt to control my desires to a defeated general who tries to prevent the enemy from attacking on their own volition by doing the following things:

He rekindles the morale lost through defeat.
He reinforces the castle wall.
He clears the fields.
He sleeps with his spear by his side.
He endures bitterness for the sake of revenge.
He urges and cautions his soldiers.

In case he does confront the enemy, he employs all kinds of maneuvers: he does not engage the enemy, employing the techniques used in quelling Western Qiang's[2] revolt. As a last resort, if he had no choice but to deploy his soldiers—what would be the right course of action? He would penetrate the wall of the castle, send in the angry cows, and with one blow crush the invading armies of the Yuan Dynasty. Or he would act like Sun Bin who distracted Pang Juan by engraving his name in the tree before killing him instantly with arrows and catapults.[3]

Even if you were confident—endowed with a fighting spirit and with the resources of many armies at your beckoning call—if you constantly fought against a strong foe in the heart of the battlegrounds, the general would grow arrogant and the soldiers would grow lethargic. If military discipline grows lax and the soldiers fraternize at will, you may be able to win one battle through luck and rest peacefully for a night; however, when you wake up the next day, you will discover the enemy gathering everywhere. If these circumstances repeat, how will the soldiers not grow weary and how will it be possible for them *not* to lose morale?

If you were to devise a strategy, it would be a weak strategy and you would end up asserting a mixture of peaceful and retaliatory measures. You would pull troops from the capital city and have them defend the distant Xin Dynasty or you would have to save Fu Pi's starving soldiers by moving military supplies to Fangtou.[4] Then, you would not be able to trust the courage that jumps over wagons and I worry the armies pestering the state of Chu will capture the capital, Ying.[5] The best plan for you will be to cross the river, burn your ship, break the kettle, burn your house down, prepare three days ration, and show your troops that you do not plan on returning alive.[6] Only then will you be able to distinguish yourself.

I had the opportunity to read the *Annals of the Wuyi Mountain* during some free time. At that time, I read the responses from various people regarding the "Wuyi Rowing Songs." None of them grasped the profound meaning of Zhu Xi. I read Bie Zhi's *Commentaries of the Rowing Song Poems*. In this book, he interprets the first and the last of the nine turning streams poems to symbolize the steps starting with the studies and eventually entering the *dao*; however, when I quietly pondered this, I realized Zhu Xi's original meaning was not this narrow in scope. Recently, I met Seongon Byeon from Mujang who said he had learned from Haseo Gim. He came a long way to visit me and showed me the Wuyi style of Chinese verse by Haseo, which as expected, followed the meanings expressed in the *Commentaries of the Rowing Song Poems*. I am not sure but how have you perceived this matter?

In addition, there was an occasion when I wrote a poem in response to the "Rowing Songs." Although I knew I was being very impudent, I could not hide the poem from the people around me. I transcribe it, send it to you, and ask that you examine it carefully and comment. Amid the poem, I wrote two poems regarding the ninth turning stream:

One written long ago adhered to the *Commentaries of the Rowing Song Poems*.[7]

The second, I reconsidered the usage of words like "visits again" and "not this world" and deemed them incorrect. Therefore, I have written another piece.

Among the two, which should I keep and which should I discard?

The last turning stream is discovering the path towards finding the best place; there is hardly any description of beautiful scenery. If one mentions, "the tour is finished" because there is no good scenery, then all enjoyment is lost, the meaning becomes obstructed, and the sceneries that have been passed thus far have been witnessed in vain. Then, the meaning of the last verse recited by Zhu Xi is his advice: if people already outside seek earthly paradises as do fishermen, they will discover the joys of another world. If you do this, you will have reached the end and everything you have seen up to this point will have not been everything. Then, you will reach another stage after devoting all your talents, taking one-step from the last extreme. From this stage and the eighth turning stream, Zhu Xi says:

> Do not say this place does not have beautiful scenery
> From here travelers seldom visit

He is using this as a metaphor for the profoundness of the studies.

However, in the *Commentaries of the Rowing Song Poems*, the annotator interprets the eighth turning stream to be very close to low-level studies. He interpreted the "Nine Turning Streams Poems" to progress from shallow to deep, mentioning when one arrives at the eighth turning stream, the place is still comparable to low-level studies. If this is the case, what about everything that was learned previously? In the annotations of the ninth turning stream, it states:

> Although one has entered the level of the sages, he reaches a common *dao* originally used by people in everyday life. Therefore, why would he leave people, sever himself from the world, and what would be so difficult about following something that is supposedly so lofty and far removed?

These words are beautiful but do not fit in with phrases like "visits again" and "not this world." What will you do about this?

Following the phrase, "The fisherman visits again," he would not say this is the reality of our studies—he is referring to a group of people who live in obscurity and yet practice wonders. It seems plausible if he said this to say those people were wrong and to enlighten us. However, the main annotations say, "Man cannot reach this stage easily," which does not fit. Foolish as I am, I do not know what to follow. Please teach me.

---

   1. Cheng Hao thought his problem of enjoying hunting (as he liked hunting from childhood) had vanished since he had devoted himself to his studies under the tutelage of Zhou Dunyi. However, one day twelve years later, he sensed joy in his heart when he saw hunters. This meant to guard against the easy wobbling of the human mind. See the *Reflections on Things at Hand*, Chapter V: "Correcting Mistakes, Improving Oneself, Self-discipline, and Returning to Propriety." Refer to Clause 21.
   * Or *myeongsi*; refers to poems kept close to the heart and poems adopted by a person as a principle of behavior.
   2. Refers to one of the five barbarians in the Jin Dynasty period; this Tibetan nomadic tribe lived in the western edge of China.
   3. Beating off the plunderer of Yuan by using mad cow refers to Tian Dan who drove the Yuan army away when Yuan attacked Qi during the Warring States Period of China. A soldier of Qi, Sun Bin killed the general of Wei, Pang Juan, who was pushed into a corner. These two examples meant to lure the enemy to drop their guards by using artificial ploys before defeating the enemy by delivering an attack with one blow. See the *Shi ji* 82, "Biographies" 22, "The Biography of Tian dan"; *Shi ji* 65, "Biographies" 5, "The Biography of Sunzi."
   4. Picking out soldiers from the capital city and letting them stay in the garrison refers to King Ping of Zhou who divided the soldiers in the capital city and then dispatched soldiers for Xin which was plundered by Chu. Relieving the starving soldiers of Fu Pi refers to the ruler of the Former Qin, Fu Jian, who shared scarce provisions with his son, Fu Pi, and his armies. These examples teach that escaping the immediate crisis results in more difficulties, that is, this refers to a wrong strategy. See *The Shih King*, Book VI: "The Odes of Wang." Ode IV: "Yang che shwuy"; *Book of Jin* 115, "Fu Pi."
   5. Refers to when Wu attacked Chu and toppled the capital Ying in the Spring and Autumn Period of China. See *The Chun Tsew with the Tso Chuen*, "Duke Chaou" Year XXX.
   6. After Xiang Yu consolidated his power in Chu, he dispatched 20,000 soldiers to Julu but as the war was not going in his favor, he went to war himself. He acted in this manner to make clear his intentions that he would not return unless victorious. See the *Records of the Grand Historian* 7: "The Basic Annals of Hsiang Yu."
   7. The ninth turning stream of the "Wuyi Rowing Songs" is as follows.

Eyes open brightly when reaching the ninth turning stream
I see a flat river, a mulberry and hemp field wet with rain and dewdrops
A fisherman visits again the road to Utopia
Not this world but another world

See *The Complete Works of Zhu Xi* 9.

[Letter #11 Gobong Writes Toegye]

After Receiving Various Letters and Words

Dear teacher, Toegye:

The early summer weather turns hot suddenly. How is your health? My respect for you grows with each passing day. I have been able to preserve my decrepit self thanks to your most generous favors. While keeping close to my heart the letter, which I received after September 10, I was overjoyed to receive during the end of November your handwritten letter; your reply to the debates; the response poems composed in accordance to the rhymes used in the "Rowing Songs"; and various other motto poems you had written.

The year has passed.

Spring is gone.

I hope you find aid in cultivating the *dao* and pass the time in peace.

I have brashly written my opinions about the *Four-Seven Thesis* in my book. I wanted to send this to you a long time ago but could not find a courier to deliver it. I am sending this through the respected sir of Bonju[1] who is visiting; please look over it frequently if possible. As we live far apart, I am saddened that I can only write letters.

I implore you to cherish yourself for the *dao* and the times.

I respectfully bow. The letter is not as polished as I would have liked.

Jiajing (The era of Shizong of the Ming Dynasty)
April 10, 1561 (the Year of the Chicken)
Junior scholar, Daeseung.

Regarding Your Transcription of the "Poem Advising Self Caution Written after Seeing the Theme on the Wall of Mr. Hu of Meixi's Tavern"

I received the two passages of Huian's "Poem Advising Self Caution Written after Seeing the Theme on the Wall of Mr. Hu of Meixi's Tavern," various collections of motto poems, and the two characters "Jon Jae," which you had written in oversized letters. Precise, neat, and generous, the works possess a quiet, leisurely temperament and a solemn formality. The more I looked at them, the more I was impressed and the more profound my understanding became. In your last letter, you mentioned how difficult it was to force yourself to do work. Although I knew it would be improper for me to burden you with my requests, I have received everything I wanted. How happy and relieved I was! I apologize and worry that you have expended needless energy because you were unable to refuse the request of someone so insignificant.

While cautiously and calmly reiterating even the most detailed of parts, you were occasionally very stern and resolute regarding your method of restraining desires.

Your teachings propel people to action—

> *Avoid having your spirit thwarted and becoming a member of a dispirited group that falls into the storms of life.*
> *Be cautious starting from the smallest work.*

I will abide by these teachings.

It was very thoughtful of you to use the war analogy to move and inspire my flimsy temperament. You mentioned as the strategy for victory the perspicacity to surmise and gain control of the enemy. Truly, you will not be able to discover the crux or even the outline of a (successful strategy) with flippant thoughts and a flimsy scheme; people will say you are far from achieving victory.

I have not been able to exert a total effort even regarding this one aspect. Consistently failing in my daily life, I tried to be contrite but shamed and upset, I was unable to escape failure. However, after receiving your detailed guidance regarding this matter, I tested it in my everyday life. I realized I had gained enormous strength. Relief filled me, as expectations rose I would be able to avoid the indignity of falling and being buried in a pit.

Annex
Regarding the "Response Poems Composed in Accordance to the Rhymes Used in the Wuyi Rowing Songs"[2]

I could not hold back my admiration for many days after receiving ten poems[3] from the "Response Poems Composed in Accordance to the Rhymes Used in the Rowing Songs," the one verse you rewrote, and your additional teachings. In the *Huian Poetry Collection*, I found various poems and prefaces regarding the Wuyi Jingshe Academy and ten poems of the "Rowing Song Poems." I glanced at the poems and understood them superficially; however, I was not aware of *Annals of the Wuyi Mountain* nor did I know the complete meaning of the "Rowing Song Poems." In 1553—the Year of the Cow—when I was in Seoul to take an exam, by chance, I had the opportunity to look over the *Annotations of the Rowing Song Poems* while staying at an older cousin's abode. The work enticed me. I kept turning the pages but I did not dare to read the entire book and ended up closing it.

I have always thought as follows:
Zhu Xi in his ten poems of the "Nine Turning Streams Poems"[4] expressed his feelings through the pleasures arising from inanimate objects. The meaning of the metaphors and the other revealed meanings are pellucid, lofty, gentle, hearty, profound, plain, and pure: its mirth resembles the spirit of washing in the River Yi.[5] He was not simply devising the chronological steps towards entering the *dao* by adding and describing secretly a covert meaning in the interior of the "Rowing Songs of the Nine Turning Streams"! I am guessing the minds of the sages and wise men were not this complicated.

However, the annotator adds to distance oneself from sexual appetite at the Jade Maiden Peak of the second turning stream.

He adds to lay down your life for righteousness at the boat shaped coffins suspended between cliffs in the third turning stream.

He also mentions, "A man who is studying can learn the *dao* only after distancing himself from sexual appetite and discarding his own life." I have no idea what this means. It is truly a common worry among scholars that man will come to lose virtue by enjoying women and harm righteousness by coveting life; however, man can distance himself from sexual appetite and discard his life *after* he has completed his studies—it is hard to in the beginning. If I should embark upon my studies after eliminating such worries, I fear I would never be able to study. Are these the words of a Confucian scholar! This is the theory of Zen Buddhism. After making up my mind in this manner, I did not want to think about that book again.

Although I intended to examine this thoroughly after receiving your guidance, I could not get a hold of the annotations as I live in the remote country. I have heard that teacher, Haseo, was particularly fond of these annotations, but I have not had the opportunity to converse with him. Furthermore, I do not dare bring up the matter and question him because we possess differing views. I have always harbored doubts about (these annotations). I cannot recollect anything because a long time has passed since I have seen these annotations. I can remember offhand one verse from Haseo's poem, which reads as follows:

> I might know the waters and moon of Jinji
> Doubts suddenly arise about the forest where it drizzles

This seems peculiar. If he considered true, "The moon fills the empty mountains, the water fills the ponds," why would he doubt, "The long drizzle darkens the forests"? Although the ancient ones said if man doubts, he would comprehend the studies, how can a man harbor such prodigious doubts after reaching a certain level of understanding! He does not make any sense.

In my view, since the Wuyi Jingshe Academy is located in the fifth turning stream, we can say, "There is a traveler in the midst of the forest" is a metaphor for the self. Therefore, while arousing mirth because of the drizzling rain, the author speaks figuratively that man hides himself, concealing his talents; therefore, this does not mean harboring doubts about the studies. Looking at *The Complete Works of Zhu Xi*, in the epilogue where Yang Zizhi recites a quatrain regarding Wang Caichen,[6] it states, "I truly love this poem from Wang Moji's 'Wangchunqiyuanshi':

> Although the ancient ones were not wicked officials
> They postponed matters of administration
> By chance, they clung to their humble government posts
> Stammering under several trees

I have told others about it but I have not found anyone who shares my enthusiasm. However, after reading Zizhi's poem, I was moved while reading the 'Valleys of Mount Nanshan.'" He mentions Yang Zizhi's poem at the end, which reads as follows:

> Mount Nanshan is high and bright
> Below are deep valleys
> A spotted leopard appears and hides as he pleases
> He bathes all morning in the descending fog

This seems to evoke the same meaning as the one revealed in the fifth turning stream poem, but I cannot be sure.

Although we cannot obstinately speak metaphorically of these ten poems and arrange them one by one. As there are certain places where there is increased significance, he uses metaphors to reveal his ideas. From the first turning stream poem:

> No news after the rainbow bridge has been severed
> Steep mountains and deep valleys are submerged in blue smoke

There is a clear meaning here.

How can anybody claim Zhu Xi had written this while tristful because the *dao* had been buried and lost! For the most part, he writes in response to the scenery unfolding before him. Therefore, if his thoughts and his surroundings are true, naturally, his words will evoke profound flavor, which is the reason why this is *Zhu Xiesque*. However, if he had decided to describe simply the scenery but then intended the scenery to be a metaphor for the *Learning of the Way*, as well, he would have been guilty of possessing two minds. While reciting these poems, I fear not only losing the properness of nature and feelings, but also a small disparity will transform into a big mistake when proceeding with the studies.

That is not to say the second and third turning streams are void of any meaning; I contend that their meanings do not coincide with the forced interpretations of the annotator.

The same goes for the fourth turning stream.

The sixth and seventh turning streams along with the first are candid and worth savoring. However, as my views are shallow and weak, I cannot brazenly expose and contemplate the places of significance.

The eighth and ninth turning streams are with meaning, as well. In the eighth turning stream poem, it says:

> Do not say this place does not have beautiful scenery
> From here travelers seldom visit

Although there are no spectacular or phenomenal sites, there is enough scenery to enjoy a quiet stroll. As it mentions those people who step outside and look for this quietly will absolutely discover a *taste*, even though it may be a bland taste, we cannot say this (part) is without meaning

> Eyes open brightly when reaching the ninth turning stream
> I see a flat river, a mulberry and hemp field wet with rain
>   and dewdrops

When reaching this point, with a lucid and pure spirit, we know his soul and significance transcend words. There is something all the more meaningful here. The annotator says, "Although he has entered the level of the sages, he reaches a common *dao* originally used by people in everyday life." Phrases like this are long-winded at best.

The following phrases where the fisherman is mentioned are simple metaphors that mean *to caution*. The meaning is as follows:

> After finishing your visit to the ninth turning stream, the scenery unfolds before you—rain and dewdrops fall on a mulberry and hemp field, blanketing the flat river; this will be the pinnacle of your excursion, a fresh and secluded place with flat and wide borders. If you are not satisfied with this place and want to seek utopia, this is another world, not something that exists in this world.

People who step outside should be cautious not to seek (Utopia) elsewhere while discarding this place. What I have mentioned thus far have been my everyday thoughts.

I worry about defiling the *dao*.

I worry about harming the teachings of Confucius.

I originally intended to refrain from speaking cumbrously; however, since you asked questions that exceeded my abilities, I had no choice but to audaciously answer with all my heart.

Your poems composed in response were exquisitely beautiful and outstanding; however, I did not understand many parts, which I attribute to my ignorance of the Wuyi. Regarding the new poem and the letter, I dare to say that I think they were wrong. However, the words you wrote citing, "To live in obscurity and yet practice wonders,"[7] were reasonable. Furthermore, I have difficulty believing the annotator's comment:

> This scenery cannot be reached easily in this world.

However, in the past, the *Lianzhushige* included these poems and this sentence in its annotation. At the bottom, it noted, "People had slandered Zhu Xi for writing these poems." I hope you can tell me the reason why people slandered him.

Lately, people write commentaries about the works of our predecessors, and some personally author books of their own ideas. People are chaotically circulating these books, which create confusion regarding what is right and wrong. The scholars are making it hard to determine which books to read. In addition, these scholars dislike the books accessible in everyday life and instead seek what is novel, struggling to adopt those kinds of books.

This is truly lamentable.

Furthermore, regarding the *Hunmongjeolgu*, which is being circulated in the secular world, I have harbored doubts about this book from early on, and when I met you in Seoul, I asked you about these suspicions, and you mentioned that it did not appear to be the authentic work of Zhu Xi. I was enormously relieved when I heard you say that. I sigh as most scholars consider it authentic and are busy acquainting themselves with this book. I apologize as I have let my brush move at will in my desire to learn.

---

1. Refers to the local magistrate of Gwangju, Gyeongsim Ryu.

2. Refers to composing a verse in response using the rhymes in another poem.

3. See *Toegye's Collections* 1, Poetry section: "Ten Poems Which Were Composed by Using the Rhymes in the Nine Turning Streams after Reading *Annals of Wuyi Mountain* with Leisure."

4. See *The Complete Works of Zhu Xi* 9, Poetry section: "Composing Ten Poems of Wuyi Rowing Songs for Fun and Dedicating Them to My Friends for Laughter While Staying in a Leisurely Way at the Academy in February During the Chunxi era, the Year of the Dragon."

5. Confucius asked his pupils what they would do if a ruler were to recognize and acknowledge their abilities. All the pupils expressed their ambition to govern the nation in the proper way. However, Zeng Xi replied in this manner: "In this, the last month of spring, with the dress of the season all complete, along with five or six young men who have assumed

the cap, and six or seven boys, I would wash in the I, enjoy the breeze among the rain altars, and return home singing." See the *Confucian Analects*, Book XI: "Hsien Tsin," Chapter XXV.

6. See *The Complete Works of Zhu Xi* 84, Epilogue section: "An Epilogue in the Quatrain Where Yang Zizhi Talks About Wang Caichen."

7. "The Master said, 'To live in obscurity, and yet practise wonders, in order to be mentioned with honor in future ages: this is what I do not do.'" See *The Doctrine of the Mean*, Chapter XI.

Response to the Letter I Received Last Autumn

I was extremely grateful and comforted when I received one letter and one annex of your teachings through a courier making his way back last September. After carefully studying your lessons, which were very explicit and cordial, I most assuredly will adhere to them sincerely. I will not lose sight of them. I have not dared to trouble you by writing an urgent response; please take this under advisement. However, I have an earnest request and have no choice but to ask—it is difficult to cope with your honorable treatment, which is burdensome. It would be a relief if you considered this.

Wang Yuanze is the son of Wang Jiefu. His name was Pang. Please refer to book 130 of the *Classified Conversations of Master Zhu*. I am unceasingly ashamed and apologetic after receiving my (old) letters, which you had copied and sent back to me. Regarding what I informed you near the end of my *Four-Seven Thesis*, I do not have a copy of the paragraph that includes the words "the principle is empty and has no counterpart." Could you copy this and send me a copy? I am even more apologetic that I have asked you to do such a trivial task.

Daeseung respectfully bows and offers this response.

[Letter #12 Toegye Writes Gobong]

No Time to Read Your Letters

I reply to you, Myeongeon.

I could not remain reticent after receiving your teachings; I haphazardly stated my narrow-minded views. However, when reflecting, I was overcome with fearful thoughts, perspiring, as some parts were remiss and off the mark, but surprisingly, you did not disregard them but wrote and responded to every thought, one by one.

I was pleased and relieved.

I was unbearably overjoyed to hear that you felt mentally relaxed and physically tranquil. Temperamental and old, my illness lingers and grows fiercer by the day. I encountered extreme difficulties conducting myself during the spring, but fortunately, indebted to the king's lenient forgiveness, I am ignobly hiding here but I pass each day wrenched in anxiety, as certain matters remain unresolved. Most likely, wise scholars will disown me because of this matter. However, I sense your magnanimity, your ability to tolerate all things, as we continue to debate through exchanging correspondences.

It was a holiday and I had just gotten on my horse to visit the graves of my ancestors when I met the courier you had sent. I went back inside, sat, and as I began writing my response, I realized I did not have time to glance at even one or two parts of your letter. I am overwrought with shame that I could not thank you properly for your consideration in teaching me through your letter. On a later date, if I come up with something worth conveying to you after savoring and further examining your letter, I will send it through the Gwangju local magistrate's household courier. This will reduce the risk of the letter being lost in mid delivery.

The distance between us is far and rugged; we cannot sit face to face and ask questions; and, we can only depend on written correspondences. I fear our debates will never end and people will end up ridiculing and maligning us.

I believe Gyejin Gim[1] has returned to Chilsang. How is he doing? I asked the courier you had sent about him but he had no idea. Because I have been so busy, I could not send a brief letter inquiring about his well-being. If you see him, could you please convey these thoughts? I will send a letter if I come across a courier. Please take this under advisement.

I could not write even the slightest fraction of the things I wanted to say.

Hoping you continue to preserve yourself for the *dao*, I respectfully bow and send this brief letter.

May, 1561 (the Year of the Chicken), two days before the Danyang.[2]

Respectfully bowing,
Hwang.

---

1. Refers to Jeong Gim.
2. The Dano festival was held (on the fifth of the fifth month of the year according to the lunar calendar).

[Letter #13 Gobong Writes Toegye]

After Receiving Word of Elderly Chuman's Passing

I respectfully reply to teacher, Toegye.

How is your health? My respect for you grows deeper with each passing day. Although I am impudent, I am barely getting along thanks to your concerns.

I received your letter around May 20 and was comforted and grateful after learning in detail of your intentions; however, I am truly frustrated because I am unable to respond regularly, as you are far away, blocked by mountains and streams.

I assume you have already looked over my arguments. I ask you for your guidance regarding these matters. I cannot restrain my eager anticipation.

Unfortunately for the *dao*, elderly Chuman passed away quite unexpectedly sometime after our last correspondence. After hearing news of his passing, I was overwrought with grief. Last year, teacher, Haseo, passed away and this year we grieve for Chuman. The heavens have unleashed a ferocious wrath: how can they be so cruel? Where can somebody like me seek virtue and ask about the studies? My heart is torn. Respectfully thinking about it, as you fostered a deep relationship with him based on moral principle, undoubtedly you must be bereaved.

Thankfully, I am currently residing in a peaceful place and can focus on my studies; however, when I look back on my life, shame fills me, as I have been bewildered by a chaotic, secular world. On top of that, as I approach the time to enter my government office, I know I will have the audacity to be continuously busy. I cannot begin to describe the anxiety and worries I will encounter in future days. What can I do? I implore you to guide me through this. Although I have many things to say to you, I shall end my letter here. Please excuse me.

I bow and respectfully close this letter.

Year 40 of the Jiajing (The era of Shizong of the Ming Dynasty)
July 21, 1561 (the Year of the Chicken)
Lowering my head and bowing,
Junior scholar, Daeseung.

After receiving the notice of Chuman's passing, I was shocked and overcome with unbearable sorrow. To express my emotions in words, I wrote an eight-line poem. I showed this poem to younger students who shared my grief, and I have written it for you. Please glance over it.

> Last year we lamented for Haseo
> This year we grieve for Chuman
> Good men have passed without break
> The *dao* has left and has no place to return
> My narrow-minded disposition—
> To whom shall I look?
> Lonely, lying in a dark room
> The brook futilely dribbles by

In your letter to Jajung Jeong, you wrote, "Although I have already written about those points unclear in my arguments, I do not have time to transcribe them for you." Most certainly, I think Jajung would have inquired about this, but did he? I would be relieved to hear your teachings regarding this matter.

Gyejin Gim is currently residing in Chilsang and is getting along fine without any major difficulties. However, unfortunately, our paths did not cross because of various matters, and I could not meet him for a long time. I have not been able to relay your message to him. I am ashamed and filled with sorrow and regret.

Hwasuk Bak has retired from his government post and has returned to his native village. He is currently living in Seochon, Geumseong.[1] He is taking care of himself. Not too long ago, we met on several occasions. Please be advised.

I respectfully bow and inform.

---

1. Present day Naju, Jeolla Province.

[Letter #14 Toegye Writes Gobong]

Learning a Short Time Remains before You Come to Seoul

I respectfully reply to your letter, Myeongeon.

After reading the letter you sent through the Gwangju local magistrate, I was extremely relieved to hear you were living tranquilly these days. With my heart inclining towards you, I was greatly comforted.

Desiring to respond promptly to the letter you sent last summer, I failed to proofread my letter and feared I had written it very carelessly. While suffering from illnesses, I read your arguments periodically whenever I had time and noticed they were profound and more precise. How lucky for an old man to be hearing such opinions!

However, occasionally, I disagreed with some of your points. While unable to liberate myself from past guiles, newer doubts arise more than ever. Although it would seem reasonable to question you about those one or two points now, it makes more sense to ask after I have prudently looked at the assertions laid out in the book you sent, which I must get back from Jajung Jeong, who borrowed the book. As Jajung spends his summer in Seoul, in the near future, I think he will be visiting his native village, but he has yet to come. For this reason, I could not write a response in this letter to the arguments you sent last time. I am guilty of foolishness as well as laziness. My shame has no limits.

Letter #14

Chuman died before he was old. I am stricken with immeasurable grief. Although I shared a deep friendship with him, I could not brush my hand against his coffin because I live so far away. My shame and sorrow will never dwindle. Recently, I sent along with my son, who was going to Seoul, things needed for the memorial service; I asked him to pay condolences to the departed. After reading the poem you sent, I realized your demeanor was ardent. You treated him with affection as a true companion in the *dao* would. The courier was busy to make his return and I could not write a response poem that depicted my trivial feelings.

I hold back the tears, caress your poem, and make pledges for the future.

Regarding what Jajung said, I am not sure to what he refers, as I did not consult with him while writing my arguments. When I see him, I will find out what he meant and of course, I will tell you about it in the future. I have not exchanged any letters with Hwasuk Bak after he left. I cannot express my joy when hearing of his good news. As the courier was busy to return in this case, as well, I was unable to send him a letter. Please convey my best wishes when you see him. In addition, please concentrate on your studies while you have the time, and appease my heart that worries from a distance. I would be greatly relieved.

Jeong Gim has also sent me a letter.

Learning a short time remains before you come to Seoul, I congratulate you. As I place this paper in front of me, I can do nothing but worry because I was unable to express all my concerns. In the future, when we leisurely exchange long letters and refine our studies, I worry things will not be the same as when you are in the remote country. I close this letter by asking you to preserve yourself for the *dao* and the ages.

August 4, 1561 (the Year of the Chicken)

Hwang.

Although I have endless questions to ask, I have concluded with these several words. Please understand.

[Letter #15 Gobong Writes Toegye]

On My Way to Seoul in the Spring

Dear teacher,

The yearend cold seems to be twice as fierce. How are you getting along? Barely able to care for myself, I have nothing to say. Starting from the autumn and extending through the winter, I suffered hardship as worries congregated and diseases inflicted. I received your letter through the Gawngju magistrate. The kindness you showed me was courteous and extreme. I was overcome with comfort and relief.

I respectfully ask to view your established theories regarding the *Four-Seven*.

Since I have recently received royal orders to enter a government post, I must go to Seoul in the spring; however, poverty and disease rotate their inflictions upon me. I agonize that I will have no alternative but to imitate others woefully. However, if I go to Seoul, I will be closer to you. We will be able to maintain contact frequently—this is a relief.

Respectfully, I ask you to be advised of this.

I feel I have rushed to write and send this to you through a passing monk; hence, the letter seems insufficient. Please excuse me. I respectfully bow twice.

November 15, 1561 (the Year of the Chicken)
Bowing, yours truly,
Junior scholar, Daeseung.

1562-1565

Sharing the Difficulties of Conduct

[Letter #16 Toegye Writes Gobong]

Difficulties in Making Arguments about the "Four-Seven"

To Myeongeon:
When you are in Honam, I am in Yeongnam, and when you are in Seoul, I am in the local regions. Our correspondence continues to remain blocked even as days and years pass. Jajung has returned but I have not had a chance to meet him.

You have left your family; you have started at a new government post;[1] and you are working hard for the affairs of the state—how are things going? Have you noticed any unstable aspects as you test your moral training in the real world?

It may seem a relief that I am still sequestered in this remote place when appraising my foolish status; however, age moves quickly along with time, and disease follows age growing in severity.

I sensed the withering of my spirit and energy.

Finally, I understood that I had no choice but to move hastily regarding my studies. The broad-minded scholars will assuredly ridicule me for my inability to show remorse even while being so foolish and sluggish.

Although I halted our exchanges regarding the *Four-Seven* debates, we had not reached any concrete conclusions. I had several thoughts I wanted to finish. Upon reflection, the revelations of moral principle needed to be precise and erudite beyond measure; however, when reflecting on my essays, my logic was not clear, my sentences were loose, my opinions were not broad, and my knowledge seemed short in places.

Every time I sensed this, I picked up theories from past Confucian scholars and implemented them into the weak spots of my replies to your arguments. What is the difference between doing this and somebody who walks into the examination area to take the civil service exam, looks at the subject of a poem, copies all the historical allusions and then proceeds to answer each clause! Even if my response employing this technique was appropriate, it would be useless to someone devoted to the studies; therefore, the futile quarrels would result in the violation of important taboos of the exalted studies. Furthermore, I am in a position that is anything but reasonable. Thus, I refrain from courageously responding as I did in the past, but I write and send you a quatrain for your amusement alluding to the metaphor you used of two men loading supplies on a horse:

> The two men moving their loads (on a horse) quarrel
>   over the weight
> Thinking about it, whether the high end or the low end
>   the (total) weight remains the same
> If you press down on this side, the other side goes up
> When will the weight of the load balance out?

Ha-ha.

I wrote in the annex what I did not understand while reading a book. This does not compare to the debate we had last time; I look forward to your response. I will relay the rest to Jajung. I respectfully bow.

October 16, 1562 (the Year of the Dog)
From Hwang.

Inside the *Supplement to the Complete Works of Zhu Xi*, amidst "The Answer Given to Cai Jitong,"[2] it states:

> If we open up all the warehouses in the world, the regretful act of *yongzhiguoluo* suffering damage will occur.

I do not know what it means when it says *yongzhiguoluo* will suffer damage.

In *Yuanyuanlu's* "Xiexiandaoyishi,"[3] it states:

> Please write in *Liuwenyiguanbi* in particular to teach us. Will it not be good to pacify this person's heart?

To what does *Liuwenyiguanbi* refer?

A person from the following generation wrote in "Tiwuyiqingseshi":

> The moonlight shines on the sparse field, the monkey weeps
> Dust rises from the bamboo desk, a pheasant flies by

However, no source is indicated and I have no idea what the pheasant means.

Letter #16 61

When Zhu Xi toured Mount Tiantai, in his "Poem Written While Staying Overnight at Fangguang and Hearing of the Death of the Elder Shourong,"[4] he says, "Doing the act of *geundu* in midair." What does it mean to do the act of *geundu* in midair?

In many of the writings, the "mun" character replaces the "jang" character in "jon-jang." At first, I thought it was a mistake and made revisions whenever I came across it; however, later, when noticing that this continued to occur, I realized it was not a mistake at all. Could it be possible that people used something "mun" in place of "jon-jang"?

Amidst the *Annotations of Heart Sutra*,[5] it says, "One forgets the *dao* because of desire." In the annotations, Mr. Hu's theory says regarding this, "It says Ban Bo is the root of lasciviousness." Who is Ban Bo? In what period did he live? In what book does his story appear?

Regarding the Fangweng's[6] affair in "The Answer Given to Gong Zhongzhi,"[7] Zhu Xi says, "Although Hu Shun suffered confusion on the Tianjin Bridge without reason, on the contrary he created the "*daiersancangxijian.*" What does this mean?

I am not sure what "Yizuxunlong," which appears in the "Liugongshendaobei," actually is.

---

1. The king promoted Gobong to historiographer of the Office of the Recorders of the Royal Command and appointed him the official writer of the Office of the Recorders of Political Affairs in May.

2. See the *Supplement to the Complete Works of Zhu Xi* 2, Letters section.

3. The *Yuanyuanlu* refers to *Yiluoyuanyuanlu*, a book which Zhu Xi wrote about the words and behavior of the 46 pupils of Cheng Hao and Cheng Yi who came after Zhou Dunyi, and he explained the origins of (their) studies. See Book 9: "Xueshi," "Xiexiandaoyishi," *Yuanyuanlu* Book 9.

4. See *The Complete Works of Zhu Xi* 5, Poetry section.

5. In this book, the Confucian scholar of the Ming Dynasty, Zhen Minzheng, commented on and supplemented Zhen Dexiu's *Heart Sutra* by collecting the opinions of several scholars. Toegye made appended notes to difficult characters and phrases in the *Heart Sutra* and he later compiled and titled it *Explanations on Heart Sutra*. The theory of Mr. Hu refers to the opinion of Mr. Hu of Zhitang and is mentioned in the commentary of Book 2, Chapter 5 ("Jinziledao") of the *Annotations of Heart Sutra*.

6. Refers to the pen name of the Southern Song poet, Lu You.

7. See *The Complete Works of Zhu Xi* 64, Letters section.

[Letter #17 Gobong Writes Toegye]

Like a Caged Monkey and Bird

To teacher,
I respectfully inquire about your well-being. How is your health? I miss you unceasingly.
Spring gradually blooms.
The remaining cold begins to dissipate.
I hope this helps you and you grow more peaceful with each passing day. I am able to preserve myself barely because of the affectionate graces you have bestowed upon me.
Last spring I returned to Seoul and the path of government service. Immediately, I was appointed a historiographer, which I did without pause from summer until winter. My mind and body grew fatigued, and I doubted whether I could continue to maintain control of my body. Therefore, I received permission to visit the graves of my ancestors and traveled to the country sometime around October 30. However, it was cumbersome to cross over mountains and rivers and an old sickness suddenly returned. Finally, I risked shame and sent a letter to the provincial governor, requesting the king to replace me.
The king shed his grace. He immediately gave me time off, ordering me to recuperate. As a lowly vassal from the remote country, needless to say, I was apologetic and dumbfounded by the undeserved hospitality. I immediately dragged my sick body (back to the royal palace), and it has already been a month since I have returned. However, my sickness amasses and on top of that, I have become busy again with work. My mind grows hazy and I feel like I have gone insane—I have become an idiot. I am very worried this will become an inveterate illness of the heart.
I received your letter from Jajung Jeong. I read it three or four times. Grateful, ashamed, and comforted, my heart has broadened immeasurably. However, I could not respond to you for a long time. I blame myself for being so consistently negligent and lazy. However, because I have been isolated in the royal palace, I could not send word to you because it has been difficult finding people coming and going. Furthermore, I intended to send word through Jajung when he returned to his native village, but he left for Yeong-

neung[1] to probe for impropriety.[2] How can I make amends for my foolishness? I feel ashamed to no end.

During our past exchanges, I roughly expressed my opinions because I did not dare hide them from you; however, I was not claiming to be correct. After receiving your letter and reading what you have taught, I cannot overcome my wary and fearful heart. You stated:

> Our faults arise from contesting each other with just words instead of genuine study. If we realize this disease and attempt to cure it, all will not have been in vain.

Spoken from somebody of your stature, this is truly a humble statement, but for me this is medication for my disease. I am relieved to have learned this. I feel blissful.

I did not know the answers to many of the questions you posed in your annex. Merely, since I responded to only three clauses, I hope you will look at it.

I am not somebody who has studied from an early age; I have confidence solely in my vigor and writing skills. I tried to adhere to the words of the sages and wise men later on in life but since I have been accustomed to doing what I want for a long time, I have not been able to discipline myself according to the laws of the *dao*. How could I have cultivated myself to any degree! Because I have suddenly embarked on this path of government service and must attend to it, not only am I unable to cure this old disease, but also everything I touch seems to go wrong. I cannot put my mind to rest because fearful thoughts press down upon my heart, and everything I do ends in failure. Using a metaphor, I am like a caged monkey or bird that simply sits in its cage wasting time. Not only this, I am in the condition Zhu Xi referred to when he said, "I cannot lift my head and stand. I want to move my body but cannot. Increasingly, I cannot endure the situations I encounter."

What can I do?

I crave for your guidance regarding this matter. I will end this letter, although I have many things to say. I ask you to be lenient while looking at this. I respectfully bow and offer this letter.

February 12, 1563 (the Year of the Pig)
Bowing, yours truly,
Junior scholar, Daeseung.

Annex [Letter #17]

Yongzhiguoluo appears in Liu Zhihou's "Tianshuo."[3] I am not sure of the details but this is probably the meaning, right?
Ban Bo appears in the *Book of Han's* "Xuzhuan."[4]
Geundu refers to a jester standing upside down. Early on, I met a monk who said, "A long time ago, there was an elder who attended a Buddhist ceremony who spoke standing upside down after reaching understanding, and these words appear in the *Chuandenglu*." I am not sure but this appears to be the meaning, right?

---

1. Refers to the mausoleum of the Joseon King Sejong, which was located in Yeoju, Gyeonggi Province.
2. Or *cheokgan*; this meant probing for irregularities or wrongdoings.
3. Liu Zhihou refers to Liu Zongyuan (773-819), a poet who lived in the Tang Dynasty period. "Tianshuo" is in book 16 of his collected works, *Liuhedongji*.
4. "Xuzhuan" of the *Book of Han* was a biography written about Ban Gu's family line. Ban Bo was his great uncle.

[Letter # 18 Toegye Writes Gobong]

The Three Obstacles to Truthful Studying

I reply to you, Myeongeon.
I received your letter from Gyeongseo Gu[1] who delivered it to me on his way home. Starting from last year and continuing through the present, as your letter detailed many favorable conditions, the frustration I felt for being so far away and secluded was resolved more refreshingly than if ice had melted away and fog had been lifted. I was greatly comforted.
Living on a secluded mountain, I rarely hear news from Seoul. I did not know the details but discovered through your letter that you had left your government post due to illness and returned to your native village only to return to Seoul after the king had appointed you to a new post. I can only imagine what you must be feeling, as your attempts have been unsuccessful. This is the hardest aspect about maintaining a government post and the reason peo-

ple of today do not measure up to the people of old. You will come to understand with more insight as you gain more experience.

Old and lowly, due to my illness I am passing the time in relative leisure thanks to the king's royal favor, which is as lofty as the heavens. However, the king has yet to dismiss me from my *Dongjijungchubusa* position. I requested my release when I received the royal summons last spring but after that, I have not dared to submit another request; therefore, not only am I uneasy, but also it appears as if public opinion is critical of me for not resigning from the *Dongjijungchubusa* position. Although such public opinion is natural, I am very cautious and coiled because of the difficulties I encountered during my past resignation. I do not dare reveal my thoughts to resign but wait for the Office of the Censor General and the Office of the Inspector General to impeach and dismiss me from office. It seems shameless and disloyal, but what other alternatives do I have?

When Jajung visited me last winter, he had already mentioned the reason you could not respond to my letter. Competition based on eloquence seems fruitless; to study faithfully but intermittently puts me in agony. When I ponder why I am unable to study continuously without constantly stopping, I can think of three reasons:

Biased personal habits and temperaments—
Cloaking of worldly desires—
Being trapped by world affairs—

Fortunately, living in the mountains, "cloaking of worldly desires" and "being trapped by the world" are less significant; however, I have had difficulties amending my biased personal habits and temperaments. While wandering in the front courtyard, I imagined receiving the aid of a virtuous friend, but I have yet to meet such a person. I felt like I had discovered a great treasure when receiving your letter. I was amazed as I opened and read your letter.

I will not give up solely because I am old and befuddled.

Although I know you regretted living an unbridled lifestyle in the past, people continue to adore you! People continue to imagine what kind of person you are! Although you are not in the position to act freely, I hope you will not be too hard on yourself.

In your annex, you alerted me to much of my foolishness.

I realized I must read every book in the world! I feel relieved.

I have sent this letter through Gyeongseo who was traveling back. I end my letter here and ask that you be advised of this.
I respectfully bow and write this reply.
February 24, 1563 (the Year of the Pig)
Hwang bows his head.

---

1. Refers to Bongryeong Gu. His pen name was Baekdam and Gyeongseo was his pseudonym. He was Toegye's pupil and wrote *Baekdam's Collections*.

[Letter # 19 Gobong Writes Toegye]

Becoming the Seungji of the Royal Secretariat

I respectfully reply to teacher, Toegye.
Jeongja Gu visited the royal palace upon his arrival. When I heard you were in good health, I was overjoyed and comforted; after reading your letter several times, I was overwrought with concern.
I am in a position where it is impossible to budge, even slightly. Since I had nobody to care for me, I wanted to live together with my family. Last month, I planned to have my wife and children move to Seoul, to prepare a home, and to live more comfortably. However, near the beginning of this month, I became the *Seungji* of the Royal Secretariat and ended up working many nights. Distressed, I felt stifled and did not know what to do, as the work was prodigious and I felt annoyed.
A few days ago, although I had a chance to reread the works of the sages and wise men, it looked commonplace, which resulted in me simply flipping the pages. I did not study faithfully because I failed to concentrate on the words of the sages and wise men, and I lacked any experience in familiarizing my body to those words. Although I am confronted with the events of the world today, I cannot garner any strength whatsoever, and I have no place to appeal these fearful thoughts.
In your last letter, you taught about the worries of studying intermittently: those words were earnest and extreme. The three obstacles you mentioned unfold chaotically before my eyes.

I slice them out but they fail to disappear.
I chase them away but they do not leave.

I do not know how this will all conclude. What can I do since I cannot make any more friends who will help and exert an effort on my behalf?

Since your expressions of discomfort were earnest and extreme, you incited lament and unknowingly put me into a stupor. Today, passing through this barrier is my worry in the world; however, it breaks my heart to say that. What can I do?

I ask you to research this important task and supplicate that you will bring glory to the *dao*. I have not been able to say everything I am thinking, as I have roughly written this letter. Thinking about the spring garden where you reside, I am filled with sorrow from afar.

Please understand.
I respectfully bow and offer this letter.
March 21, 1563 (the Year of the Pig)
In the night, junior scholar, Daeseung, lowers his head in reverence and bows twice, writing this concise letter under the lamp during night duty. I am in awe and ashamed to no end. Please excuse me.

[Letter #20 Gobong Writes Toegye]

Regarding Appropriate Conduct

Dear teacher, Toegye,

Time passes quickly. Spring has already passed. Are you comfortable and healthy? I am still near the king and since I pass the time in an absentminded daze, my illness grows worse, my spirit grows haggard. I am worried about maintaining my energy level but at the same time, I cannot quit—I can only tremble in fear.

When I received your letter and respectfully studied your ideas, on one hand, I was comforted, but on the other hand, I felt enormous lament, unable to take my mind off what you had said. I was relieved to hear you were abundantly enjoying yourself while accomplishing your aspirations in times of leisure. However, I did not realize that staying home while maintaining a government post could be so uncomfortable.

My knowledge is short and deficient.

I am ashamed beyond measure.

However, when I subsequently thought about it, as you mentioned in your letter, those difficult points do exist. When writing my last response, I was extremely busy and could not answer all the questions you asked. I am filled with sorrow and regret.

A scholar has no place to move around while living in this world. However, you do not dare to think about requesting to leave your government post but wait to be impeached, dismissed from office. I am not sure when you will be able to leave. However, if you request to leave office, I worry you will fail. If you do not leave office, you must be ready to suffer the shame of ignobly seeking only comfort. Instead of remaining in office and always feeling uncomfortable, it would be better to resign even if you encounter awkward situations, whereby avoiding the harboring of regrets regarding your original intention. Furthermore, present day resignations are different from those of the past: if you submit, with the utmost of earnestness, a resignation on the grounds of old age or disease, and repeatedly submit such a resignation, it is possible you will succeed!

Foolish and ignorant, I feel I have committed a grave sin against a man of virtue by haphazardly discussing the way a man should conduct himself. However, I have always believed in you and relied upon you.

I worry about you.

I could not dare ignore your situation.

Although adopting unpretentiousness as a virtue and concealing yourself is the way to behave, establishing yourself in life and believing in the *dao* is truly the way to resolve the issue. Although this is a situation when adopting a course of action may be difficult, your appropriate conduct will send a message to future generations. If you consider this while making your final decision, you will realize what is trivial, what is valuable, and what you should discard and what you should keep. Our generation will not be the only ones who look up to your *dao*.

I have always thought your dao will be a model for future generations.

Place yourself in the *dao* and avoid being tied up by the details of daily regulations. As my heart overflows with devotion, I may have spoken impudently, not knowing where to stop. You might chuckle as you read this.

Please send me your correspondence through the courier and open my eyes regarding my delusions. I cannot endure my sincere anticipation. While asking you to look over and consider this, I respectfully bow and offer this letter.

April 2, 1563 (the Year of the Pig)
Bowing, yours truly,
Junior scholar, Daeseung.

I was barely able to finish this letter, as I am so foolish.

[Letter #21 Toegye Writes Gobong]

The Difficulties in Offering My Resignation and Retiring

I reply to you, Myeongeon Gi.

Just as I finished reading the letter dated April 2, which Jajung delivered, Gyeongseo brought me your response dated March 21. Having had a chance to read both letters, I recognized your sincerity in teaching me: you sent me a second letter after realizing some parts of your first letter were deficient. My heart is expressed in the sayings, "A man of noble character loves others through virtue and does not change his treatment of others according to circumstances for his own comfort" and philosopher Zeng's saying, "When transacting business for others, do it faithfully."

I was deeply moved.

In your letter, you stated in so many words, "Instead of not resigning from office and always feeling uncomfortable, it would be better to resign even if you encounter awkward situations, whereby avoiding the harboring of regrets regarding your original intention." These are truly fervent, extremely logical words. If you had said these words to somebody who had *never* offered resignations, your advice would have set righteousness straight; it would have ended up exemplifying the *dao*; and, it would have been good because (your advice) would not have been something where benefit and loss needed to be weighed. However, in my case, I have already offered my resignation. I offered it with all my heart, even suffering in an embarrassing event because of it. I cannot offer my resignation again because I am wary of this.

Regarding the ancient ones, retiring from government posts due to old age and illness was as commonplace as eating and wearing clothes. For this reason, those seeking retirement had their wishes fulfilled and nobody thought strangely of it. However, today, this procedure faded and died off. We could only see in writing an old minister of the state professing he wanted to leave office according to customs; however, most vassals do not even know this happened.

Unfortunately, I have received enormous favors even though I am a foolish man. Because I have risen to high government offices despite my inveterate illness, I have not been able to spend a single day in peace for the sake of loyalty.

Resigning from office is not an easy option.

For dozens of years I have written countless numbers of words.

I have explained countless number of moral principles.

I have revealed my innermost thoughts and repeatedly informed the king of my woeful situation using historical facts.

However, I did not know that I would be turned down, forced to stammer at my government post, and that men of high virtue would mockingly scorn me.

Not only was I unable to resign, but also (the king) assigned me to a higher government post. Although I declined on five or six occasions, (the king) kept promoting me to higher posts. Powerless, with no place to hide in the world, I submissively went along without uttering a word. You advise in your letter that it would be better for me to resign and not regret forsaking my original intentions. But what choice do I have? In addition, you mention in your letter, ". . . present day resignations are different from resignations of the past." This has much credence. Nothing has changed from the past to the present regarding my old age and illness; my genuineness regarding resigning was not recognized. Although I am older and sicker now, how can I count the added years and compare degree of sickness in hopes the king will accept my resignation!

A senior official from our district, teacher Nongam Yi,[1] retired from office when he was seventy-five and died when he was eighty-eight. When he returned to his native village, he maintained a position in the Office of the Royal Command, which he kept until his death. In the beginning, although he offered his resignation at least once or twice a year, (the king) flatly rejected him often and instead, granted him royal favors by giving him special prizes from time to time. Later, he decided not to submit his resignation. He said:

> Resignation is something not even worth talking about and the most uncomfortable aspect is the subsequent bestowal of royal favors. It is better not to resign.

Although at the time I thought Nongam had not been entirely faithful in his duties regarding resigning, I agreed with him after going through it personally.

I have heard that a long time ago, Zhu Xi declined the prefect of Nankang position but his refusal was not accepted. He told Lu Bogong:

> Although I want to apply for a resignation again, many people tell me, 'Even if a minister of the state or a statesman takes charge of the local military camp,[2] make sure you offer your resignation a year later.' They blame me for not knowing my place and being presumptuous. Therefore, I have no choice but to follow the advice that I should wait a little longer and submit my request after winter passes and one year has elapsed.

According to these words, it would be indiscreet to submit resignations continuously to be replaced while staying in the country. Instead of doing this, if I follow the example to offer my resignation once a year, my plea would appear trivial to the king and my request would be unquestionably denied. I have pondered these details at great length and I have observed such cases on many occasions. Therefore, I declined the position at the Board of Public Works during the Year of the Sheep and I declined the king's calling in the Year of the Chicken. Outside of these two cases, it has been five years since I have submitted my resignation from my position at the Office of the Royal Command.

I continue to pass the days in sickness.

Having the title of government official while living in the mountains is not what our ancestors had in mind. What could I say in my defense to those people who might interrogate me about this in the future! I struggle to sleep, thinking about this every night. While reading your letter, I came across this sentence:

> Although this is a situation when adopting a course of action may be difficult, your appropriate conduct will send a message to future generations.

You also say, ". . . place yourself in the *dao* and avoid being tied up by the details of the daily regulations."

These are truly magnificent words.

A man can be considered heroic only after he has conducted himself in this manner.

Even amidst turbulent times, during the ban against the heretical studies,[3] Zhu Xi left only after (the king) accepted his resignation and departure.

I personally think that as someone born without any talents necessary to the world, I was afflicted with illness early in my life. I collapsed several times before reaching middle age. I was able to garner those things that had been scattered and replenish those things that had been lacking only after growing old. I would be satisfied if:

> *I could reduce my mistakes.*
> *I could end my life doing the things I had always wanted to do.*

However, without looking back and forth or without surmising my personal abilities, if I would solely return to the *dao* regarding one aspect—that being entering a government post—this would be like having one short leg and one long leg. How could I avoid the calamity of falling down? Although I know there are certain duties to accomplish as a man, I would rather hesitate and refrain from brashly claiming I will take charge of that work by exerting an effort and marching forward. Why am I so inflexible in my attachment to old views! Your letter moved and prompted me to think profoundly. Furthermore, I will look at the times, consider righteousness, and submit my request again. How can I say that I will not do this! After all, I am able to reply at length in this manner because of your benevolent kindness. Please be advised.

In addition, hoping you will preserve and take good care of yourself, I respectfully bow and offer this response.

April 17, 1563 (the Year of the Pig)

Hwang bows his head.

1. Refers to Hyeonbo Yi (1467-1555).
2. Refers to a military camp, which was stationed in the regional province.
3. In the Song Dynasty under the reign of Ningzong, Zhu Xi reported to the king about the treacherousness of Han Tuozhou who was a power holder at the time. He boar a grudge against Zhu Xi and removed him from office by denouncing the *Learning of the Way* as a heretical study. He also banned the appointment of those people who studied the *Learning of the Way* by denouncing them as a heretical group. See the *History of Song* 429, "Biographies" 188, "Learning of the Way" 3, "The Biography of Zhu Xi."

[Letter #22 Gobong Writes Toegye]

Difference in Conduct

Dear teacher, Toegye,

The heat swelters and the rain pours continuously. How is your health these days? While missing you without end, I was shocked and worried to hear through friends that your condition had deteriorated.

I hope you enjoy your life.
I hope you will exert greater efforts in practicing the dao.

Impertinent, I am able to preserve myself solely thanks to the generous concern you have shown me from afar. I am working at a military related post because I scored poorly on my evaluation of merits. Consequently, I have been able to avoid the agony of working from dawn to dusk. I am leading a very stable life and have learned that when something is lost, something is also gained.

Because of the last letter you sent to me, I unabashedly inquired about one or two matters but the tone of the letter was quite flippant and rash—I worried you would scold me. Jajung delivered your response on his way back. I read it. You unraveled, carefully examined repeatedly, and generally discussed the principles of work. I read your letter slowly, savoring every bit. Although older generations may have shown perfect form regarding their social duties in entering government posts, since times have changed and the work is different, the method of proper conduct has changed as well.

Precise reason must fit properly with its usage. However, since I have no way to meet and personally learn from you, my yearning grows more profound with each passing day. In addition, near the end of your letter you mention, ". . . having one short leg and one long leg." I felt something enormous stir inside of me when I read this metaphor. My views in the past were wrong in this regard.

When confronting everyday situations and encountering inanimate objects, man carefully considers the *inside* and the *outside*, as well as other aspects. Man acts sequentially only after he conforms without obstructions. Otherwise, man does not think as he pleases; man does not force himself to act beyond his limits. This seems as if he has not set high aims in his life and is repressing himself; however, when self-examining his mind and body, neither mind nor body is guilty of committing any great transgressions and they both progressively gain strength. Hence, it seems possible he will discover significance. I am looking at your teachings and you seem to be saying this. When Zhuangzi said, "We will meet between morning and night,"[1] how can this necessarily mean to wait another thousand years? I am comforted and relieved to no ends. Although I want to inform you of many things, I could not include them because I was busy with my tedious work. Please excuse me. I respectfully bow and offer this letter.

June 28, 1563 (the Year of the Pig)
Bowing, yours truly,
Junior scholar, Daeseung.

I have something to add. Carefully listening to public opinion, people are saying your forthright exit from public office was commendable and that the imperial court should grant royal favors to praise you by awarding you with a prize. I have no idea how this discussion will conclude; however, you will be put in a more awkward position than previous if these discussions arise while you have submitted your resignation (for the other post). What will you do? I know you have already made your decision regarding this matter but I felt I needed to tell you what I have been hearing. Please be advised of this.

Because of my illness, I am leaving from my *Juseo* position at the Royal Secretariat[2] and moving to the *Bonggyo* position at the Office of the Recorders of the Royal Command.[3] Therefore, I am unable to leave the office because I must familiarize myself with the work. Please excuse me. I respectfully bow and inform you of these details. Daeseung bows his head.

---

1. "Those who dream of the banquet, wake to lamentation and sorrow. Those who dream of lamentation and sorrow wake to join the hunt. While they dream, they do not know that they dream. Some will even interpret the very dream they are dreaming; and only when they awake do they know it was a dream. By and by comes the Great Awakening, and then we find out that this life is really a great dream. Fools think they are awake now, and flatter themselves they know if they are really princes or peasants. Confucius and you are both dreams; and I who say you are dreams,—I am but a dream myself. This is a paradox. Tomorrow a sage may arise to explain it; but that tomorrow will not be until ten thousand generations have gone by. See the *Chuang Tzu*, Chapter II: "The Identity of Contraries."

2. A senior with a 7th official rank in the Royal Secretariat who handled the king's order.

3. A senior with a 7th official rank in the Office of the Recorders of the Royal Command, who drew up papers under the king's directions.

[Letter #23 Toegye Writes Gobong]

Standing Face to Face Against a Steep Cliff, Straight as an Arrow

I respectfully reply to you, Myeongeon.

After reading your letter, I realized that being relegated to a less important post and enjoying leisure time can be a very good thing. Truly, your new position at the Royal Secretariat, which allows you to consult with the king freely, is a good place for a person. Lately, I suffered for many months as I suddenly met one illness after another. Thanks to the help of friends who supplied me with various kinds of medication, I am just healthy enough to function. Nevertheless, as I am much weaker than I was previous, I do not have the energy to study again as I did in the old days!

Although in midlife I was fortunate enough to realize my mistakes and formed new resolutions, I have already grown old since then. I do not know how much success I will have. Furthermore, my body is once again impoverished; how can I expect any results from training myself? I am truly worried.

Your comment, "Since times have changed and the work is different, the method of proper conduct has changed as well" and the metaphor I used about the long and short leg is principally correct. However, in my last letter, I wrote everything based on my own situation. I had no choice but to speak from a low standpoint. I could not deceive others and myself by speaking of lofty things while being in such lowly circumstances. I am not satisfied with what I said, and I worry that virtuous people will reject me in their discussions. In your letter, why did you speak as you did, without rejecting or scolding me?

> *When standing face to face against a steep cliff, some act straight as an arrow.*

In your case, you are at the starting point of a long journey—has anything happened that you had not planned? I know that possessing lofty and luminous ideas, you probably have a clear view of things. I know you did not speak those words offhand by plagiarizing somebody else's words. However, regarding our debate, if I were to ask a pupil of Zhu Xi, what would he say? Would he scold us by saying:

> How is that you stand face to face against a steep cliff but have no intentions that are straight as an arrow? How is that you have learned to engage in a debate that bends one's will[1] for the sake of self profit?

I fear he would chastise me more heavily as I started the whole affair by uttering the first words.

Ha-ha.

I thought Jajung would be peacefully recuperating after being appointed the county magistrate.[2] I assumed he got what he wanted, but I have learned he has no leisure time since the county is in such a decrepit state.

I could not express everything I wanted to say; I am dizzy and tired because I have just recuperated from my illness. Preserve yourself for the ages and make an effort to study more profoundly, loftily.

I end my letter here.
I respectfully bow and write this reply.
Jiajing (The era of Shizong of the Ming Dynasty)
August 5, 1563 (the Year of the Pig)
The old and diseased Hwang bows his head.

Letter #23

Regarding what you mentioned in your additional writings, how could that possibly happen? Even if this were the case, there are those who should receive royal favors and then there is me! If I should somehow receive those special favors by mistake, this would be an affront to those who made such suggestions. Not to mention, words would not be able to describe my embarrassment. Behaving in this manner without considering the opinions of people in high and low positions will undoubtedly incite people to rise up and object.

If you are in the position to exert some influence between these two sides, I implore you to make people realize I am not worthy of this. Others are but I am not. This is how you help someone who has fallen into a pit! Cai Jiefu wrote to Dong Mou saying it was wrong for him to scheme having Zhang Fengshan enter government service.[3] That being said, what more do I need to say about myself!

    I sent the above letter and a brief attachment on August 5. I asked my nephew who lives in Seoul to deliver it to you. Before he had a chance to deliver it, you had left for the south. He returned with my undelivered letter. Soon after, I heard news that you had entered the Office of the Recorders of the Royal Command. I wanted to send this letter again but my nephew had not returned to Seoul. My friends in Seoul warned me not to give letters to just anybody; therefore, I could not find anybody suitable to deliver the letters. Even the courier who had delivered letters to me had stopped coming—I could not hear news from Seoul. I left the letter, not knowing when you would return to Seoul. Three winter months had passed and the year had already changed.

    My son has become an official at a horse relay station[4] and I had a chance to send this letter through him when he left for Seoul. I hope you will realize through this letter that those were my opinions at the time. When thinking about it, I have already tested the reactions of those around me regarding the concerns I had for you in the past and my personal concerns expressed in this letter. If this is the case, from now on, how should we continue our discussion at the appropriate times while surmising our situation? In my foolish opinion, I think we should hold fast to what we cannot change, keep loftier and more profound what we must conceal, and since we cannot surmise the other things in advance, I have not raised each point, one by one. I behave in this manner because we are still in the spotlight even though this comes after the king has decided to expunge an evil group.[5]

Please do not show this letter to others.

When my son returns, please send a few words about how you are doing. It would be an enormous relief if you appeased my stifling heart.

---

1. "By bending only one cubit, you make eight cubits straight" is mentioned in Book III, "Tang Wan Kung," Part 2 of *The Works of Mencius*. Mencius' pupil, Chen Dai, tried to persuade Mencius that meeting the prince was an insignificant matter but governing with the prince was a significant matter, which meant that by bending only one cubit Mencius could make eight cubits straight; however, Mencius criticized this as meaning compromising intentions and garnering benefits.

2. At that time, Yuil Jeong became the head of the Jinbo-*hyeon* in the Gyeongsang Province.

3. Cai Jiefu referred to Cai Ging, a scholar from the China Ming Dynasty period. His pen name was Xuzai. Zhang Fengshan referred to a contemporary scholar, Zhang Mao. When Dong Zudao asked the Emperor to engage Zhang Mao and give him a high post, Cai Ging wrote a letter to Dong Zudao saying: "Teacher Zhang has no intention of coming out at all and he will not adhere. Not only is his will firm, but also if you are a disciple who understands him, you should strongly tell the powers above not to treat the teacher like this." See *Xuzai's Collections* 2.

4. Toegye's first son, Jun, became the *Chalbang* of Angi-*do* in the Gyeongsang Province.

5. Refers to the removal of Ryang Yi and his company. Ryang Yi was a chief vassal during King Myeongjong's period and a maternal relative. He once wielded power by owning the confidence of Myeongjong but he was impeached for plotting the purge of the Confucian literati and then was ruined. Gobong was also included among those people he wanted to purge.

[Letter #24 Gobong Writes Toegye]

My Second Son Has Died from Illness

Dear teacher, Toegye,

I respectfully inquire about your current health. My respect for you grows to extremes. A short time ago, I received your letter and met your son, the *Chalbang*. I was happy and comforted to hear you were in good health. I am barely getting along thanks to your beneficial kindness.

After being dismissed from my government post last autumn and heading south, I thought I had finally achieved what I wanted. However, I received orders to return to government service soon after. For the sake of social duty, I could not remain complacent. I came to Seoul around October 20. I feel enormous lament as I have dragged my family and tried to settle in a strange place—things have not gone as I planned. On top of that, in early December my second son died from an illness.

He was loveable.
He was just seven years old and quick at learning new things.

At his sudden death, my heart suffers unbearable agony. After that, my youngest son was also in danger of losing his life, but we barely managed to save him. After worrying for such long periods, I feel as if I have lost my wits; I am only skin and bones. Since my moral training is not firm, I feel oppressed, as I realize I cannot maintain control when confronting hardships.

I carefully perused line by line everything you taught me. I think you are correct when you mention that bending your will for the sake of self-profit is an ill practice of modern day scholars; I must embrace and never forget this. I will not reiterate anything about the rest of your teachings. Our present circumstance is like this:

We are crossing a vast ocean in a boat that leaks water. It has a leaning mast. The oars are broken. Strong waves take turns smashing against the boat. Can anybody save the cargo and survive?

There are still people who point their fingers at us. I do not know how this will all end. However, as things have turned out this way, I will not pitifully devise schemes to save myself.

Because I have not reacquainted myself with the studies and have failed in cultivating virtue, I cannot fulfill my duties as a vassal and devote myself to the spirit of the late king.[1] I will worry about this until my dying day. Please understand.

While I read books and settle matters, I confront a mountain of skepticism and doubt that has built up inside of me. I sigh that I cannot meet you in person and ask you about these matters.

With the wind brushing against my face, I look far off into the distance with a melancholy heart. I earnestly miss you in vain. While begging you to glorify the *dao* after attaining a more abundant virtue, I end this letter.

I respectfully bow a hundred times and offer this letter.
Jiajing (The era of Shizong of the Ming Dynasty)
February 1, 1564 (the Year of the Rat)
Bowing, yours truly,
Junior scholar, Daeseung.

When the *Chalbang* returned the last time, I could not write a letter because I was working night duty at the government office. I apologize. Please excuse me.

---

1. See *The Book of Historical Documents*, Book VIII: "The Charge to the Viscount of Wei."

[Letter #25 Toegye Writes Gobong]

Worries until My Dying Days[1]

I respectfully reply to you, Myeongeon.

By the time I received your letter on February 2, summer and autumn had already passed but I still had not sent word, which strayed from proper etiquette. At the time, you had just started your newly appointed office, which coincided with the enormous tragedy of your son's death. I failed to comfort you, although I knew you were suffering unbearably. Although bogged down in disease, was that any excuse for not observing proper decorum?

When I—a rustic old man—heard news that you had returned to Seoul, I could not put my mind to rest. With the arrival of the cool autumn, I wonder if you are getting along fine embracing a joyful, gentle temperament and a posture that becomes renewed with every passing day. I have become an idle man, my old body stacked with diseases. These days, since every bone in my body aches due to the humidity, I drag my leg and even hobble around, which worries me even more.

Although I cannot erase the thoughts I hold deep inside of me, I have nowhere to turn when I have questions. When I think about the past, I remember how we raised our voices in heated discussion. Do you think we will ever do that again?

In your letter you mentioned, "I will worry about this until my dying day." How can I brazenly discard such insightful advice! I roughly write this letter and send it through my son who is going to Seoul. I finish my letter here and respectfully reply.

Early September, 1564 (the Year of the Rat)
Hwang bows his head.

---

1. This letter was not in *Toegye's Collections*.

[Letter #26 Gobong Writes Toegye]

Apprehension and Worry Entangle My Body

I reply to you teacher, Toegye.

As I was very busy and many things had occurred from spring until the fall, I could not send a letter inquiring about your well-being, but I missed you. The warnings you mentioned in your last letter were very effective. My concerns subsided and I was extremely comforted. However, I was worried to hear that you were suffering because of the humidity. Please take care of yourself and recuperate.

Impertinent, I am barely getting along thanks to your affectionate graces. Lately, I was in pain, as household calamities continued to strike in succession. I was very busy with the funeral procession. Only recently have I finished all the tasks. I think I can pause and catch my breath.

During the spring, I was replaced earlier than expected due to my illness.

Apprehension and worry entangle my body.
My body grows tired and my heart agonizes.
I have lost the yearning for the studies.

   I am more apprehensive because I fear I may disappoint you. I implore you to cherish yourself. I will tell the rest in detail to Ijeong Gim.[1]
   I respectfully bow and write this reply.
   October 6, 1564 (the Year of the Rat)
   Bowing, yours truly,
   Junior scholar, Daeseung.
   I have haphazardly written this letter because it is troublesome to write this while I am working night duty. I apologize.

   I respectfully inquire about your health. I revere you unceasingly. Impertinent, I have been able to leave my government office thanks to the king's affectionate favor. However, I had forgotten my studies while busy with trivial tasks. I have nothing else to say. I am ashamed and fearful. Please excuse me.
   I respectfully bow and offer this letter but I fear it is horribly lacking.
   November 12, 1564 (the Year of the Rat)
   Bowing, yours truly,
   Junior scholar, Daeseung.

---

   1. Refers to Chwiryeo Gim. His pen name was Jamjae, and Ijeong was his pseudonym. He was from Ansan and he was Toegye's pupil.

[Letter #27 Toegye Writes Gobong]

One Passage from Han Yu's Poem

   I bow and write this reply to you, Myeongoen.
   Ijeong Gim delivered your letter but I could not write a reply. Some time ago, my son delivered another letter on his way home. Since Ijeong Gim is in this area, I can frequently hear of your news. I learned that things were going well with you. Not only

was I touched, but also I was happy and congratulatory beyond expression.

The sudden death of Mr. *Pannyun*[1] (the mayor of Seoul) is related to the misfortune of the times. How sad and full of grief you must be! Will you be able to accomplish the goals you have always set for yourself (to leave your post and return home)? If you do, I am guessing you will not stay there for long. When will you come down south? You must feel invigorated and overjoyed that things have gone as planned. I worry these days that you will be stuck like a hooked fish, dragged around despite the fact the time limit has expired. However, you can only adapt to the situations unfolding before your eyes; how can you plan for anything else!

As old age and illness afflict me with one symptom after another, I have my hands full just taking care of myself in this mountain valley covered with snow and ice. This year was a bad harvest year and poverty runs rampant. The only fortunate thing:

> *The aroma of the sages permeates thicker than orchids amidst the dust, moth covered book.*

Mr. Han gave somebody a poem[2] in which the following passage appears:

> What have I done with all that time
> Without warning, another year fades away

I have always loved this passage. I repeat these words and the more I savor them, the more it appears as if he had me in mind when writing this; they are powerful enough for me to forget my worries and troubles. If you discard your government post and return home, I will have more to lose than you, since what I have to gain from being here (in the country) will be nothing more than insignificant and pitiful! From time to time, I implore you to send word of how you are doing and enlighten me on the things you have grasped.

I am not sure how far away Gwangju is from Nagan, but the magistrate, Buin Gim,[3] is from my locality. He has a courier who travels back and forth, and I think you will be able to send letters through him. If that is not possible, send your letters to Seoul and have them entrusted to Ijeong after he returns to Seoul. The letters will be delivered undoubtedly. Therefore, please send letters. Although Ijeong made a mistake by coming to me and ended up staying for a long time, he was a rare individual. However, because he has never read with much profundity, he possesses many insufficient points when observing righteousness.

The year changes.

I hope you will progressively reveal your endowed virtue and righteousness.

I wish you many good things.

I end my letter and respectfully bow.

December 27, 1564 (the Year of the Rat)

From Hwang.

When my son went to Seoul, I heard you met him on several occasions and came to the door to see him off. I am thankful and overwhelmed with gratitude.

---

1. *Pannyun* refers to the mayor of Seoul and Gobong's elder cousin, Daehang Gi. See the *Annals of Myeongjong* 29, December 12, 18th year, the Day of the Dragon.

2. Refers to the first poem from the "Six Xielus Which I Present to Yuan Shiba Independently" written by the scholar from the Tang period, Han Yu. See the *Changli's Collections* 6.

3. Buin Gim (1512-1584) was Toegye's pupil. His pseudonym was Baekyeong and his pen name was Sannam.

[Letter #28 Gobong Writes Toegye]

Like a Trapped Fish Caught on a Hook

I write this letter to my teacher.

I respectfully inquire about your well-being. How is your health? With the coming of the new year, I would be happy and overjoyed if you devoted yourself even more to your studies. Impertinent, I am preserving what life I have left thanks to your affectionate grace. I am worried because it has been two months since I have been able to go out; I caught a cold in early December, which turned severe. I was not able to take care of it for a long time and grew weak. I became afflicted with all kinds of illnesses.

Letter #28

A short while ago, Ijeong Gim delivered your letter. I was pleased and comforted after studying your words, which opened my eyes. Nothing can compare to the feeling of having my worries cleanly washed away. Adding to the disturbances incurred by my illness, I am falling deeper into the trappings of the secular world. I am having a difficult time climbing out, and I am flustered. You once again guided and presided over me; however, I am filled with the utmost of shame and embarrassment because I fear I will be unable to repay your kindness.

Furthermore, I am not used to the work here; things have not been going as I had intended; and, the two chances I had to leave government service have slipped away forever. I thought about using my long-term illness as an excuse to resign, but people would see right through such a scheme; and to make matters worse, the situation would be harder to resolve on a later date. When I think about it, I foresee much inconvenience with such a plan. While living as if a trapped fish caught on a hook, I can never break free from my shallow scheme of just receiving my stipend. I can only sigh when looking back on my life.

If the strength of our learning is not solid and our relationships to the secular world entangle us, ultimately, we will fail to walk in the footsteps of the ancient ones even though we make an effort. Using the following analogy:

> *One pulls back on the string of a bow.*
> *One can pull back the string to the point one's strength allows, nothing more.*

It is not strange that a person acts feebly following the secular world and is untidy regarding entering and leaving government service.

When I imagine your beautiful posture as you are far away from me, savoring the *dao* in times of leisure, and imagine your happiness as you enjoy the brief yearend sunlight, I unknowingly become excited, my mind leaning to you. However, since I cannot meet you, I have difficulty repressing words of lament. What else can I do but to lift my head and gaze into the distance?

I wanted to write frequently and send you at least brief letters inquiring about your well-being and at the same time, I wanted to reacquaint myself with the old studies by asking you questions; however, I am needlessly busy, not to mention I am having difficulty finding a courier. Because I was unable to do this, a sense of futility fills me. From the moment I stepped into government service, since people have turned their eyes to me—although this may be a foolish and unpolished thinking—I have always been very afraid. I did not want to harm such a distinguished teacher as yourself, by haphazardly sending you letters again. Can you understand this? Can you empathize with me?

I still keep close to my heart your previous warnings about becoming the object of people's reverence while holding an important position. However, I realize I am falling into that trap, and I do not know how to cope with the future matters that will arise. Please understand this, as I am filled with profound fear and lament.

I have sent several kinds of royally distributed medication.[1] Please consider keeping this medication as first aid for the country villagers.

Mr. Gim has traveled a long way to study under you and it is an opportunity that is hard to come by. Since somebody associated with Mr. Gim died unfortunately, how can we overcome our uneasiness and sorrows? I am worried because I have heard Mr. Gim was too poor to bury the person properly. Please be advised of this.

I respectfully bow again and offer this letter.
Jiajing (The era of Shizong of the Ming Dynasty)
January 23, 1565 (the Year of the Cow)
Bowing, yours truly,
Junior scholar, Daeseung.
My writing was not as neat as I would have liked it to be. I am having trouble holding the brush as my right arm is in pain. I apologize.

---

1. Refers to medicine, which the king gave vassals on the *Nabil*, which was the third *Miil* (the Day of the Sheep) after the winter solstice, and it was a day when the imperial court among others held memorial services for royal ancestors, the guardian deities of the state, and common household ancestors.

[Letter # 29 Gobong Writes Toegye]

I Have Entered the Library[1]

To teacher,
    I respectfully inquire about your health. I sincerely miss and respect you. Impertinent, I have been barely able to preserve what is left of my life thanks to your affectionate graces. On the eighth of the previous month, I was appointed to the *Jwarang* position at the Board of War, and I frantically worked days and nights to accomplish my allotted tasks; it was difficult to bear, as this was after I had been ill for a long time. However, yesterday, I moved after notifying the king it was my turn in the rotation to enter the Library. I am relieved because now I can rest. I heard news of your life through Ijeong Gim, and I was comforted to know my letter had been delivered to you. However, I am unclear about your final thoughts about what I had mentioned. Please be advised and write a response. On the seventeenth of this month, Mr. Gim moved the casket to Ansan and finished the funeral service. Everything worked out well. Please be advised. Negligent and careless, I could not fully prepare this letter.
    I respectfully bow and offer this letter.
    March 28, 1565 (the Year of the Cow)
    Bowing, yours truly,
    Junior scholar, Daeseung.

---

    1. Or *Dokseodang*, was an organization established by the state, where young civil vassals read and studied, and it was also called the *Hodang*. When someone entered the *Dokseodang*, he could study without attending to other troublesome duties.

[Letter #30 Toegye Writes Gobong]

While Submitting an Appeal, the Nation Mourns the Passing of Royalty

I bow and reply to you, Myeongeon.

The teachings revealed in the letter you sent on January 23 were beautiful and precious. In addition, you asked questions in the annex, but I have remained reticent, daring not to respond flippantly because my shallow insights and squalid opinions are not sufficient. Furthermore, I could not write a reply letter because of my illness. The magistrate of Uiheung, Mr. Gim, delivered your letter, which asked me questions again; I was embarrassed and burdened.

My footsteps never seem harmonious with the world, and the world continues to obstruct my path. Although I had been unable to resign brashly from government service, recently, I risked possible turmoil and presented the king with an appeal for my resignation. While taking this appeal to the king, I heard news the king's grandmother had passed away, and I think it will be impossible to submit the appeal.[1] I cannot run to the funeral procession. Since I cannot plead my case, I cannot settle down as I am depressed, afraid, in agony, and worried. I feel like the metaphor you used in your previous letter, when you said you felt like a hooked fish because you were inexperienced in handling the work.

Everybody knows I have become feckless because illnesses have been festering inside of me for a long time; however, things have not gone smoothly and I am having difficulties leaving government service. Will it be easy for you to retire from your post when none of these conditions applies to you! I have always expressed my concerns that you had miscalculated; however, you did not take (my concerns) seriously. Today, I think you finally understand the great pains this old man endured while forging through the world. This is my greater fear: one way or the other, you will not be able to avoid the trials of the world even though you may change your past attitudes by kindling your indigent heart and planning to safeguard your household without trouble. You will undoubtedly confront this. What do you think?

I was relieved to hear you had entered the Library from your *Jwarang* position at the Board of War. My only worry is that they will call you back to service, considering there is much work these days.

Letter #30

I was heartbroken over Ijeong Gim. While staying here, some place far from home, he encountered the death of a close relation in vain. I heard that Ijeong could not hold funeral processions for this person; however, I heard you helped enormously in making the funeral happen. I was relieved and filled with admiration.

The *Jocheon* Ceremony[2] is one of the major ceremonies, and the ceremonies widely performed today are different from those of the past. I could not refrain from writing all my points of suspicion in the annex. I ask you to look over each one of them and reply. I am very thankful for the royally distributed medication you sent. As Ijeong is in another place, I think it will be more difficult to find a courier. I am sending this letter through somebody in the village who is traveling to Seoul. I am not sure if this letter will make it to you safely. Although I have many things to say, I end my letter here.

I respectfully bow and write this reply.
April 23, 1565 (the Year of the Cow)
From Hwang.

I would be greatly relieved if you gave *Jwarang* Yi the enclosed letter sent to *Sapyeong*[3] Iseong Yi and asked him to deliver it. I heard he was robbed. I worry since he does not seem to be very well off.

---

1. At that time the Empress Dowager, Yun, passed away. See the *Annals of Myeongjong* 31, April 6, the 20th year, the Day of the Monkey.

2. Toegye used *Jocheon* interchangeably with *Checheon*, which meant that the *Choejangbang* took the ancestral tablet to his house to perform an ancestral sacrifice when a descendant's line died out. *Choejangbang* referred to the highest degree of kindred among four generations, and the tablet was moved to the next highest degree when the highest kin died. When the *Choejangbang* no longer existed, the tablet was usually buried in front of the tomb, and this was called the *maean*.

3. *Sapyeong* refers to the senior with a 6th official rank in the *Jangyewon;* they handled documents regarding slaves and legal cases.

[Letter # 31 Gobong Writes Toegye]

During the National Mourning for the Passing of Royalty

My response to you, teacher.

I was relieved to hear through your letter dated April 23 that you were getting along fine. I felt as if a heavy burden had been lifted after reading your detailed explanations. Impertinent, I have been barely able to preserve my sick body thanks to your affectionate graces.

I was overjoyed to hear that you had submitted your written appeal for resignation. If the heavens support your amassed sincerity and you fulfill your lifelong wish, the *dao* would shine even more. Unable to compose my reverent heart, I wanted to write you a congratulatory message, but I could not send my regards as I was frantically busy handling the national mourning for the king's grandmother. In addition, I could not find a suitable courier. Time continued to pass and I had not sent a single letter. I am ashamed and full of regrets.

As I am so impertinent—although I am working in a relatively easy office—I am still associated with the Board of War. As you correctly pointed out, I laboriously attend obligatory formalities and spend my time ignobly. What can I do about my agonizing heart! Starting a few years back, I had difficulty spreading my hands and feet as I acquired an illness because of the long lasting humidity, which had me exhibit symptoms of physical numbness. Even today, my knees ache, and I have difficulty extending my leg as I feel strain. The symptoms grow progressively worse. Considering my medical condition, needless to say, I cannot ride a horse and I fear it will be difficult for me to live long. Even with this being the case, my ties to secularism continue to ensnare me, and I continue to abandon my original intentions.

I reflect on my life and naturally grow sad. How can I not take to heart the warning "planning to safeguard your household without trouble"? Will it be possible to inform you of everything outside of this? I have no way of inviting and talking to you personally; my futile dejection and yearning grow to extremes. I ask you to look over and consider this.

Regarding the letter you sent to *Sapyeong* Yi, I gave it immediately to *Jeonjeok* Yi and he has told me he has already delivered it.

I will follow your warnings to be cautious in delivering letters. Although I have some questions regarding the *Jocheon* Ceremony among others, I could not write them all as I was busy. I will ask you when the time is right, and I ask you to be advised of these matters.

    I respectfully bow twice and offer this letter.
    May 27, 1565 (the Year of the Cow)
    Bowing, yours truly,
    Junior scholar, Daeseung.

[Letter #32 Toegye Writes Gobong]

Asking About Several Suspicious Clauses

    I bow and write my reply to you, Myeongeon.
    Ijeong Gim's courier delivered your letter and I learned of your news through your letter dated May 27, and in your short letter that arrived soon after, I learned that you had left the Board of War and moved to the Royal College. What a relief! A short time ago, I sent a letter through Jajung Jeong who was going to Seoul. I am not sure if he will deliver the letter on time.
    In your letter, you mention the symptoms of being unable to spread your legs and the tightening sensation were light in the beginning but grow progressively worse. I implore you to be careful and to take the necessary precautions. I also thank you for taking the time to pass along my letter to *Sapyeong* Yi.
    Fortunately, since the king has released from service those government officials living in hiding in the country, this is the time to focus on the *dao*; however, I am ashamed in front of my ancestors for being so old and foolish. Merely, I have left all my friends and I am alone. I think profoundly about the day when I can recite "Youhuaifu," but I sigh, as it will be difficult to go a long distance to meet friends. I would be grateful if you resolved the doubts I have regarding several of the articles in the letters you would send through future couriers. I end my letter here. I respectfully bow.
    June 24, 1565 (the Year of the Cow)
    From Hwang.

What is the fist name of Mr. Wang of Shiliang who appears in the annotations of the *Classic of Rites*? In what period did he live? From where was he? What kind of person was he?

The first name of Mr. Xiong, whose pen name was Wuxuan, was Gangda, and this person wrote an annotation to *Xingliqunshu*. The first name of Mr. Xiong, whose pen name was Tuiji, was He, and his pseudonym was Qufei. This person wrote *Hanmuquanshu*. The two Mr. Xiongs mentioned above are most assuredly two separate people. Early on, Xiong He wrote *Kaotingshuyuanji*. Later, while Qiu Xi wrote *Chongxiuji*, he cited Xiong He's saying, "The two writings of Wuxuan and Mr. Xiong." We can find this in the supplement of the last volume of the *Annals of the Wuyi Mountain*. In addition, in *The Supplement to the Great Compendium on Nature and Pattern*, under the last names of various Confucian scholars, I remember both names (Xiong) being used interchangeably. I do not have this supplement and I cannot remember clearly; please research this matter and inform me of your findings.

Chenbo of Nantang, whose pen name was Maoqing, wrote "Fengxiangyemeizhen." Although this person's studies were above average, he is not mentioned anywhere else; therefore, I do not know in what period he lived nor do I know what kind of person he was.

1566-1567
BETWEEN SEOUL AND UIJU

[Letter #33 Gobong Writes Toegye]

Theory of the Human Mind and the Dao Mind

Dear teacher,

I respectfully inquire about your well-being. I have not stopped worrying about your health, and I have been unable to focus on anything else. Impertinent, I am getting along moderately fine thanks to your concern although it has been difficult. Recently, I heard that you declined the king's calling due to illness but that he appointed you to a higher government post. While admiring you, I was both happy and afraid. After receiving *Jikgang* Jajung Jeong's letter, I learned that you had been replaced; I wanted to comfort you. I missed you more profoundly because the details of what had happened to you were unknown to me. I respectfully wish you good health and hope you attain the highest virtue.

On the way home last winter after receiving a temporary furlough, the cold journey damaged my body. This has progressed into a serious illness, and I have regressed in my studies. Since I was liberated from my government post, I had hoped to be hoarded up in the country, not involved in any kind of work. However, starting from the spring and lasting until summer, disease and anxiety afflicted me continuously. Due to this long-term distress and agony, I was dejected and grieved: I did not find the time to reacquaint and manage the studies I had pursued in the past. I have been lethargically passing time.

The tightening symptoms in my wrists and knees continue to degenerate as time passes. I want to receive acupuncture and moxibustion* therapy. As I have wantonly taken the *Nangjung* position at the Board of Rites, I was shocked, afraid, and at a loss for action after receiving the appointment. However, I am not fit to enter a government post. I will seek moxibustion therapy, wait for my condition to improve, and laggardly look for the proper way to conduct myself. I am extremely concerned as it will be uncomfortable to travel back and forth. I do not know how I should conduct myself. I hope you will guide me towards the best course of action.

After receiving your letter dated June 24 last autumn, I was moved and overcome with comfort. After that, not only was I too busy because of cumbersome tasks to write a letter, but also I had difficulty finding a courier to deliver even a single letter inquiring about your well-being. I have still not written a reply although it approaches a year since I briskly moved back south. I cannot begin to express my shame and abashment. Making matters worse, I am planted in the outskirts of Honam, which is far away and couriers are rare—how can I possibly convey to you how much I miss you! I truly feel a sense of futile loss.

I could not carelessly inform you regarding the clauses of Mr. Xiong of Shiliang among others because I did not have access to the appropriate sources. What I can say is Wuxuan and Tuiji seem to be two different people, but once again, without any sources, I cannot say this with absolute assurance. In your letter, you mentioned that you had sent a letter through Jajung who was on his way to Seoul, but when I asked Jajung, he said he had not received a letter from you. I feel perplexed since I do not know what happened. I add another letter and ask for your guidance. I hope you will offer detailed comments about my opinions.

The weather is getting hot. Please be mindful of your health as the seasons change and put at ease the hearts of those people who apotheosize you.

I respectfully bow and offer this letter.
This letter has many shortcomings.
May 1, 1566 (the Year of the Tiger)
Because of a painful wrist, junior scholar, Daeseung, barely wrote this letter and informed his teacher of his thoughts. I apologize.

From the very start, since Master Cheng and Zhu Xi did not have any special thoughts regarding the theory of the human mind and the *dao* mind, this theory is best represented in the preface to Zhu Xi's *Commentary on the Doctrine of the Mean*.[1] If scholars would carefully study this, they would understand, at least, half of that theory. Regarding the book I have been reading lately, *Kunzhiji*, written by Luo Zhengan, I have heard that his assertions are different from the theories of Master Cheng and Zhu Xi; however, I am not so sure about this. I carefully examined Luo Zhengan's idea, and I learned he really had no choice but to make such assertions because he regarded principle and material force to be one. Truly, you could say he committed "silgyeon's mistake."[2]

While Master Cheng and Master Zhang[3] made clear in their theories that nature is good, they discussed physical nature saying:

> Nature is good because of the principle and the reason it is occasionally not good is solely because of the movement of material force. The theory regarding the human mind and the *dao* mind is similar.

This is the reason I mention above "they did not have any special thoughts" regarding this matter. However, Zhengan viewed as one, the principle and material force and said Zhu Xi's words, "the reason for" were incorrect. He goes on to say, "If you use the word 'reason,' that is implying they are two." Therefore, he could not separate and attach the human mind and *dao* mind to principle and material force.

Although it seems easy to discover the bias of this kind of theory, why does the elder, Gwahoe No,[4] accept that theory wholeheartedly? While Iljae Yi strenuously objected to Zhengan, he also derided Gwahoe; however, Gwahoe did not budge from his original assertions. Iljae's theory also lost sight of Master Cheng and Zhu Xi's original intentions. Early on, although I thought Zhengan was wrong, I also thought Iljae's theory was groundless, as well. Iljae said:

> Yao and Shun transcend the human minds. Superior wisdom comes after what one knows from birth. Because Yu and Yen Hui are one grade below the sages, they have human minds. When Emperor Yao lost his reign to Shun, he did not mention the theory of the human and the *dao* mind. When Shun lost his reign to Yu,[5] he did mention it because Yu possessed a human mind.

Looking at these several clauses, I have no idea about what he means.

I can only sigh.

Nothing here is worth rigorously investigating.

The elder Mr. No strenuously asserted Luo Zhengan's theory to the point of discussing this with people while showing poems he had written. I was always unclear about what he really thought, and I had regretted not visiting him and asking him about this matter. However, last winter, while following a royal decree to move to a new place of exile, Mr. No passed by where I lived.[6] I rushed to meet him while he passed, and tentatively asked him about the theory.

He was just as I had heard he would be.

I asked:

"According to the views of a renowned elder such as yourself, why did you say that feelings were dangerous?"

"Feelings are dangerous because they can be good and evil," he replied.

I asked again:

"Zhengan's theory clings to that assertion because he views principle and material force as being one. In your opinion, do you think principle and material force are two separate things or are they one?"

"Although the ancient ones gave them separate names, *principle* and *material force*, how can we say they have two different meanings?" he replied.

By that time, because Mr. No was very inebriated, I could not make forceful arguments; however, after I returned, I thought about it and could not help but to feel lament as his words were so odd.

When considering Zhu Xi's words, "We can only say man's feeling was originally good. We cannot say it was evil." Although this is a sound, irreversible argument, Mr. No said, "Feelings are dangerous because they can be both good and evil." How can this be correct when it claims anything is possible without basing it on any sort of established reason? In my opinion, we cannot say principle and material force are two, but if we say they are one, there would be no demarcation between the *dao* and the *bowl* that holds the *dao*. However, Mr. No claims, "Although the sages and wise men named them differently, they do not have two meanings," which implies that from the beginning the sages and wise men gave them phony names—*principle* and *material force*—without any substance. I cannot help but have suspicions about these two items.

Mr. No also said, "Because pupils transcribed the *Classified Conversations of Master Zhu*, there is really no need to look at it. Furthermore, there is no need to read the collected commentaries of the *Four Books* and the *Five Classics* because later generations edited and put it together." Because these theories go contrary to reason, I am very worried his ideas will gradually proliferate and corrupt those who study.

However, besides being lowly and speaking rashly, my knowledge is short and immature. I did not dare to argue and persuade Mr. No to turn back to the good side. What if you rigorously analyzed this issue and opened the eyes of scholars? This is truly the duty for one who is responsible for the *dao*! Teacher, you cannot continue to decline this calling! Would you consider sending a letter to the elder Mr. No, helping him to realize his mistake and aiding his return to the right path? Impertinent and rash, I have committed an egregious sin. I earnestly hope you will examine and consider this. I respectfully bow and inquire.

Postscript: I want to ask many things, but starting a few days ago, my strength has been wavering and my mind has been remote. I lament to great lengths, as I have not been able to convey all my thoughts, struggling to write this letter. Please understand.

Because the day when I will keep you company is remote and unscheduled, it is becoming difficult to harbor my reverence from afar. What can I do? I respectfully inform you.

---

* A type of therapy where moxa is burned or cauterized to the skin.

1. "Since the mind's 'being empty and spiritual' and 'the ability of knowing and perceiving' are one, the difference between the human mind and the *dao* mind arises from the mind's uniqueness of physical form; and also originates from the properness of human nature and the heavenly mandate; and from the differences in knowing and perceiving. Accordingly, it is uncomfortable because it is perilous and it is difficult to look at it because it is subtle." See Zhu Xi's *Commentary on the Doctrine of the Mean*, Preface section.

2. Refers to the fault when people see only truth without considering both sides of emptiness and truth in balance.

3. Refers to Zhang Zai. His pseudonym was Zihou and his pen name was Hengqu.

4. Refers to Susin No. His pen name was Sojae, Ijae, Amsil, Elder Yeobong, and so on, and Gwahoe was his pseudonym.

5. "The mind of man is restless,—prone to err; its affinity for the *right* way is small. Be discriminating, be undivided, that you may sincerely hold fast the Mean." See *The Book of Historical Documents*, Book II: "The Counsels of the Great Yu."

6. Susin No who had been dismissed from his office and had been exiled to Jindo by way of Suncheon; he was moved to Goesan after 19 years.

[Letter #34 Toegye Writes Gobong]

Although I Have Left Two Government Offices

I respectfully bow and write this reply to you, Myeongeon.

During the end of last winter, Jajung sent me a letter and he mentioned you had traveled south and would not be returning for a while. I wanted to send a letter inquiring about your welfare, but I hesitated because I did not know where you were. My respect and longing for you did not leave my heart for a single day. I learned of the various situations that arose after returning south from Jajung who had given me your letter; while feeling stifled, how could I explain in words the manner in which my concerns were cleared and my worries were lifted! However, before you had fully recuperated, I learned that you had received word you should fill a government post. I worry that you will waver while deciding whether to go or not; however, you still have time to decide whether to enter the post or not. Please act after considering the prognosis of your illness. Of course, you should not stubbornly stick to one course of action without flexibility,[1] but how can you discard a small duty for a big one?

From the past, since my conduct has been anything but proper and I grew in fame and deceived the king, can you imagine how difficult and anxious my life has been from the beginning! I considered it an enormous relief to be narrowly pardoned from continuing in my government post. I mentioned that an issue with which I had been wrestling with for thirty years had finally been resolved; however, how could I have imagined the kinds of things that transpired this year would happen again![2] As you well know, I am very foolish.

I am ill.

I am old and weak.

How can I be expected to handle such an important position!

Granted I can be a thoughtless person, but how can I immediately turn around and accept such a big and important post after declining to the end smaller and lesser important government posts? This is why I requested to resign at the risk of dying. Unexpectedly, the king was lenient with his royal favor. Not only did he not punish me, but also he released me from two other government posts[3] I had held. I was thankful, grateful, and embarrassed beyond measure. I have one office remaining: the undeserved government

Letter #34

post at the *Jijungchubusa*. I asked the king to replace me. It seemed as if I had made my decision prematurely, and public opinion regarding this matter spread scandalously. I heard many scolding remarks. As I continue to forsake the wishes of the king, I fear events will not turn out the way I want. Therefore, I am staying quiet, avoiding confrontation and carefully observing the situation from the outside. I do not know how things will turn out. I have had no choice but to act in this manner; I leave the rest to the heavens.

Scholars should celebrate the fact Gwahoe No has moved some place closer to us. When I heard you waited for him and then met him while he passed, it rekindled thoughts of the past. I carefully looked over all the various assertions you mentioned in the annex. Although it would be appropriate to address each one of them, my circumstances being the way they are, forbid me from doing that. In times like this, people who witnessed or heard two people debating through correspondences in this manner would undoubtedly gossip about it. Furthermore, such behavior would be improper in light of reason; therefore, I will temporarily refrain from responding to you. I will not forget to respond later.

Most of what you wrote in your letter was reasonable. Last year, by chance, I had the opportunity to read two verses by Gwahoe regarding the human mind and the *dao* mind; I was filled with enormous suspicion and since we are aware of his views now, my colleagues are very concerned. I have heard that many people in Seoul are concerned with this matter and most of their opinions and arguments are similar to yours; however, if we try to compare and elucidate each point, we will end up in conflict, fighting amongst ourselves. We will find ourselves in the same situation where Bian Zhuangzi seized an opportunity.[4] At the same time, if we do not act, we will end up disheveling the *dao* while studying the *School of Principle* in name only. This is not a trivial matter. What will be the best course of action?

I think Jajung will definitely return to his native village in the fall. While he was still in Seoul, I asked somebody to give him this letter to deliver. I have informed you about these several matters.

My illness makes me tired.
I end my letter here.
I respectfully bow and write this reply.
June 16, 1566 (the Year of the Tiger)
Hwang bows his head.

1. A phrase mentioned while playing the *geomungo* (a Korean harp) with the bowstring bridges glued; this refers to being too serious and lacking flexibility.
2. Refers to Toegye being appointed to the Minister of Public Works in February.
3. At that time Toegye was the *Dongjisa* of the Office of the Royal Command, the Minister of Public Works, and the *Jehak* of the Office of the Recorders of the Royal Command at the same time.
4. When Bian Zhuangzi was going to stab a tiger, Guang Xuzi dissuaded him and said, "Now two tigers are eating one cow and they will surely come to fight; if they fight, the bigger one will get injured and the smaller one will die. Then, if you stab the injured one, you can kill two tigers with one effort. Zhuangzi listened to his words and waited; before long, the two tigers fought each other as Guang Xuzi said and he caught both tigers at once. See the *Shi ji* 70, "Biographies" 10, "The Biography of Zhang Yi."

[Letter #35 Gobong Writes Toegye]

Giving You the "General Summary" and "Postscript Explanation" of the Four-Seven Thesis

Teacher, I reply to your letter.

Although I asked Jajung, who was very far away, to deliver a letter I had written in the beginning of May, we lost contact and I could not inquire about how you were doing. As my reverence for you did not cease, I wrote another letter and wanted to send it through another person, but again, I failed to send it. However, recently, I received Jajung's letter and your letter, which he delivered. When I broke the seal, opened, and read the letter, I was overcome with comfort and gratitude. I was relieved and pleased to learn you were more than just getting along fine. My only complaint can be that after you sent your correspondence, a sandstorm blew in and it has become very hot.

Have comprehensive aid in nourishing yourself and in your training of the *Learning of the Way*.

Take care of yourself.

I prostrate myself before you and hope you will be more complete in your practice of the studies.

Letter #35

Fortunately, I have been able to avoid illness thanks to your affectionate graces, which watched over me. As I quiescently reside in the remote and desolate country, I am generously thrilled when I unexpectedly reach an understanding regarding certain matters while occasionally reacquainting myself with and researching my old studies. However, since I do not have a teacher or friends to sharpen and refine my studies, I am still uncertain about many things. That is when I think of you, so far away and without warning, my heart agonizes.

Previously, I received notice of an appointment to a government post; however, time to fill the post elapsed and somebody else filled the post because illness prevented me from going. Just a few days later, a messenger rushed in and announced the king had appointed me to the same government post I had been appointed to in the past. As I hosted the messenger, I was engrossed with all kinds of thoughts. My lament grew deeper. Although I have recuperated slightly, I have still not recovered my energy. I do not think it will be possible for me to disregard my physical condition this time as well and return to the path of government service.

I was filled with enormous respect, as I prostrated myself and carefully read your detailed reply. You truly read my mind when you said, "Of course, you should not stubbornly stick to one course of action without flexibility, but how can you discard a small duty for a big one?" Judging from the comprehensive views of my colleagues regarding this matter, their opinions paled in comparison. Although people may have avoided stubbornly asserting one course of action, they discarded smaller duties for bigger ones. I have been heartbroken because of this; however, I could not solve this problem on my own. After receiving your guidance, a concealed problem has been lucidly resolved.

My views remaining unclear, I worry I might not be able to make definitive, correct decisions. A virtuous man enters government service for the purpose of righteousness; then, how can it be that the teachings of the old sages were words spoken to deceive us! They said:

> Although man must not put in disarray the ethical conduct of being faithful to the king in order to purify himself, man must not seek government service while forgetting righteousness.[1]

In addition, after learning through your letter in detail how you were conducting yourself, my heart leans to you in extremes. I prostrate myself before you and implore you—somebody who has embraced an exalted virtue and a great task—to select your methods in advance and avoid distressful situations. You were very accurate regarding the obligation of entering and leaving government posts. You were completely reasonable when you said in so many words, "I will do my best and leave the results to the heavens." However, between the extremes of working or not working, and working for a long time or withdrawing quickly,[2] I ask you to consider this again profoundly. What do you think?

Although you did not send any eye-opening teachings regarding the theory of the human mind and the *dao* mind, I was deeply relieved and relieved again that you had already acknowledged that I was correct. Line for line, although you were correct when saying, "We may do this in the name of the *School of Principle*, but we will end up disheveling the *dao*," this does not seem like a trivial problem. Although we should refrain from loudly disputing each point, we should, by all means, examine, discriminate, and make an effort to seek the truth. While doing this, it would be right to say we should watch carefully over one or two scholars, waiting for future sages to come into being. This reminds me of the words of Zhu Xi who said, "Although present day people do not believe in this theory, unquestionably, some people in later days will recognize this theory, and it will change the minds of a few people."

To avoid clamorous suspicions, how can we not stand up and fight when they are wastefully demolishing the hearts of people by popularizing at will such vicious assertions!

In the past, while I was in Seoul, I met the respectable Mr. Taehwi Heo[3] by chance. His assertions were so askew that I could not debate every point. He went so far as to divide the *bieun* (reaches wide and far and yet is secret) in *The Doctrine of the Mean*[4] and attached it to the things that transcended the physical and the things that were bound by the physical. I tried my best to refute him. I read in Jajung's letter that Taehwi still stubbornly sticks to his assertions. Taehwi's assertions were so biased I feared there was no way to correct them. However, I deeply sighed when I heard the rumors that Gwahoe's theory resembled Taehwi's theory.

In *The Great Treatise*, it states, "The *dao* refers to that which transcends the physical, and material force refers to that which is bound in the physical." In *The Doctrine of the Mean*, it states, "The way which the superior man pursues, reaches wide and far, and yet is secret." Accordingly, the *dao* transcends the physical originally. How can he think to divide and attach that which is bound to the physical? These are easily distinguishable like beans and barley; however, this says much about his studies, if he cannot even make this distinction!

In most cases, this is a result of carelessly reading in his everyday life, of enjoying speculations and conjectures. Furthermore, when questions are posed, he cannot simply confess and say, "I do not know." He fabricates words through speculation and conjecture.

He fools himself and others.

What kind of disposition and reasoning is this!

On one hand, I am repulsed and on the other, I am fearful. I prostrate myself before you and implore you to sharply examine this and develop a strategy to put to rest all these evil and crooked assertions. This would be an enormous relief.

In the past, regarding the *Four-Seven Thesis*, I told you all my narrow-minded views without taking into consideration how contemptible and occluded my thoughts may be because I wanted genuinely to learn the truth through your guidance.

There were occasions during our correspondences when we did not agree. This happened as I expressed my opinions; it was not my intention to create chaos deliberately. Early on, after receiving a quatrain in your reply, I felt remote and did not think I would have the opportunity to ask you; consequently, I did not inquire about it for a long time. As I think about it, even while passing the time in leisure, you are probably delving deeply into your studies and have become more precise and detailed. Most likely you have become increasingly enlightened.

I am using these tranquil times, as well, and after brooding and examining again, I have encountered many points in my previous contentions about which I had not considered. Therefore, I boldly wrote one "Postscript Explanation" and one "General Summary." Although I intended to deliver them to you, I could not find a courier. I send them to you now and I would consider it an enormous relief if you inspected them.

I am finding it difficult to ask people to deliver letters because Honam and Yeongnam are so far apart, and entrusting the letter to somebody for delivery to Seoul has not been easy, as well. Because I cannot convey the extent of my heart, which inclines toward you, I sigh because I am at a loss. In the letter you sent last year, you mentioned I could deliver letters by asking the Nagan magistrate, but it is a two-day trip from here to Nagan. I could not contact you for a long time, as it was difficult for me to indiscriminately visit and ask him for such a favor. I do not know him that well. I have not been able to inform you of the rest.

While beseeching you to preserve yourself for the sake of the *dao*, I respectfully bow and offer this reply.

July 15, 1566 (the Year of the Tiger)
Bowing, yours truly,
Junior scholar, Daeseung.

While I was here, I wanted to talk to you every time a fervent thought overcame me. However, I knew that would be too presumptuous and impudent. Therefore, I refrained from brazenly rushing and telling you. However, I felt uncomfortable keeping these thoughts enshrouded and I boldly intend to tell you about them once again.

As I quietly ponder, I think you should not act lightly in times such as now. Since the king has already fostered you, I think you must go at least once and express your appreciation for his kindness. If you inform the king of your thoughts, but he does not agree with you and you return, it would be acceptable in light of righteousness. However, if you continue to refuse sternly and if the king, once again, rescinds his fondness for wise people which he has developed, in the broad scope of things, I worry and fear harm may come. Although you are not faced with ideal circumstances—did you see the sages and wise men ever give up? I prostrate myself before you and ponder: if you have already considered everything I have said thus far—you must be delaying moving forward and vacillating because there is some other perplexing issue, right?

Although I am foolish, stubborn, and rude, you did not rashly consider me ignoble; it has been several years since I have received the kindness of your affectionate guidance from time to time. There is not a day when my loving and yearning affection ceases. I have always worried about your affairs as if they were my own.

Although I did not intend to hold these views—without knowing if these views are right or wrong—I have dared to ask you about them. It is my hope but could you guide me regarding this matter?

---

    1. "To take office meant to perform righteously between the sovereign and the minister. As to the failure of right principles to make progress, although he is aware of that, he may not retire from office. If it is considered righteousness, naturally there is a point not to be ignoble in success and failure of work, entering (government service) and retiring. Therefore, even though one may not allow the great relation to come to confusion by wishing to maintain his personal purity, he may not pursue only government service while forgetting righteousness." See Zhu Xi's commentary of *Confucian Analects,* Book XVIII: "Wei Tsze," Chapter VII.

    2. "When it was proper to go into office, then to go into it; when it was proper to keep retired from office, then to keep retired from it; when it was proper to continue in it long, then to continue in it long; when it was proper to withdraw from it quickly, then to withdraw quickly: that was the way of Confucius." See *The Works of Mencius,* Book II: "Kung-sun Chau," Part I, Chapter II.

    3. Refers to Yeop Heo. His pen name was Chodang and Taehwi was his pseudonym. He was Gyeongdeok "Hwadam" Seo's pupil.

    4. See *The Doctrine of the Mean,* Chapter XII: "The way which the superior man pursues, reaches wide and far, and yet is secret."

[Letter #36 Gobong Writes Toegye]

While Moving from Many Government Posts

Dear teacher,

    I respectfully inquire about your well-being these days. I cannot overcome my longing heart. During the beginning of last month, a royal decree appointed me to the *Gyori* position at the Office of the Royal Lecturers and soon after, I was appointed to the *Heonnap* position at the Office of the Censor General. After receiving two official orders from the king, I considered it my moral duty and could not side with comfort. I risked illness and headed on my way; however, I was moved again to the *Geomsang* position at the State Council. I barely made it to Seoul, as I was exhausted from riding the horse. On that day, I could barely resemble human form thanks to the benevolent grace of your supervision.

While in the country, I was extremely comforted after hearing of your news through Jeong "Chilgye" Gim. However, I could not send word to you, as you were far away, blocked off by mountains and streams. While revering and missing you, I futilely worry to extremes. I pray that only good things will befall you and end my letter here.

Please be advised. I respectfully bow and offer this letter.

The leap month of October 11, 1566 (the Year of the Tiger)

Bowing, yours truly,

Junior scholar, Daeseung.

I hope you will carefully examine the assertions I sent to you last time and teach me. I could not express everything I wanted to say as I have written this in-between my busy schedule. I will wait for a future courier. Please understand this, as well.

[Letter #37 Toegye Writes Gobong]

Comprehensive Good View of the "Four-Seven Thesis'" "General Summary" and "Postscript Explanation"

I respectfully bow and write this reply to you, Myeongeon.

Last autumn, while Jajung was in Seoul, he sent your correspondence dated July 15; however, as I was ill, I delayed writing a response, which made me feel disquieted. During the winter, I had heard that you had been appointed repeatedly to (different) government posts. I was doubly concerned because I was unaware as to whether you had accepted and entered these government posts. Yesterday, Jajung delivered another letter and I learned that you had followed the king's decree and came to Seoul, then changed posts and entered the State Council. Although this situation does not match your original intention when you left your government post in the past, you cannot help but make changes to cope with this situation and conduct yourself to suit the times since things have happened in this manner. This is exactly what Master Cheng meant when he said, "Follow the *dao*."[1]

Although it would be insufficient to use myself, someone so lowly, as an example: before I became so old and severely ill, I dashed to the king every time he called. In the span of eight or nine years, I dashed to the king on three occasions. Not to mention your situation is different from mine, but what excuse will you have to assert yourself stubbornly and make plans to avoid entering service? Although I grew older and my disease deteriorated after the Year of the Horse, the king bestowed his royal favors more extensively; I cannot begin to describe how hard it was accepting government posts while braving illness. Although I audaciously avoided his royal favor on several occasions, things progressively turned foul and I have arrived at this present awkward situation.

However, the king revealed his intention that he would wait until I had recovered. The king did not press me, although I did not show sings of improvement in my illness. However, scholars ranging from high-ranking officials on top, down to the scholars without government posts wrote nearly every month without exception, rebuking me. Each of them made an effort to distinguish what was right, and they informed the king; however, when they realized that the king would not accept (their suggestions), some people even talked of pushing me out. What could I do? I was worried and frightened. It made me forget I had ever rested! Although I have spoken about this in detail in my letter to Hwasuk Bak, I have not received a response and do not know what he is thinking.

As I was lost and wandering, I was extremely grateful for your attempt to set me straight in your annex to the letter dated July 15. However, those words were not appropriate for my circumstance. Why is that? Your words were reasonable if I were a kindhearted man who conformed to the king's requests; however, since I was never a man of great administrative ability nor a man fit for the ministry, I know I cannot repay even the slightest fraction of the king's grace. After this, how can I enter a government post empty handed, clutch onto a lofty government post, garner all the glory and profits from that post and then at once, want to return and plan for personal peace?

This cannot be proper in light of the assertion to make distinctions between personal gain and sense of duty that we have tried to polish and refine in our everyday lives.

Later, when I go to my grave and meet my ancestors, I will have nothing to say in my defense. For this reason, I cannot do as you suggested. What can I do?

Your arguments regarding the *Four-Seven Thesis* in your "General Summary" and "Postscript Explanation" are very lucid. I find no defects to attack recklessly. Since you possessed a comprehensive good view that was just and proper, I can say you alone witnessed a lucid and broad foundation. Furthermore, as you make distinctions regarding the smallest differences we held in our previous opinions, you immediately revised your assertions and followed your new understanding. This is very difficult for people to do.

Your resolve is admirable.

However, in your arguments regarding my assertion about the "Sages and wise men's joy, anger, sorrow, and pleasure" and about "each of these has an origin," earnestly, the arguments you made regarding these parts made me feel uncomfortable. I will take some time and rethink these points. In addition, regarding your theories of the human mind and the *dao* mind among others, it will be proper to receive your guidance after I rethink and reread these theories on various levels. However, I was only able to cover up to this point, but on the day Jajung goes to Seoul, I will respectfully request to be taught point by point.

It has gotten cold. Imploring you take care of yourself proper to the season, I respectfully bow and write this reply.

The leap month of October 26, 1566 (the Year of the Tiger)

Hwang bows his head.

---

1. "Follow the *dao* changing according to the time." See the Introduction to *Treaties on the Book of Changes*.

[Letter #38 Toegye Writes Gobong]

Arguments Regarding the Human Mind and the Dao Mind

I reply to you again, Myeongeon.

Recently, Jajung delivered the letter you had sent after returning to Seoul. I immediately wrote a reply and asked Jajung to deliver it to you. I am not sure if it has reached you on time. The winter weather has been severe, and I suspect you were quite busy with your public duties after we had exchanged letters. I am not sure how you are getting along. You have illustriously moved to a higher government post at the State Council—what more could I possibly do for you! In the future, only good things will happen, as you form relationships with people of the imperial court. Except for my chronic internal sicknesses, I hear the wind in my ears and I see stars sparkling in my eyes. I spend each passing day in this dizzy state. I am severely concerned that I will be unable to polish my studies!

I am going over again and thinking profoundly about the two theories you sent regarding the *Four-Seven Thesis*. The ancient ones did not say in vain:

> Although opinions can be serrated and therefore different in the beginning, in the end they brilliantly come together in one place.

Although I mentioned this roughly in my last letter, since I wrote that without heavy contemplation, I fear it accomplished nothing more than to defile your ears. I intend to say now what I did not have a chance to say before.

Although the phrase, "We place joy, anger, sorrow, and pleasure as partners to humanity, righteousness, propriety, and wisdom," seems plausible, it is not complete. In the past, in the "Diagram of the Heavenly Mandate," because they possessed similar points, in one way or another, I tried to divide and write them down by way of experiment. However, I truly did not designate them to be partners, as if the *four virtues* had been partnered and combined to *humanity, righteousness, propriety,* and *wisdom.*

You said, "Principle is manifested solely through the principle, and material force is manifested through a mixture of principle and material force." I once said regarding these words:

"Although the origins are the same, the ends are different."

This is truly similar to my view and I have always said:
"The origins are the same."
You use this as the basis for your argument. You said:
"The four beginnings and seven feelings cannot be separated and attached to principle and material force."
I have said in response:
"The ends are different."
However, if the opinions and arguments you have sent in the past were as clear and tidy as the two theories you have just sent, how could I say something like, "The ends are different"?

From early on, I made a book of the arguments we have exchanged and occasionally look at them to make corrections. However, I regret not being able to organize and record some things. Furthermore, I cannot remember a phrase you mentioned. Can you tell me what it was in your next letter? I truly have many suspicions regarding the theories various people have of the human mind and the *dao* mind. I have the theory of Iljae Yi, which Gangi Yi[1] sent to me early on. I will send you Gangi's letter and two of my theories. Please look at it and tell me what you think in your next letter. I respectfully ask you not to show it to other people. I am afraid they will make a big fuss out of nothing.
November 6, 1566 (the Year of the Tiger)
Hwang bows his head.

Annex [Letter #38]

In the past, people said, "Gwahoe enjoys the subtle taste of Zen Buddhism." Meanwhile, although I had also heard that Gwahoe revered and believed in the *Kunzhiji*, I did not believe it. When I saw the two quatrains he had written, "Reciting the Human Mind and the *Dao* Mind," while being very suspicious, I thought Gwahoe would not have gone this far and that somebody looking to stir trouble had stolen his name. However, I read in the letter you had just sent that you had met him personally and asked him about this matter. If this is truly what he meant to say and these are his real thoughts, I am filled with sorrow and disappointment. I do not know what to do.

In the big picture, although it is safe to say Zhengan had gained some understanding of the *dao*, he thought incorrectly about the root, the crux of the matter. Although he may have been principally correct in many parts in the remaining minor discussions, it would be hard to consider them of any value. I never imagined Gwahoe to be so careless, considering he had spent so many years making an effort in his studies. Unexpectedly, I discovered his theory to be closer to Zhengan's theory; his theory deviated from the Cheng-Zhu philosophy line.

In Iljae Yi's letter to Gangi Yi, he had discussed Zhengan's faults. Gangi sent this letter to me. Iljae's opinions were not very accurate and many assertions were incorrect—it was as you pointed out in your letter. However, I have heard this old man does not read books thoroughly and rashly believes only in himself; therefore, his mistakes do not necessarily arise from some origin. It seems as if Gwahoe's errors arose from going down the wrong path by studying the *School of Mind*: what you heard the last time were not words said in vain. Therefore, as you mentioned in your letter, he does not accept books like the *Classified Conversations* or *Collected Commentaries*. He dislikes the tediousness of thoroughly examining principles and heads straight for the simple and expedient path, which is a prodigious worry.

However, if I wanted to clarify the reason for this, the explanation would become quite lengthy. You have already grasped the main points in your letter. Why do you need my unenlightened opinions? However, another aspect that is hard to understand is if Gwahoe already considered principle and material force to be one, he would have considered the *dao* and the bowl holding the *dao* to be one, as well. However, in his poem he also says, "The original *dao* and bowl do not intersect." It would seem here that he separated the *dao* and the bowl, each one not interfering with the other. Regardless of how much I think about it, I cannot think from where this mistake originates. It would be a relief if you enlightened me.

I give to you, Jonjae, a reply I sent to a friend called "Words Commenting on Learning."

"Words Commenting on Learning"

I have noticed a problem in Mr. Zhan's[2] studies while looking at his book, *Baishaji*. I had the chance to look at his *Gewutong*, but I disliked him when I discovered he enjoyed aberrant views. In several clauses of the books I have just mentioned, he says, "*Mindfulness* is equal to 'Let not the mind forget its work, but let there be no assisting the growth of that nature.'"[3] In my presumption, it would have been correct if he had said, "I adopt not letting the mind forget and not assisting the growth of nature as a means of moderation to cherish *mindfulness*." However, it is wrong for him to say this phrase (which is expressed in four Chinese characters) is equal to *mindfulness*. What is worse, he interpreted "peril" to be "rampant" and "hazy" to be "disappearing." He went so far as to say, "If man's desire spreads rampantly, the heavenly principle declines and eventually disappears." There is no point in discussing its meaning or reason; his interpretations are so off based, there is nothing to deeply examine.

In Mr. Luo's *Kunzhiji*, it states:

> The human mind is feelings, the *dao* mind is nature. The exceedingly pure substance is subtle because we cannot see it; the endless, changing functions are perilous because we will be unable to surmise them.

Although his theory appears to be quite phenomenal and Mr. Zhan's theory pales in comparison, nevertheless, it is still all the more harmful. In general, if he limits the *dao* mind to exist only before the manifestation of emotions, that *dao* mind cannot exist along side of the functions of the heavens. Then, nature has a substance but can exude no function. If we decide that the human mind occurs only after the manifestation of feelings, the human mind will not have originated from human nature and the heavenly mandate, which are the foundations. Then, feelings can only be evil, void of any good. As mentioned above, between the words, "we cannot see the exceedingly pure substance because it is subtle" and "this is perilous because we will be unable to surmise," either a wide gap will form or they will mix. Therefore, the more we attempt to closely examine this, the wider the gap grows and the more we try to keep them as one, the more mixed they become. What would happen if we compared this to Zhu Xi who pierced through and spoke extensively without fail regarding the preciseness and scarcity of the substance and function and the effectiveness of studying?

> Although scholars must unquestionably know about nature, they do not need to cultivate their minds.

I cannot understand this theory at all. While arguing, "Benevolence is man's mind, and righteousness is man's path," Mencius always concluded the argument by seeking the lost mind.[4] However, according to Mr. Lou, it is sufficient to know benevolence and righteousness. What reason would he have to seek the lost mind? While Mencius discussed the *proper goodness of the mind*, he first mentioned benevolence and righteousness.[5] However, while discussing receiving its proper nourishment and losing its proper nourishment, holding it fast for it to remain and letting go to lose it, he did not mention nature again, but talked of the mind.[6] In places where he discussed that a man who has exhausted all his mental constitution knows his nature, Mencius always concluded that the mind must be preserved and that nature must be nourished.[7] The mind governs nature and feelings. If he cannot nourish the mind, it is because nature cannot be preserved on its own. Not to mention, nobody exists in the world who can know nature truly without cultivating the mind.

The saying, "Good and evil are the names of the heavenly principles" is not proper because this phrase is so vague. In the past, while discussing Guishan's[8] words, "Man's desire is not nature," He Shujing[9] questioned, "I do not know from where this man's desires come." Zhu Xi said:

> "This is a very important question. Man's desire comes exactly from opposing the heavenly principle. You are correct if you say man's desire was formed by the heavenly principle. However, it would be wrong to say man's desire is also a heavenly principle. In general, man's desire was not originally among the heavenly principles. Merely, if it trickles out and forms a gap, man's desire is formed for the first time. Master Cheng said, 'Good and evil are all heavenly principles.' Zhu Xi says in his main notes, 'This passage has a very strange meaning.' What we call evil was not originally evil. In the main notes, he says, 'This phrase is completely upside down.' Evil comes from being too extreme or lacking. In the main notes, he says, 'When people ask me from where man's desires originate, I answer with this passage.' One cannot help but call the evil quoted here to be nature, as well, and the meaning would be so."

The above mentioned are all Zhu Xi's theories.

I also want to say that good and evil are the names of the heavenly principles. Comparing and examining these several theories[10] of Master Cheng and Zhu Xi you can resolve the views about which you had suspicion in your letter. Although Master Cheng said, "Good and evil are all heavenly principles," he explains it again two passages down.[11] In addition, while citing this paragraph, Zhu Xi interpreted this with more clarity; he cleanly washed his hands of (Master Cheng's) previous theory that stated evil became principle, and he set out to create his own spotless theory.

You have not done this. You have vaguely and ambiguously lumped everything together. How can this not amount to you spoiling yourself, as well as others? ["Although scholars must unquestionably know about nature . . ." These two clauses were not the views of Mr. Zhan and Mr. Luo, but something discussed among fellow members while being asked by friends.]

(End to "Words Commenting on Learning")

I had frivolously replied in this manner to a friend in Seoul who asked about several articles in a letter he had sent to me. After receiving your letter, which discusses the human mind and the *dao* mind among other things, I shuffled through old drawers and found a copy of this letter I sent to friends. In one paragraph, I discussed Zhengan, but I am not sure if that discussion will help in the significance of this dialog and elucidate matters. I send this letter and I would be greatly relieved if you pointed out what was unreasonable and what was wrong in the other paragraphs outside of the one where I discussed Zhengan.

---

1. Refers to Jeong Yi. He was Toegye's pupil; his pen name was Guam and Gangi was his pseudonym.

2. Refers to Zhan Ruoshui, a scholar of the China Ming Dynasty period; when he was young, he learned from Baisha Chen Xianzhang. He had studied with Wang Shoulen but later they divided into two different schools each asserting their own views. See *History of Ming* 283, "Biographies of Confucian Scholars."

3. See *The Works of Mencius*, Book II: "Kung-sun Chau," Part I, Chapter I. As Confucius replied to Kung-sun Chau who asked what was passion-nature, he said not to forget to nourish the passion-nature and let there be no assisting the growth of that nature.

4. See *The Works of Mencius*, Book VI: "Kao Tsze" Part I, Chapter XI: "The great end of learning is nothing else but to seek for the lost mind,"

which is in the last part of the phrase, "Benevolence is man's mind, and righteousness is man's path."

5. See *The Works of Mencius*, Book VI: "Kao Tsze" Part I, Chapter VIII: "And so also of what properly belongs to man; shall it be said that the mind of any man was without benevolence and righteousness? The way in which a man loses his proper goodness of mind is like the way in which the trees are denuded by axes and bills. Hewn down day after day, can it—the mind—retain its beauty?"

6. See *The Works of Mencius*, Book VI: "Kao Tsze" Part I, Chapter VIII: "Therefore, if it receive its proper nourishment, there is nothing which will not grow. If it lose its proper nourishment, there is nothing which will not decay away. Confucius said, 'Hold it fast, and it remains with you. Let it go, and you lose it. Its outgoing and incoming cannot be defined as to time or place.' It is the mind of which this is said!"

7. See *The Works of Mencius*, Book VII: "Tsin Sin" Part I, Chapter I: "Mencius said, 'He who has exhausted all his mental constitution knows his nature. Knowing his nature, he knows Heaven. To preserve one's mental constitution, and nourish one's nature, is the way to serve Heaven. When neither a premature death nor long life causes a man any double-mindedness, but he waits in the cultivation of his personal character for whatever issue; this is the way in which he establishes his Heaven-ordained being.'"

8. Refers to the scholar of the China Song Dynasty period, Yang Shi. He was Master Cheng's pupil and Guishan was his pseudonym.

9. Refers to a China Song period scholar, He Hao. His pen name was Taixi and Shujing, his pseudonym.

10. Cheng Yichuan's remarks and Zhu Xi's commentary are mentioned in *Reflections on Things at Hand*, Chapter I: "On the Substance of the Way."

11. Before a man is born, we cannot say man is with nature and when we can say man is with nature, man is already without nature. Before man is born, man is with principle and not with nature; we can say man is with nature for the first time after man is born. Since principle already exists in physical form, we can say it is not the substance of nature. See Chapter I: "On the Substance of the Way," *Reflections on Things at Hand*.

[Letter #39 Gobong Writes Toegye]

No Time for a Momentary Break

Dear teacher,
I respectfully prostrate myself and inquire about your wellbeing. How is your health? My reverence for you is immeasurable. Impertinent, I am barely making my way on this path of government service thanks to your affectionate grace. However, after returning to Seoul, not only did my illness and concerns continue without end, but also tedious works pursued me and I had no time for a momentary break, as I was extremely rushed—my mind is in immeasurable chaos.

Jajung came and delivered two letters, which you had written, and "Reply to a Friend." I cannot begin to express how happy and comforted I was to receive the letter you had sent to various people. However, as I mentioned before, because tedious, boisterous work entangled me, I could not send a thank you letter for a long time. My lament only grew.

I am guessing you are getting along more peacefully these days. Another year ends. While hoping the new year brings you more blessings and hoping all your endeavors are abundantly realized, I respectfully end this letter.

Please be advised. I respectfully bow and offer this letter.
December 29, 1566 (the Year of the Tiger)
Bowing, yours truly,
Junior scholar, Daeseung.

Although Jajung has gone to Yongman[1] to serve briefly as the royal emissary for inspections, he should be returning shortly. Since he plans to return to his native village around February, I plan to inform you in detail at that time. Furthermore, I am sending you some medication distributed by the State Council[2] among several other things. Please be advised.

---

1. Refers to Uiju in the Pyeongan Province.
2. Or *Bonsa*; refers to the State Council where Gobong served.

[Letter #40 Gobong Writes Toegye]

Although Many People Claim to Study The Way

Dear teacher,

I respectfully prostrate myself and inquire about your well-being. How is your health? I miss you more with each passing day. These days, spring is in the air and the weather grows steadily warmer. I hope you are doing well and that all your endeavors are abundantly blessed. Impertinent, I am barely making my way on this path of government service thanks to your affectionate grace. After returning to Seoul, however, I have been unable to catch my breath as I am dizzily replaced from government posts. My body and mind grow fatigued and I am having difficulty sustaining myself. Now, I have taken on another position as the *Jongsagwan* and am heading for Yongman. I can only sigh as eight or nine out of ten things I am doing do not turn out the way I plan.

Last year, I was filled with enormous happiness as you lucidly opened my eyes. Although I thought about relaying my thoughts once I had some leisure time, I have not been able to do this as I continue to be bogged down with tedious works—I feel incredibly ashamed and can do nothing but sigh. You cannot imagine how relieved I felt to have received recognition from you regarding my two theories on the *Four-Seven Thesis*. However, I have thought about many things since then but did not dare to ask you about them lightly. I am waiting for the possibility that several modest views may come to mind. I transcribe a phrase and send it to you. As we collect our writings and make a book of our continuing correspondences, I hope we can decide what to put in and what to remove. What do you think about this?

Last autumn I had the opportunity to read Zhengan's book. After digging up its shortcomings, I wanted to analyze aggressively each fault and write a chapter about each of them, but I have not been able to write anything because I have been unable to focus. It might take as long as a year or two to finish this.

In your letter, the several provisions to which you opened my eyes were detailed and reasonable. These days, while many people stake their names, claiming to study *The Way*, they end up harming the *dao* with views that are distorted and incorrect. What can we do as it has reached the point there are so many of them they are hard to distinguish! On top of that, it is a mystery as to whose theory claimed, "Although scholars must unquestionably know about nature, he does not need to cultivate his mind." I am shocked and I can do nothing but sigh. When a person's views are this distorted, how can we argue with words! I am truly worried and frightened.

I had a chance to read your letter, which you had sent to Hwa-suk Bak, when I visited his home. I respectfully understand your intentions. What else can I say as your intentions are already set? I am not sure what you think, but I believe you do not need to explain yourself extensively to all the scholars, ranging from the three ministers in lofty government posts to scholars without any posts regardless of what they might say.

Regarding what I had informed you of in the past, all I did was to ask you about my views as they came to mind—it was not my hope that you would accept those views. I feel incredibly obliged that you took the time to reply personally and diligently. Although I wanted to tell you of more than just several matters, I could not inform you of everything, as I am so needlessly busy. I only ask that you exert more of an effort in savoring the *dao* and cherish yourself more for the ages. As we have no set plans to meet in the future, I cannot begin to express my sad and reverent heart. I prostrate myself and ask you to understand this. I respectfully bow and offer this letter.

January 24, 1567 (the Year of the Rabbit)
Junior scholar Daeseung bows.
I also send you two letters from Iljae and Guam and ask you to accept them.

[Letter #41 Toegye Writes Gobong]

Eliminate the Book in Circulation That Steals My Name

I respectfully bow and reply to you, Myeongeon.
We have not been able to correspond these days because of various circumstances. Besides missing you, I was very worried and saddened. I was inflicted with an illness before the end of the year and my condition grew worse in the beginning of January. I was in agony; not only did I cough and excrete phlegm profusely, but also various symptoms transpired. Twisting and turning my body be-

cause of the pain, it has been several months since I have been bedridden. My vitality has declined and my energy has all but dissipated. I do not know what is going to happen. What can I do?

Meanwhile, I heard that people from the Junghwa County of the Pyeongan Province had engraved books entitled, *Yonghakseogui* and *Eorokseok*. People tell me both are my theories. I was overcome with shock and distress when I heard that news. I do not know anything about *Eorokseok*. However, regarding *Yonghakseok*, after realizing all the various theories from the people of our country regarding *The Doctrine of the Mean* and *The Great Learning* were too confusing, I collected the various theories. I examined and edited them, considering what should be added and deleted; I tried to seek the original meaning and gather them into one assertion. However, since my views were not clear, I gathered various theories from time to time but could not decide what to eradicate and what to keep, and occasionally I only argued without ever reaching any conclusions. In short, everything was jumbled, confusing, and incomplete; hence, it was insufficient to show others. However, going against my intentions my children showed it around, and I was extremely embarrassed and afraid by its wide circulation in my native village. How could I have known something like this was going to happen again?

Although Wi An, the magistrate of the Junghwa County, has good intentions, he is inflicted with a sickness that has him enjoy stirring trouble. Although the name of the instructor, Myeonggae Mun, is well known in writing, he is also someone with many problems. They have carried out this act, and I know both men. Therefore, I want to send them letters severely reprimanding them, and I want to tell them to get rid of these xylographic books. However, if I ask them to get rid of these books voluntarily, I worry if they will actually do it. I have looked everywhere for friends who can see to it that this is executed, but I have nobody to whom to turn.

At that time, I had heard you had left for the Gwanseo district to meet the Chinese envoys. As I think about it, you are the only one who can do this work for someone as old and near death as me. Therefore, I have urgently written this letter and have revealed my innermost hope. I prostrate myself before you and humbly ask that when you arrive in Junghwa County, put all your busy work aside, immediately seek out these xylographic books, and *witness them being burned in the courtyard before you leave*. If I do not ask you but merely ask the county magistrate to burn these books, undoubtedly, it will not be done properly at the end. I ask you again for this favor; please do not treat this matter lightly. Because I was ill, I had somebody else write these several lines. I could not mention many other things I wanted to discuss. Work hard in everything that you do and I implore you not to disappoint the expectations of the ages.

I respectfully bow and inform you.
February 5, 1567 (the Year of the Rabbit)
From Hwang.

[Letter #42 Gobong Writes Toegye]

Your Sickness Remains Unchanged

I respectfully reply to you, teacher.

While missing you terribly, I received your letter written on the fifth of this month. As you mentioned your sickness remains unchanged, I am filled with worries from a distance. Has your condition ameliorated since sending word the last time? I am sincerely hoping that you have improved and have already recuperated. Impertinent, I am barely preserving myself thanks to your affectionate grace. However, after my mother passed away, my younger brother was at home in mourning. His body fell ill, as he felt excessively bereaved. Unable to recover, he passed away, as well. When I heard the news, my heart ripped apart; no words can describe the pain I endured. I felt like I was in a dream as I had lost my wits.

I am guessing you have already received my letter, which I had sent though Jajung, when he was on his way back. How could I not keep in mind your request to eliminate those xylographic books? However, because the *Jangnyeong* position[1] has been added to my place of services, it is possible I will not be able to make it to Gwanseo in view of the circumstances. Some people have said I must be moved from my *Daegwan* position[2] to become the envoy to the ambassador. I am not sure how this will all unfold. Meanwhile, the three ministers informed the king and the king gave orders to meet you. When your health is not good, I worry profusely that anxiety will overcome you, as convoluted thoughts entangle you. I prostrate myself and respectfully think: you are high in virtue and distinguished in service; you will not encounter distress if you form a plan of action in advance. If you rest at the right times, you will most assuredly enjoy leisure.

I beg you again to take care of your illness and recuperate, and please do not disappoint our meager desires. I end this letter here. Please be advised. I respectfully bow and send this reply.

February 19, the First Year of Longqing (The era of Muzong's reign of the Ming Dynasty)

Bowing, yours truly,

Junior scholar, Daeseung.

I am not sure if you have received the royally dispersed medication which I wrapped and gave to the *Hyeonjeoin*[3] for delivery. Please tell me whenever you need more medication. I will be able to prepare it for you. As chaos fills my heart and I have been able to write only a few lines, I can do nothing but fear.

---

1. Refers to the senior with a 4th official rank at the Office of the Inspector General, an organization in charge of commenting on politics and inspecting government officials.

2. Refers to the *Jangnyeong* of the Office of the Inspector General; *Daegwan* refers to the official of the *Eosadae*, and this was another name for the Office of the Inspector General.

3. Refers to a type of *hyangni*; he was dispatched from the *Hyeon* village of the local regions to Seoul to mediate office work and maintain correspondence.

[Letter #43 Toegye Writes Gobong]

Everybody Is Making an Effort Just to Win

I respectfully reply to you, Myeongeon.

Jajung delivered your letter dated January 24 when he visited last month, and soon after, I received your letter dated February 19 through another courier. I truly appreciate all the concern you showed me. I was shocked and saddened immeasurably to hear that your brother had passed away while in mourning. I know that you were especially close to him and it must have been unbearable as your heart was torn with grief. However, from afar, I hope you will possess a lenient heart and suppress your sadness. My best wishes are all the more profound.

When going to Gwanseo, it would seem appropriate to change government offices even though you are at the post of the Office of the Inspector General/the Office of the Censor General. In addition, recently, I heard that you had already been replaced from your government post. As I am far away, I do not receive accurate news and have not heard yet to which post you have moved. What I know is that, undoubtedly, you will leave for Gwanseo, and I believe with all my heart that you will take care of eliminating the xylographic books in one swift blow. If you cannot help regarding this situation, I do not think anybody else will be able to resolve the matter according to my wish. Therefore, I beg you earnestly to take care of this matter.

I would be tremendously relieved if I could read your clarification and examination of the certain parts that needed reconsidering in the *Four-Seven Thesis*. Today, Zhengan's writings have poisoned many people. In your letter, you state that you wanted to add an explanation to his writings, pointing out the fallacies, whereby showing people the path out of the darkness; this is my wish as well.[1] I am very worried when I hear about the circulation of theories proposed by various people. On top of that, everybody makes an effort to win over others, seemingly unconcerned about returning to the right path. As this is the case, do you think it will be necessary to argue with them and have other people point fingers at us? Rather, the wisest thing will be to advise those people to speak less and eliminate the worries of Bian Zhuangzi continuing to scheme.*

In your letter, you mention you had a chance to read my letter at Hwasuk Bak's house. I had no choice but to act the way I did while caught between idle fame and the king's abundant grace. I roughly wrote what I had always thought in that letter. When the envoys arrived and notified me I was not included in the *Choseon*,[2] I was moved by the king's generous royal favor. However, suddenly, people not only pulled me in again, but also they blocked my way out, leaving me helpless. Extremely awestruck and in a distressed predicament, what would be the best thing for me to do? After mentioning I would be unable to handle the king's abundant grace, it would make me feel uneasy to turn around and decline yet a formal call to temporary service. However, I cannot go immediately because I have not recovered from my major illness yet.

While recovering through medication, for a moment I considered following everybody's wishes; however, this would only amount to a scheme to avoid dealing with the urgent affairs right before me. To some extent, I mulled the possibility of going. However, I reconsidered when realizing once I returned to Seoul, it would be hard to leave again. I would reach an extremely awkward position after being in the position to respond to every matter I came across—regret and disparagement would grow daily. As I was extremely worried that something unexpected might happen because of my lowly plans to avoid this uneasy situation, I thought this would be worse than adhering more steadfastly to my original intention.

Although the ancient ones said that determining one's course of action is not something to discuss with others, after surmising the times and carefully considering the situation, I was hoping you would show me—somebody who is lost—the way because you possess such warm affections for me. As there are many worrisome events, it is not easy to write about them haphazardly.

Be prudent.

Be truthful and do not disappoint me, someone who is so far away.

I end the letter here and respectfully bow.

March 18, Longqing (The era of Muzong's reign of the Ming Dynasty)

From Hwang.

I received the medication and brushes sent last year on December 29 while you were stationed at the State Council. In addition, I heard that you had sent a letter inquiring about my well-being, as well, but I do not what happened to it: I received the medication and the brushes but not the letter. I mentioned briefly in my response letter sent to the State Council that I had not received the letter, but upon contemplation, I realized you would have already left that place by the time my letter arrived. However, recently, a friend in Seoul delivered that letter, which I had thought was lost.

I was grateful beyond measure for your letter, which brimmed of your good faith. I am also grateful for your offer to send more medication upon my request. However, since several close acquaintances in Seoul have been sending me medication and since my grandson is in Seoul, I do not think I will run out of medication. It will be unnecessary for me to trouble you with this matter.

I have heard from someone that lately, you have acquired the evil habit of drinking alcohol excessively. I am not sure if this is true. If you have developed such a habit, then most assuredly, that is *not* the way to raise virtue and watch over your health. What do you think?

---

1. Gobong wrote "Gonjigiron" (discussion about *Kunzhiji*) which criticized Zhengan's *Kunzhiji*. See *Gobong's Collections* 2.
* Refer to Letter #34, Endnote #4.
2. *Choseon* refers to a process where the ministers of State Council and senior officials with the 3rd official rank or above in the Board of Personnel gather and select people to serve as royal lecturers or as *Jeopbangwan*. As envoys of the Ming Dynasty were dispatched, Toegye was summoned to Seoul to serve as a *Jesulgwan*. Just at that time, King Myeongjong passed away and Toegye dedicated a biography of Myeongjong and then was appointed the Minister of Rites. See the *Revised Annals of Seonjo* 1, July 17, the year of accession, the Day of the Horse.

[Letter #44 Gobong Writes Toegye]

If You Come to Seoul after Recuperating

I respectfully inquire about your well-being. How is your health? I miss you terribly. I was enormously relieved to hear through Ijeong Gim that your condition had improved. I am barely preserving myself, thanks to your affectionate grace. However, this wayfaring lifestyle is uncomfortable and since my family must follow me around, my lament grows because the work conflicts with my original intentions. In addition, I am not sure how I will settle this problem.

As I think about it quietly, you have already received the king's calling. If you come to Seoul after recuperating, I will be able to meet you again and ask you personally about things that are suspicious and ambiguous. In my life, this would be truly the most fortunate event! I am overcome with anticipation.

I end my letter here. Please pay close attention to your health according to the seasons. I prostrate myself before and ask you to consider this. I respectfully bow and offer this letter.

March 21, the First Year of Longqing (The era of Muzong's reign of the Ming Dynasty)

Bowing, yours truly,

Junior scholar, Daeseung.

[Letter #45 Gobong Writes Toegye]

According to Social Duty and Destiny

I respectfully reply to your letter, teacher.

I respectfully inquire about your well-being. I am curious. Are you passing the time peacefully? Are you managing your illness? My respect for you has no limits. Impertinent, I am barely getting along thanks to your affectionate grace. On the fifth day of this month, I moved from the *Jangnyeong* position to the *Eunggyo*[1] position, and on the following day, I left for Yongman.

Jajung delivered your letter on his way here the last time. I had difficulty fathoming my own gratefulness and fearful heart as I read your detailed remarks. How can I—someone with such superficial and dark views—dare to discuss the course of action to be taken by a man of virtue such as yourself? However, when I think about it, you must have had a plan set in advance. What about making a decision based on social duty and destiny while surmising your new circumstance and after considering what is right and wrong?

Following popular opinion to ignobly escape hardship not only goes against the will of the sages and wise men, but also worries about slander and unexpected events will be harmful in establishing a proper principle. Master Cheng's saying, "If you do not go when called, the country has its own regulations," means that not accepting the king's calling means not fulfilling one's social duty; however, when consulting Zhu Xi's case, he hesitated entering government service. If he had asked to earnestly retire by submitting a request to leave, how could there not have been something reasonable between those two alternatives?

These two teachers lived in different times, and because their eventual course of actions were appropriate according to their times, their actions were never biased; I am not sure what this means. I have haphazardly commented on their footsteps without profoundly knowing the social duties by which wise men of old conducted themselves according to their respective times; I am cautious and filled with great fear. I prostrate myself before you and ask you to consider this.

Furthermore, I will take into deep consideration your warning about enjoying alcohol. In fact, I have had this disease from an early age. Although in agony, I have not been able to cure it. What greater fortune in my life would there be if your chastisement could cure this sickness!

It was of incredible solace to me.

I respectfully end my letter here.

I beg you to live healthily through the changing of seasons. Please consider this. I respectfully bow and offer this reply.

May 11, the First Year of Longqing (The era of Muzong's reign of the Ming Dynasty)

Bowing, yours truly,

Junior scholar, Daeseung.

I wanted to write a response for the longest time but could not achieve my wishes, as I failed to find someone traveling back and forth. I write this letter hastily and give it to Ijeong for delivery before I leave to travel long distances. Please excuse me. As I think about you repeatedly in my mind, on one hand, considering the time, it does not seem right for you to come out, but on the other hand, when considering social duty, you might have to come and thank the king for his grace.[2] Depending on the state of affairs, perhaps you can come and meet the king sometime in the fall. Kindly explain to him that you are old and sick. If you could courteously refuse the government post and retire, you would not feel any regret regarding the times or your social duty.

I ask you consider this leniently.

I shall eradicate the xylographic books as you ordered. Please be advised of this.

1. Refers to the senior with the 4th official rank at the Office of the Royal Lecturers, an organization in charge of books and papers and answering the king's questions.

2. In the last year of King Myeongjong's reign, he offered Toegye government positions on five occasions without Toegye being nominated by others and urged him to come up to the capital.

[Letter #46 Gobong Writes Toegye]

I Burned the Xylographic Books in the Courtyard

Dear teacher,

I respectfully inquire about your well-being. How is your health? I am overcome with longing for you. I left Seoul on the twelfth of this month and yesterday I stayed at the Saengyang Inn.[1] I am staying here because something has come up. Thanks to your concern, I am getting along fine without much trouble after starting my journey. I am leaving for Pyeongyang tomorrow.

Previously, you had asked me to eradicate the xylographic books and upon arrival to my official residence, I immediately sought out the xylograph. I discovered only twenty-four pages published from six printing blocks. Although I gathered all these books and burned them in the courtyard, all the government officials and friends were very regretful, and I was very sad, as well. However, because you had made the request so fervently, I had no choice but to adhere. Please be advised.

While I was in Seoul, I briskly wrote a letter and gave it to Ijeong to be delivered. I will not tediously repeat everything. Please consider this with a lenient mind. I respectfully bow and offer this letter.

May 22, the Longqing (The era of Muzong's reign of the Ming Dynasty)

Bowing from the Saengyang Inn, yours truly,

Junior scholar, Daeseung.

---

1. (The name of) the inn at the station in Junghwa County.

[Letter #47 Gobong Writes Toegye]

Resolving an Old Burden

Dear teacher,

This morning, you sent a person to inquire about my well-being and soon after, I received your letter. As I revere you, I was moved, as well as being comforted.

Earlier, I had a chance to sit before you and bow in your presence, and I resolved an old burden; I was enormously comforted. However, it was late at night and because I could not find a quiet gap in time, I barely managed keeping you company and we could only talk tenderly for a short time.

> *I felt enraptured.*
> *It felt like a dream.*

I wanted to go back and meet you again, but I sighed as I was unable to because I was busy with work. However, I was able to see you from afar while you were at the Royal College. I watched you carefully and was very worried as you seemed so emaciated. Prostrating myself before you and pleading, I ask you: how about putting aside all work and concentrating on taking care of your health? Furthermore, I have something apologetic to say:

Although you did not completely disregard my notion that it would be difficult to retire hastily from service based on social duty as the funeral affairs had yet to be completed, you have not changed your thinking in the least. After leaving your presence and pondering, I felt stifled and filled with suspicion. What do you think about reconsidering? Mencius once said, "I cannot make such a request in times of continuous wars."[1] Although Mencius wanted to leave because he did not get along with the emperor of the Qi Dynasty, he said it was difficult to request leaving while war raged in the Qi Dynasty. Comparing your present situation to the one just mentioned, it would seem more difficult for you to make such a request to leave briskly. I cannot be sure, but what do you think about this?

Please pay attention to this.

I know I have been rash and rude in speaking so carelessly; however, I could not help but tell you what I could not understand. Please excuse me with a lenient heart.

I respectfully bow and offer this letter.
July 20, 1567 (the Year of the Rabbit)
Bowing, yours truly,
Junior scholar, Daeseung.

I have written this letter hastily under a lamp at the Byeokje Inn. I apologize. I erased many spots in this letter while writing it. I am deeply ashamed.

---

1. See *The Works of Mencius*, Book II: "Kung-sun Chau" Part II, Chapter XIV.

[Letter #48 Toegye Writes Gobong]

Some Parts upon Which I Could Not Agree

I respectfully reply to you, Myeongeon.

I see you are sending me news while busily entertaining envoys. When I saw your son who delivered your letter, I saw the beauty of orchids and jades illuminated in human form—my melancholy thoughts subsided.

Pushing all your busy work to the side, when we talked through the night the last time you visited, it was more helpful than reading books for ten years! I was very grateful and obliged. However, there were some parts of your requests in your last letter with which I did not agree. Although I read the letter two, three times after receiving it, I was at a loss and did not know the best course of action to take. Even in such a special relationship that we possess, you have not been able to consider leniently the appropriate course of action for me to take. What can I expect from other people!

Furthermore, while saying you were worried that I had grown so emaciated, why did you try to stop me from leaving? If I do not leave, I would end up coveting personal profit and forgetting shame.

I would arrive alive and return dead.
People would point fingers at me.
They would ridicule me.
They would spit on me and curse me, suffering such scorn.

As you mentioned in your letter, there are parts of the war example you used that resemble the funeral affairs; however, Mencius and I are very different like a worm and swan. How can you make such a comparison by dragging Mencius into the picture? I do not possess any qualities, not even one, that are superior to others, and I am afflicted with all kinds of illnesses. On top of that, I have fooled the late king with my undeserved reputation. How can I steal another position and fool the new king!

Truly, I am like the person Han Yu mentioned when he says, "It was named a wooden Buddhist statue by chance!"[1] On the contrary, people today want to entrust me with more difficult-to-endure responsibilities. However, after mentioning you were planning a way for me to become a retired scholar, it might have been excessive for you to advise me to quickly run and hide. But how can you say so calmly that your advice to stay in government service was appropriate! I only hope you will leniently revise and assess with a magnanimous heart and with great insight. It would be a relief if you could help me—someone who is so lonely and lowly—to escape the ridicule of the secular world.

I respectfully bow and reply.
July 24, 1567 (the Year of the Rabbit)
From Hwang.
The new rice and side dish were delicious. I am very obliged.

It appears as if I have no particular reason to return urgently; I am sitting here as a high leveled government official. However, if I retrace my footsteps from the past, starting from when I occupied a low government post I have been requesting to be dismissed from my post for a long time and have kept my distance because of foolishness and sickness. However, today, my rise to a high government post has been the result of a vain and false reputation building up. Although I did come here to take care of this matter, I plan to return once this work is over. Furthermore, from the beginning, I had no intentions of entering a government office, managing the work, and distinguishing myself. However, unfortunately, the king has passed away and I had to stand in the ranks of the government officials. I have reached these circumstances, as I am busily taking care of the funeral affairs.

Already depressed beyond measure, my illness grows worse suddenly, and the cold weather is already antagonizing me even though the funeral procession for the king is still far away. As a vassal who had left his post because of illness for the past twenty to thirty years, would (those illnesses) have gone anywhere simply because I have reached these circumstances? If my exit is delayed, I will not be able to effectively work at the things I want to do. How desperate must I be to even mention in my letter the wooden Buddhist statue avoiding his responsibility? It is not strange at all that my latest actions shown to the world have caused the secular world to lose trust in me. However, I am filled with grief, as I feel you—someone with exalted and luminous ideas—have lost faith in me.

I heard something was wrong in my reply to the envoys carrying the royal edict.[2] Amidst my reply, I had actually written the rough draft regarding words like *simhak* and *jusu*. Therefore, I am worried when I hear such talk. However, I hope you will teach me, as I do not know which words were wrong. Among the previous Confucian scholars recorded, I attached explanatory notes under the names Eonjeok Yi and Gwangjo Jo. Was there something wrong with doing that? Furthermore, under the name, Tak U, I added to the explanatory notes, "Tak U is comparable to Tang Jie" to the part where it says, "the king losing virtue."[3] This was originally the case and later, while the teacher, Jeompil,[4] passed his native village, he recited the following poem:

> *Grabbing an axe in the red yard of the royal palace is acting like Tang Jie*
> *Studying the sacred books from a poor, white, straw-thatched cottage is acting like Zheng Xuan*

I said what I said because of this.

Although people say Tak U was never compared to Tang Jie in the biographies of the *History of Goryeo*, how can they be words not worth adopting, as the teacher, Jeompil, spoke them? If it is worth believing, it is worth adopting. Why would it be a problem, whether it is in the *History of Goryeo* or not?

---

1. This is a quotation from the poem written by the Tang poet, Han Yu. See *Changli's Collections* 9, "Name It a Wooden Buddhist Statue."

2. See supplement book 8 to *Toegye's Collections*, "Reply to Chinese Envoys."

3. Refers to the when Tak U remonstrated King Chungseon, which was comparable to when Tang Jie remonstrated Renzong without fear of being killed during the reign of Song Renzong. Tak U's advice was as follows: "As Goryeo King Chungseon committed adultery with a royal concubine, Sukchang, Tak U entered the royal place with an axe and remonstrated. As he scolded the king's vassals severely in a loud voice, the startled vassals shivered right and left and the king felt shame." See the *History of Goryeo* 109, "Biographies" 22, "Tak U."

4. Jeompil refers to Jongjik Gim. See the *Jeompiljae's Collections* 3, "Thinking Tak U Passing by Yean."

[Letter #49 Gobong Writes Toegye]

After Hearing You Had Packed and Returned East

Dear teacher,

I respectfully prostrate myself and inquire about your well-being. How is your health after returning home? I apotheosize you with more eagerness. Impertinent, I was able to return safely to Seoul on the twenty-third of the previous month thanks to your affectionate grace. However, I have not been able to complete all the difficult tasks. Because I had to report on the send off and departure of the envoy, I was tied up in tedious work, but now I have found some stability.

On my way back from Uiju, I arrived at Gwaksan, where I received your letter and two pieces which contained your annex; I became fully aware of your intentions. However, with shallow views, I failed to understand. I became filled with greater suspicions. When I arrived at Anju, I was surprised and dumbfounded when I heard you had packed your things and returned east.

My lifelong affection for you had me wanting you to be near, so that we could meet often and I could receive your guidance; however, that is not all: I was hoping you would observe profoundly the greater intentions of a man of scholarship while conducting yourself. However, when my plans went awry, I was saddened and felt stifled. I could not get over this for a long time. When I quietly reflect, I knew you had to make plans to leave. You could not stay in Seoul for a long time because of the many uncomfortable occurrences that you would confront; nevertheless, how could I have expected things to culminate like this? I am not sure, but how would this look in light of righteousness according to the ancient ones? I would be relieved if you opened my eyes regarding this matter.

Furthermore, I have heard the discussions of numerous people who say you are the one who said the former Queen, Gongui,[1] should not wear mourning attire. What did you mean? I met Hwasuk Bak and I saw something you had personally written; I was awestruck and perplexed. Mencius said, "I have not learned about the etiquette regarding princes." How can we make the final decision by applying the household etiquette of ordinary people to the affairs of the state? If you carefully take into consideration the meaning of etiquette, there were no cases when mourning attire was not worn. I perused many books looking for evidence to set matters straight. However, this was not something I could suddenly understand, which is truly lamentable. Furthermore, the memorial service for the Lady Hadong was performed incorrectly;[2] I felt they used the wrong title for the deceased. How could you not say one word to amend this! I feel uncomfortable with this. What do you think?

Your response to the envoys carrying the royal edict was inconsistent and there were many mistakes. However, because the Board of Rites did not permit any revisions, I had no choice but to submit the original contents. The two envoys were not satisfied at all. However, regarding the various articles in your rough draft, nothing was suspicious or incorrect. I gave the writings of *Chanseong* Yi and Sun Yi to the vice envoy. Since both envoys had studied the philosophy of Wang Yangming, it was difficult to talk to them. Although I have many things to say, I will end the letter here. I prostrate myself before you and implore you to consider. I respectfully bow and offer this letter.

September 8, 1567 (the Year of the Rabbit)
Bowing, yours truly,
Junior scholar, Daeseung.
I had difficulty drafting this, as I was very tired. I apologize.

---

1. Refers to King Injong's wife, Bak. This dispute arose because Injong and Myeongjong inherited the throne as brothers.

2. Refers to Lady Hadong, Jeong, who was King Seonjo's blood related mother. King Seonjo was the grandson of King Jungjong and the son of

Prince Deokheung. At first, he was conferred prince Haseong and after King Myeongjong died with no heir, he entered the royal palace and acceded to the throne. At that time, he was in mourning for his mother, but an argument ensued because there was a principle that mourning decorum for the public without formalities could not be performed during national mourning for royalty. See the *Annals of Seonjo* 1, "Chongseo."

[Letter #50 Toegye Writes Gobong]

Five Vexations and Two Concerns

I respectfully reply to you, Myeongeon.

During the gloomy atmosphere of the funeral for the king, the grieving government officials followed behind as pallbearers as the procession arrived; however, as I was extremely ill, I could not do this. I returned, and I am staying at an old temple.[1] You sent me a letter scolding me in light of righteousness held by the ancient ones—what could I say in my defense? I was deathly ashamed! I realized with further conviction that I am a small and vulgar person, a sinner.

However, regarding this matter, there is a reason I am suspicious about what you said. The whole world mocked and ridiculed me when I returned to my native village. Some people have compared me to a mountain bird, and others have rejected me claiming I am a heretic. It seems as if they will never mention me again in their conversations. However, you have refrained from scolding me, choosing to speak differently. Why is that? Do you feel pity for someone like me who has lost his way and fallen into a pit of troubles? Have you decided to adopt a conciliatory policy? Although I am worried I may be committing a greater crime by droning on about this matter, I cannot let your warm kindness go to waste. I want to write about a few things.

Do you consider me an odd person? My conduct is likewise difficult to understand. Why is that?

> *Great foolishness, acute disease, vain reputation, and undeserved kindness:*

These four vexations gather in my body. They obstruct me by collectively meddling in my affairs and creating contradictions. I wanted to live up to the ancient ones, but they did not possess the foolishness I possess. I wanted to get along with colleagues but they were free from the diseases that inflicted me. I have tried on many occasions to flee from this false reputation but it kept following me. I have tried to refuse accepting undeserved kindness but on the contrary, more undeserved kindness was bestowed upon me. It would be reckless of me to try to feed my vain reputation with such great foolishness, and it would be shameful to accept all the undeserved kindness shown to me while in such an invalid state. If I were to act recklessly and without shame, this would be unfortunate for raising virtue; this would not be good for others; and this would harm the country. What other reason would there be for me not enjoying government service and constantly leaving office?

I left because of these four vexations, which place me in awkward positions.

I left because of these two concerns, which pursue me.

Looking back, by the time I was forty-three, I was already aware of this. I planned to leave government service.

Twenty-five years have already passed.

However, because my actions have not been reliable and my sincerity anything but true, people above and below me still do not trust me. Therefore, I staggered and suffered failures while entering and leaving government posts on numerous occasions; this finally reached its climax last year and this year. In addition, as I am approaching seventy, one vexation, *old age*, has been added to the four making it five vexations. Since I have been shown more undeserved kindness as I was appointed the minister of one of the Six Boards of the Government, things have become more difficult. Even without mentioning the events of last year, just this year the king has called me into service twice. Because I turned down five calls to service last year, it would be awkward to assert myself stubbornly again. Consequently, I ignobly entered a government post and received the grace, which I had turned down previously. Therefore, I violated on my own volition one of the two worries.

I offer this as an excuse: because I was called to greet the Chinese envoys, I naturally thought I would retire once this work was completed. However, unexpectedly, upon my return, the king passed away, and I followed numerous vassals while weeping arduously. When the Chinese envoys arrived with the royal edict, my illness was already grave. Why would it be strange that it reached such a dangerous situation, as I had lost consciousness and nearly died because I had made such an effort and expended all my energy?

At about this time, receiving word I should take charge of the Board of Rites, I enjoyed prosperous benefits, as the new king embarked on a new administration. Although I was moved and wanted to devote myself entirely, it would have been impossible even in the eyes of others to handle the duties, being so critically ill. For this reason, I submitted my resignations on five separate occasions for appointments to government posts and did not enter office. Fortunately, at that time, I felt indebted as I was able to leave my post. This kind of situation did not arise with the last king; how can I hold up my head and stand among the numerous vassals after receiving this new order and turning down such kindness!

Since men of honor from ancient times were very distinct about entering and leaving office and were never careless about even the tiniest aspect, they would immediately retire from office if they had lost their usefulness even to the slightest. They would not have been able to do that if they looked exclusively at their affectionate love for the king. However, they did not forsake the proper way of leaving because of affection. It was proper they should devote themselves to their government posts; however, they would leave if they could not perform that work in the light of moral principle—only after that would they take the side of righteousness. If they had met times such as these, they would have had no choice but to submit to the moral principle of leaving office, despite possessing the affection that would have them hesitate in turning down the king.

Although I am an immoral man, as someone who has received boundless, special kindness from the now deceased king, I would not want to turn him down even though I may turn to dust. Why would I hesitate to spend several months for the funeral processions! However, my obligations as a vassal had already expired. If I clung to an empty affection and guarded my position simply spending my wages, I would have risked shame. While simply passing the time in mourning, it would be easy as a dry field burning for me—someone who is in such critical condition, someone so feeble, and someone full of fear—to wake up one morning, dead. If I had done this, what I have achieved by devoting my life would amount to nothing more than "women and eunuchs obeying but never assisting the king properly."[2] What would remain of my intentions to avoid the two worries while making such an effort and enduring hardship for dozens of years? Here lies my greatest fear. That is why I had to be quick and decisive in making plans for my return home. However, it has been a long time since the way to leave government service has been blocked. There has never been a case when somebody made the request to retire recently and it was actually accepted. Although I have thought of various ways, there seems to be no way out. Therefore, after receiving permission to leave my government post, in the span of time before the king assigned me to another post, I took advantage of this opportunity and returned home while I was free and without government posts.

In my view, everybody has completed all their assigned tasks and has poured out their affections and heart for the sake of the funeral procession. Doing this is truly a sincere desire of a vassal. I was unable to finish my duties for the funeral processions, and curbing my affections for the late king and pursuing moral principle were the conducts of a pitiful vassal, but I had no choice.

The king is like a parent.

They are one.

Since we must serve them immutably, we must lay down our lives.

Since the heavens have bound father and son, there are no formal rules on how to attend to one's father; however, a king and a vassal meet for the sake of social duty and certain formalities for serving the king must be observed. If there are no standard formalities, grace will always smother social duty and never leave. If there are fixed formalities, social duty can occasionally snatch grace and the vassal has no choice but to leave. Whether supporting a living person or sending off the dead, the rules never change.

However, we do not behave in this manner anymore. We do not care about social duty or intentions or consider what is right or wrong. We base everything on our affections. I believe the moral principle, which states fixed formalities exist for serving the king is not something so imprudent and vague. If I ignored my foolishness and illness and if I was not ashamed of being unable to perform my duties and held my position for a long time, there would be no reason for me to discard government service and leave.

Although I was an unworthy and lowly vassal, I received the late king's affectionate graces—his broad generosity and abundant virtue. Although he did not let me retire from government office on one swift occasion, eventually he leniently accepted the situation. Not only did he refrain from accusing me of committing an offense, but also he offered me encouragement. Invalid and foolish, I accomplished my wish of taking care of myself and for sixteen or seventeen years I passed the time in leisure. Since the late king had always regarded me as a distant vassal living in the mountains and fields, I am sure he would not blame me for not risking my life to follow the funeral processions!

However, I would be betraying the king's kindness if I were unable to do the work assigned to me effectively. If I did not shamelessly leave my post although my illness had reached a critical stage; if I had lost integrity; and, if I had defiled my name, would the spirit of the departed king be able to exclaim heartily:

"There was once this vassal who did not betray my kindness!"

On the contrary, I think he might come down and scold me exclaiming:

"Where is your integrity! How was it that you were persistent in refusing my orders to serve at government posts in the past?"

What could I say in my defense? Regarding this line of thinking, there are some reasonable points in light of moral principle and the state of affairs. If I continue the discussion from this standpoint, even if I were to disgrace myself by pursuing affection and disregarding moral principle, there is a reason I cannot act lightly whether I stay or go, live or die. What else could I do but leave?

However, regarding this matter, if we were walking down the same path, we would understand each other without speaking. If our paths were different, we could speak a thousand words but you would fail to understand. There is nothing left to do if you say your path is different from mine; however, if my actions occasionally correspond to the right path, how can it be that you would have to wait for my worthless explanations to know (my actions were correct) considering your position and knowledge? It is needless to say that what I will say will disagree with your opinions. Furthermore, you failed to accept what I slightly revealed the last time.

In your recent letter, you said, "I knew you had to make plans to leave. You could not stay in Seoul for a long time because of the many uncomfortable occurrences that you would confront." For several lines, it appeared as if you agreed with me, but you hurriedly attacked me during the rest of the letter. People like Hwasuk Bak, Junggu Yi,[3] Jajung Jeong, and Sukheon Yi[4] who had heard about my departure, raised their voices in greater reproach and grew even more skeptical about my departure. What can I expect from others! I am holding my breath and trembling in fear as I wait for the king's fierce rebuke.

However, when bracing myself and contemplating, the various scholars and ministers scolded me according to the general *dao* of scholars and men of virtue. They overlooked my faults urging me not to stubbornly fixate on nor shun away from one aspect but to move only after pursuing righteousness. This was quite profound of them.

> *However, the only mark I wanted to leave in life was to return home, hide, and pursue righteousness.*

I am very ashamed that I have been unable to absolve the anger of the prime ministers and everybody else's suspicions. This may be the case, but if I learned something and tried to apply it, I could have done it. However, occasionally, I would have reached very humiliating places. When knowing something because I learned it, I knew it well, but I always ended up following the world and traveling down the wrong path. The five vexations and two worries would obstruct me, which was worse than if I had just quietly kept my understanding to myself. Therefore, I wanted to retire from government service while seeking to conform to the *dao* of the ancient ones, which contradicted my devotion to the king. This is truly like a man from the Lu Dynasty saying, "I cannot do it, but I will train myself to do it as Liu Xiahui does it."[5] How can you say this is not true and not believe this? Social duty changes according to the person and according to the times.

It may be social duty for you to enter a government post but it is wrong for you to force that social duty on me. Similarly, although it is social duty for me to retire from office, it would be wrong to force this upon you.

I have heard recently Sibo Nam[6] say Yi Hwang studies for the sake of himself.

> Although Yi Hwang did not intend to study for himself, his works appear to show that he did study for himself.

When I heard those words, I began to sweat, perspiring to the point my clothes became wet. However, if we were to judge people purely on their actions, even in the olden days, while not to the extent of being Yang Zhu, would the number of people who acted for themselves be so few? Early on, Zhu Xi quoted the words of Buddha saying, "If you support many temples with this kind of mind and body, this is on the surface recompensing Buddha's grace." He said citing Du Fu's poem, "As your neighbor shoulders his plough and goes to work, will I do the same!"[7] Li Yanping said, "In times like this, hide yourself in a solemn place and only cultivate your everyday studies." [Although I cannot remember the exact quote, this is the general gist of it.]

Yang Guishan said in his poem:

> Sparsely gathered flower buds, fight gently with the snow! From inside the brightness of the moon, savor your lucidness and beauty!

This speaks of all the studies done for yourself.

Somebody once said only after being on top can one see what is straight and crooked in the people below. I am not sure, but what do you consider right or otherwise between these two points? What would you keep and what would you discard? I would consider it an enormous relief if you blessed me with your teachings.

Longqing (The era of Muzong's reign of the Ming Dynasty)
September 21, 1567 (the Year of the Rabbit)
The invalid, Yi Hwang, bows his head.

I am not sure what was wrong in my answers to the envoys. Can you tell me in your next letter? Chiwon Choe, Chong Seol, Chung Choe, and Yu An among others were ancestral Confucian scholars mentioned at the Board of Rites. I did not want to reject what people said about these scholars, but I wanted to make my own comments about them. Therefore, while keeping their names intact, amidst one of my responses, I stated plainly that Confucian scholars of the Silla and Goryeo period did not study the *School of Mind*. I did not think there would be any problems with this statement. However, now that I think about it, I regret unceasingly and want you to request that it be erased.

Outside of that, the envoys had no choice but to comment on people like Jae Gil and Jeompiljae; and among the people they commented upon, they could not exclude Sang Yun. Although the two envoys were gentle, unfortunately, the words of the *Isang* Yi[8] were probably like enemy soldiers to them if our standpoint regarding the studies was different in this manner. How could they surrender and immediately wave the white flag? What do you think about the above-mentioned words? I am sure you have an opinion about it. Please send it to me through letter. Evening has come and I briskly write this amidst the darkness.

---

1. On the day they carried King Myeongjong's coffin, Toegye stayed at Yongsu Temple because he felt uneasy staying at home.
2. This means being good at obeying but not assisting properly.
3. Refers to Dam Yi. His pen name was Jeongjonjae and Junggu was his pseudonym.
4. Refers to I (Yi) Yi. His pen name was Yulgok and Sukheon was his pseudonym.
5. "A widow of the Lu Dynasty whose house was destroyed by a storm paid a visit to the widower next door to take shelter from the rainstorm, but the widower did not open the door. The widow asked, 'Why do you not like Liu Xiahui?' The widower answered, 'Liu Xiahui can do but I cannot. Therefore, I will learn what I cannot do with what Liu Xiahui can do.'" See the *Kongzijiayu* 2, "Haosheng" 10.
6. Refers to Eongyeong Nam. His pen name was Jeongjae and Sibo was his pseudonym. He was absorbed in reading Chen Baisha and Wang Yangming's *Zhuanxilu* and through these influences he became the first follower of Wang Yangming in Joseon.
7. This is a phrase from Du Fu's poem, "Heavy Rain."
8. *Isang* (two ministers) is another name for *Jwachanseong* and *Uchanseong* and this position ranks next to the three ministers of the State Council. The letter mentioned here refers to Eonjeok Yi's letter, which was sent to Hanbo Jo.

[Letter #51 Gobong Writes Toegye]

Replying in Detail Instead of Scolding

Dear teacher,

I received your letter dated September 21. You repeated and reiterated hundreds of words to show me the error of my ways. You considered both sides and enlightened me regarding my foolish views. I was filled with endless adoration and lament after opening, reading, and rereading your letter. However, after you sent the letter, I wanted to meet you twofold since I could not check on your health. Even today, as I am so impertinent, I am barely preserving myself thanks to your affectionate grace.

There is nothing special about which to inform you regarding the various circumstances. Merely, as the king issued tolerant orders after an unexpected newness of heart, a group of people who spent dozens of years in the shadow holding grudges have come to see the light.[1] We have come to an era where we can witness the expansion of good politics. I was a vassal who simply squandered the government's money and followed others, moving in packs, but fortunately, I am moved and overjoyed because I am able to be a part of this. However, I have one worry remaining.

I troubled you carelessly with my views earlier because I wanted answers to a suspicious part—that is all. I would not dare to target and criticize you as others have. I could not have been more fortunate to have you reply to me in detail instead of scolding me.

I have resolved nine out of my ten doubts.

If we continue to seek common points in this manner, in the end, there will be a time when we are in complete consensus. In your letter, I agreed with your statements: "like women and eunuchs who obey but do not serve" and "returning home, hiding, and pursuing only after righteousness." However, I am not sure if they conform to the deeper meaning you might possess.

I am not sure if Sibo Nam really said those words. However, it will be difficult for him to avoid rebuke for speaking so carelessly. I have roughly written my thoughts about the annex. I seek your guidance again. Can you comment?

I have not been able to concentrate for long periods since difficult work continues to come my way. I feel numb when writing and feel ashamed and frightened because I have not been able to say everything I want.

Please excuse me. I end the letter here.
Respectfully bowing, I offer this letter.
Longqing (The era of Muzong's reign of the Ming Dynasty)
October 11, 1567 (the Year of the Rabbit)
Bowing, yours truly,
Junior scholar, Daeseung.

---

1. Susin No, Ingeol Baek, Huichun Ryu and so on, who were dismissed during the literati purges of the Year of the Snake, were reinstated in October.

[Letter #52, Gobong Writes Toegye]

Come and Comply with the King's Wishes

Dear teacher,
 I respectfully prostrate myself and inquire about your well-being. How is your health? I miss you endlessly. Thanks to your affectionate grace, I am barely preserving this worthless body. I sent a letter in early winter through Jajung Jeong, but I am not sure if you have received it yet.
 Recently, the king has called you to service again and since the situation does not appear to be that bad, I was thinking from a distance that you would comply with the king's wishes. Instead of waiting for the wagon to escort you, I thought you might have already made plans to come. My only concern was that it was winter and very cold. I worried twofold about how you would make such a long journey. Fortunately, orders from the king arrived later so that you should come when it was warmer; and you could make the journey without tediously making haste. I am extremely comforted and relieved.
 I have presumptuously become an Instructor[1] and I serve the king from his side. Prostrating myself before the king, I have never met somebody who enjoys the studies and virtue more than this king does. One day, he called me to his presence. I told him about the work of the sages and the wise men. In response, the king said: "Although the majority of wise men these days do not want to serve in government posts, how can it be that their original hearts do not want to serve? Is it that perhaps the king cannot appoint them to offices because the king lacks a sincere heart?"
 He went on to say:
 "If the king possesses extreme sincerity, what reason would there be for not appointing wise men to offices?"
 Later, he relayed these intentions on numerous occasions in his royal orders. As his thoughts are expansive, how can we not consider adhering? As I quietly ponder, I think you should come at once and comply with the king's wishes.
 A long time ago, when Zhu Xi declined Nam Gang's order, Donglai and Nanxuan urged him to go. Nanxuan said, "If you continue to decline firmly without change, superiors will say that the wise people do not want to be employed, and in the broad picture,

this is harmful." The meaning is very clear and I want to offer this to you. I am not sure what you will say in response. One can now prognosticate that our *dao* will be realized; I do not think you can lean to one side and stick to old assertions. I prostrate myself before you and ask you to consider this.

December has all but passed and spring is returning. If you embark on your travels quickly, in no time I will be able to serve you from your side. I ardently wait for you and in the meantime, I have written this letter. Please be advised. I respectfully bow, end here, and offer this letter.

Longqing (The era of Muzong's reign of the Ming Dynasty)
December 9, 1567 (the Year of the Rabbit)
Bowing, yours truly,
Junior scholar, Daeseung.
The handwriting is not neat, as I have written this during the night shift. I apologize.

During the royal lectures, we took turns lecturing about the four books of the *Classic of Rites* and *The Great Learning* and now that we are finished, we are carefully reading them. I was called today and asked by the king:

"In the discussions of the general principle mentioned in the commentary section, chapter ten of *The Great Learning*, only the studies are mentioned; in places where the clauses are discussed, the troubles with the studies are also discussed. What does that mean?"

Judging from this kind of royal order, the king is superior to the average person. As an insignificant vassal, I was deeply moved. Teacher, please keep this point in mind. Starting from the beginning of January, we have been informed we will be lecturing about *Confucian Analects* during the morning and lunch hour and the text, *The Elementary Learning*, in the evening. Please keep this in mind.

---

1. Refers to an official who reads and discusses sacred books with the King for the Royal Lectures.

1568–1569

THE IMBROGLIO OF SICKNESS AND RETURNING HOME

[Letter #53 Gobong Writes Toegye]

Two Agonies, Two Concerns

Dear teacher,

I respectfully inquire about your well-being. How is your health? My longing for you grows deeper with each passing day. From winter to spring, the king has called you to service on numerous occasions and the new government post is even higher than previous. However, I have no way of knowing your plans. My worry grows to the utmost. I am barely getting along thanks to your concerns.

Recently, I had the opportunity to read your subsequent letter of resignation and your written appeal to the king, which revealed your hidden intentions. Furthermore, I met the *Jikjang* Yi and heard word of how you were getting along. Because I agonized and was unable to suppress my concerns, I dare to write a few thoughts to you. I prostrate myself before you and ask you to listen attentively.

Just as the king's desire is at the brink of overflowing, his desire to meet you rivals his longing for the old sages and wise men. However, after repeatedly declining his invitations, eventually you did not come. The king feels stifled and grows lethargic in his calling. I am afraid he will change his mind. Would it not be regretful if he did?

This is my first agony.

Not only would it be good for our time, but also it would be good for all the ages if you met the king and opened his eyes with your brief words and established a trusting relationship. However, you refuse to do this.

This is my second agony.

Furthermore, you wrote in good faith and stated that your absolute retirement from government service was undoubtedly correct and significant in the light of moral principle. However, I think the more you make an effort to leave and hide from government service, the more the king will take interest in you. In the rare, ten thousand to one probability the king attempts to draw you out by offering you the prime minister position, how will you conduct yourself then?

This is my first concern.

The *dao* of the times has become very trivial and insignificant. The human mind has become blind, unable to see. Man cannot find the path. It has become difficult to plan for anything. Not to mention, if throngs of people stand by your side as spectators and turn their backs on you at will, feigning loyalty on the outside while betraying you on the inside, I do not know how you will resolve this matter even after you have returned.

This is my second concern.

Of course, it would be difficult to consider all the reasons for my agonies and concerns, but these are the major points. What do you think?

Even as I repeatedly deliberate on this issue with my foolish views I have held from before, I do not think you will be able to escape (these difficulties) by declining when considering the situations you are confronting. Therefore, I implore you to make the journey in the spring and express gratitude for the kindness the king has bestowed upon you. In addition, after repaying his good faith in the least bit by enlightening him about the learning of the sages at the royal lecture, you can cordially inform the king of your illness and old age and request to leave office as that would be course of action in light of moral principle. Then, the king would not harbor any displeasing emotions regarding your loyalty and patriotism. Although Zhu Xi also received many orders from the king, he said he was not comfortable with just lying down peacefully. We must carefully consider what this means.

Although I have more to say, I will stop here because I think saying more will be impolite to my elder. I am gracious and incredibly ashamed. I prostrate myself before you and ask you to consider this. I respectfully bow and offer this letter.

February 12, 1568 (the Year of the Dragon)
Bowing, yours truly,
Junior scholar, Daeseung.

I have something else about which to inform you. As I try to plan on your behalf, how can I be the same as the throngs of people who only talk? Although I try to exert earnestly a comprehensive effort on your behalf, I have not been satisfied. What can I do? My job is writing the king's message, but I cannot write something that might be beneficial to you according to my own whim. What should

I do? In addition, I ask to understand this. I cannot go into detail, as I have pressing business.

[Letter #54 Toegye Writes Gobong]

I Have Not Made It to Gangneung Yet

I write this to you, Myeongeon.[1]

I am thankful and relieved beyond measure that I have been assuaged of my burden thanks to the king's royal favor. I am truly sorry and ashamed that I have not been to Gangneung[2] even once. I want to visit Gangneung as the envoy who superintends the ceremonial rites, whereby attending to the upcoming Sak memorial service.[3] However, in the past, I heard they cancelled memorial services when a solar eclipse was at hand. I am not sure if they still do this. If old laws are followed and the memorial services are cancelled, are envoys still dispatched for the Wian or Seongosayu memorial services among others? Please look into this matter for me. I respectfully inform you.

From Hwang.

---

1. From this point, while Toegye and Gobong both resided in Seoul, they exchanged brief letters for a period. As they exchanged many letters during a short period, many letters with different subjects were mixed together. In addition, since they did not write the dates on these letters, it is difficult to know the sequence of these letters. As this is the case, the letter sequencing in *Toegye's Collections* and the letter sequencing in *Gobong's Collections* do not match. Foremost, I followed the sequence of *Gobong's Collections* because it seemed more accurate chronologically. However, the sequencing in *Gobong's Collections* is not entirely accurate, as well.

2. Refers to the mausoleum of King Myeongjong.

3. The royal household held a memorial service for ancestors every first day of the month in the lunar calendar.

[Letter #55 Gobong Writes Toegye]

I Will Look into and Execute Your Request

I respectfully reply to your letter, teacher.
I received your letter yesterday. I was humbled and grateful. However, I returned late in the evening and could not write a response immediately. My apologetic, lamentable heart truly grows more profound. I wonder how your health is today. I miss you more fervently. I will look into and execute your request. Please be advised. I will tell you the rest when we meet. I respectfully end and offer this letter.
Bowing, yours truly,
Junior scholar, Daeseung.

[Letter #56 Toegye Writes Gobong]

Sending You the "Ten Diagrams of Confucian Philosophy"

I give this to you.
I am sending you the *Ten Diagrams of Confucian Philosophy*. Can you send it back to me after you have pointed out and discussed the mistakes?
From Hwang. Please do not let others see this.

[Letter #57 Gobong Writes Toegye]

As the "Ten Diagrams of Confucian Philosophy" is Very Precise and Accurate

Dear teacher,
I prostrate myself and respectfully inquire about your well-being. How is your health? I miss you unceasingly. Yesterday, I stayed at home to take care of myself and today I was able to go to work. Furthermore, I have some apologetic words to convey. In the

Ten Diagrams of Confucian Philosophy, if you look at the "Diagram of the Rules of the White Deer Hollow Academy" part where it says, "the reasonableness of principle," there are circles drawn next to these words. However, you drew no circles around the two characters "ji-dang." I think you must have made a mistake while writing this down. I roughly and briskly looked through the *Ten Diagrams of Confucian Philosophy* and although I may have some suspicions about certain parts, I cannot inform you of them now. What can I do? My colleagues want to submit it immediately to the king, but I will hold on to it, as there may be parts that need further consideration. I am not sure but what if I submit it to the king sometime tomorrow? Please be advised of this. I respectfully bow and offer this letter.

Bowing, yours truly,
Junior scholar, Daeseung.

As the *Ten Diagrams of Confucian Philosophy* is very precise and accurate, it would be a relief if I showed it to the king. I would be more pleased and comforted if the "Presentation Address"[1] was even more accurate.

---

[1] Refers to "Jinseonghaksibdocha," which Toegye wrote while presenting the *Ten Diagrams of Confucian Philosophy*. See *Toegye's Collections* 7. See also *Revised Annals of Seonjo* 2, the first year of King Seonjo's reign, December 1, the Day of the Pig.

[Letter #58 Toegye Writes Gobong]

After Receiving Your Guidance

I bow and offer my gratitude to you, noble friend.[1]*

I was relieved and moved when I received your guidance. I made a writing error in not circling the two words. Please circle them and submit. I am very fortunate you caught that. Beyond that, there are probably many points about which you are suspicious. I wanted to revise it, but as I could see no end in sight if I continued to struggle with certain points, I just sent it off. If the king royally sanctions this, I hope you will make an original copy by transcribing it while various Instructors appraise and discuss it.

From Hwang.

---

1. From this letter on, Toegye refers to Gobong as *Yeonggong*. This is because Gobong was promoted to the senior with a 3rd official rank at the *Ubuseungji*. Those above the 3rd official rank were called the *Dangsanggwan* and were distinguished from those officials lower in rank.

* Or *Yeonggong*. See endnote 1 for title explanation. Translated as "noble friend" or "respected sir" or "duke," Toegye calls Gobong by this title as a sign of respect.

[Letter #59 Gobong Writes Toegye]

Yesterday, After Greeting and Meeting You

Dear teacher,

The cold grows progressively fiercer and I did not have the chance to check on your health. There is no place to set my longing heart. My cold is mollifying and my wife is recuperating as well. I was enormously relieved that I had the opportunity to greet and meet you yesterday. However, I lamented as I could not convey all of my thoughts because worries flooded into my heart and I grew tired from the alcohol. I forgot to inform you about certain matters and thinking about it later on, I arrived at some new thoughts. I wrote them on the annex. Please teach me regarding these matters. It would be a relief if you considered this.

Although I had slightly recuperated, I could not attend the Chin memorial service* on the first day of January—I felt uneasy. I intend on going to work tomorrow. Please be advised. I respectfully bow, and while I am moved and overjoyed truly,

Junior scholar, Daeseung.

---

* A memorial service attended personally by the king.

"Qian" and "Kun"

These two characters appear in the *Book of Changes*. Originally, these were the names of the eight trigrams which Fu Xi drew and he modeled them after heaven and earth, the Yin and Yang.[1]

---

1. This annexed paper is about Gobong's comments on "Diagram of the Western Inscription" in the *Ten Diagrams of Confucian Philosophy*.

"Saek" and "Su"

Regarding these two characters, there is no commentary. Although it is recorded that energy is exceedingly large and strong, and energy fills the body, the "che" character has an origin.

"Pae" and "Deok" (Preserve Disposition)

This appears in *The Classic of Filial Piety* but I cannot remember whether you had recorded it or not.

The Affair of the border-warden of the vale of Ying

As this is troublesome to write, how about deleting some parts and tidying it up?

Nature Is the One Origin of All Creation

Hengqu originally said this. How about adding a few more words as commentary?

No Place He Can Escape to

Most likely, it states in *Chuang Tzu*, "No place he can escape to between heaven and earth." Your meaning will become clearer if you quote this.

The Shen Sheng Affair

How about being a little clearer by referencing "The Tan Gong"?[2]

---

2. Refers to one title in the book of the *Classic of Rites*.

Fixing the Storage Room and Digging a Well

I am not comfortable because you cited these words as meaning exerting an effort and suffering but there is no way of knowing if such an event occurred or not.

Principle Remains Because the Words are Unfinished
This is the same as saying parts of principles remain because the words are not detailed. In other words, by not saying everything, the principle is not explained and there are parts remaining. Therefore, it means the words of Guishan are incomplete. However, since it says only that principle remains, these words are very concise and do not betray the meaning of previous wise men. How about making this clearer?

[Letter #60 Toegye Writes Gobong]

*Enlightening Me on the Lacking Parts
of the Historical Investigation*

I respectfully bow to you, noble friend, and reply.
I was extremely relieved to hear through your letter that you were fine and that your wife was doing well. I was deeply relieved that you visited me yesterday and enlightened me on the lacking parts of the historical investigation.
When I thought about it, it has been several days since the lectures regarding *The Elementary Learning* have finished. The office of Royal Lecturers waits for me to finish the historical investigation and after submitting it, they will inform the king about the beginning of the lectures; people will consider it to be behind schedule. Just as I was about to submit it, I needed to make more revisions on the original and transcribe a copy, which would have slowed down things to a stifling pace. Therefore, braving illness and working under a dull light with poor vision, I made all the revisions and finished it by morning. I did not ask you to look over it but sent it directly to the government office. However, they received your response and sent it to me. After seeing your annex, I regretted that I could not go back and make additions and supplements. I write a response to your annex in my own annex.
I thank you again.
From Hwang.

It would have been appropriate if I had interpreted the two characters, "qian" and "kun" as you did. It is a pity that I did not have the foresight to think that far.

Although the main notes regarding "saeksu" were deleted, the broader meaning has already been provided. Writing about this in detail would be unnecessary.

The two characters, "pae" and "deok," are quoted from *The Classics of Filial Piety*. There are many words from *Zuo's Commentary on the Spring and Autumn Annals* regarding "the affair of the border-warden of the vale of Ying." I wanted to delete and summarize to reveal the bigger meaning. If I delete it anymore, I worry this fact will be lost completely.

I quoted the words of Hengqu when saying, "Nature is the one origin of all creation," and I quoted *Chuang Tzu* when saying, "No place he can escape to." I sigh that I could not think of it before.

It will be harmless if we leave "the Shen Sheng affair" in that manner.

Regarding "Fixing the storage room and digging a well," previous Confucian scholars could not verify if this had happened or not. However, there should not be a problem if these words provide testimony for not delaying effort.

Regarding "principles remain because the words are unfinished," I think Zhu Xi referenced these words while talking about Guishan. By adhering to the meaning—principles remain although words are unfinished—I disclosed that the principle was as mentioned above. Furthermore, amidst the historical investigation, while writing, ". . . although the meaning remains," I did not use the "yi" character, which I believe is harmless.

Under the sentence, "It was the reverence of Shen Sheng that caused him to await death because there was no place to which he could escape," I wrote, "No place he can escape to between heaven and earth comes from *Chuang Tzu*." These twelve characters are under the "gong" character and above the "jinheongong" character.

In the postscript, under "chingmulpyeongsi," I corrected the two characters, which mean *remains* from the phrase "although the meaning remains" and changed it to "were not lost."

[Letter #61 Gobong Writes Toegye]

Guard Correctly and Highly Regard Simplicity

Dear teacher,
I respectfully inquire about your well-being. How is your health these days? I have always looked up to you and yearned for you. I felt truly frustrated because I could not say everything that was on my mind yesterday, as I had to leave abruptly. As propriety is a heavenly principle, it is lucidly distinguished; if one thread of this composition were fabricated at will, there would be no end to evil practices. Please consider this profoundly! Although the placement of one word seems trivial, I think you would regret it if there was even the slightest variation from the original meaning of the examples! Instead of being deeply worried, overly calculative and trying to add more, I am saying it would be better to gain what is proper by guarding what is right and highly regarding simplicity. What do you think? I ask you to observe and consider this. I will tell you the rest when we meet, but I have asked about these few matters in advance.
   Bowing, yours truly,
   Junior scholar, Daeseung.

[Letter #62 Toegye Writes Gobong]

Extensively Refer to the Classical Books of Previous Times

I reply.
Thank you for asking about how I was doing. What you said in your letter was truly correct. However, I have some suspicions as the proposed title and the title used in "always uses that title" will have some parts that conflict; then, one will not be able to guard correctly and highly regard its simplicity. To say nothing of the fact that there are no classical books to reference regarding this matter, how can one stubbornly say that using this title is the only way to save one's superficial honor? Since there are no books in this place, I hope you extensively refer to the classical books of previous times and make the decision regarding this important matter. I respectfully reply.
   From Hwang.

[Letter #63 Toegye Writes Gobong]

Sending the Abridged Transcript of What Jeongam Jo Had Informed the King

I bow to you, noble friend, and inquire about your well-being.

As I cringe in the face of the cold, an inescapable worry forms inside of me. I return the *Four Books* you had sent to me. I added "Xiang Dang" in the table of contents of the *Confucian Analects* and at the same time omitted "Li Ren"; therefore, the lines are crooked. I am quite embarrassed, as I am old and my wits are dull.

I send you my summary of the writings Jeongam Jo[1] had given to the king. When you have time, please carefully look over it for experiment sake. After reading his writings, I spent fifteen days and ten more days in what seemed like either a state of inebriation or sobriety. I still have not recovered. When I carefully think about it, this man knew the meaning of hardship. While knowing hardship, parts of his beliefs were wrong. However, (his failure) was not only a result of his incorrect beliefs. Although he wanted to leave for the longest time, things happened the way they did because there was no way out. Therefore, I realized the saying, "Forever a hero, soaking his towel in tears," does not apply to only one person, the deceased, Zhuge Liang.[2]

Furthermore, when looking at the circumstances of those times, even without the crisis that entailed the stripping of the *jeonggukgongsin** titles, Jeongam Jo could not have avoided yet another defeat. However, the infestation of many villainous, insignificant retainers and the ignition of astonishing schemes arose because of this one event. This was a result of many wise men not being cautious of such perilous times and simply proceeding forward violently. We must not be ignorant of this point.

I send you one book, Jajung Jeong's *Yusannok*. I am happy that his poems are slightly improving. The only fault I see is that among the many words he wrote, not even one mentioned his thoughts about the studies.

From Hwang.

Where is Hwasuk Bak's place of birth? Please inform me as I need to know.

1. Refers to Gwangjo Jo (1482-1519). His pseudonym was Hyojik and Jeongam was his pen name. He pushed on with the reformation as the leader of the *Sarim* (the literati) in the Jungjong period but was executed at the time of the literati purges during the Year of the Rabbit.

2. This expression originated from "Shuxiangshi," which Tang poet Du Fu wrote, as he longed for the minister of the Shu Kingdom, Zhuge Liang, who was an outstanding hero but daunted without having his day.

* A title given to those vassals who helped in the enthronement of the new king, Jungjong, subsequent to the dethronement of a wicked king.

[Letter #64 Gobong Writes Toegye]

Comparing the Present to Jeongam's Time

I reply to you teacher and offer this letter.

After respectfully receiving your word, I was unfathomably happy to realize the letter was endowed with your gratefulness. It was precious and momentous that you personally went through the trouble of making the changes in the table of contents of the *Four Books*. Regarding the incorrect parts you wrote in the table of contents, I greatly benefited that you clearly enlightened me on the fact that even the tiniest flaw in a gem cannot be hidden. Regarding the two writings you had sent me, I expect to learn profound teachings piecemeal after looking over them from start to finish. I respectfully weigh the fact that the heavens did not help the deceased Zhuge, although he took the right measures. We should make a distinction, as the shocking events that occurred a short time ago, happened because Jeongam took incomplete measures. He wanted to leave but there was no way out. As events began to unfold in an odd manner, he should have been cautious and fearful without pause; however, he haphazardly created new problems and rushed calamity his way.

This was a chronic disease of that time.

Even today, we must sternly observe and be very cautious. What do you think? I cannot say all the rest without meeting you. Please excuse me.

I respectfully bow and offer this letter.

Bowing, yours truly,

Junior scholar, Daeseung.

Hwasuk Bak's place of origin is Chungju. Early on, Nulje referred to himself as Mr. Bak of Jungwon.

[Letter #65 Gobong Writes Toegye]

I Presented the "Ten Diagrams of Confucian Philosophy" and the "Presentation Address" Yesterday Evening

Dear teacher,
I respectfully prostrate myself and inquire about your well-being. I wonder about your health. My reverent, longing for you grows twofold. Although I presented the *Ten Diagrams of Confucian Philosophy* and the "Presentation Address" yesterday evening, it has not come out yet. Recently, I lament as I have been unable to visit you. I have been bogged down with work. I will end this letter here. Please be advised.
Respectfully bowing, I offer this letter.
Bowing, yours truly,
Junior scholar, Daeseung.

I have some apologetic words to add. Amidst the statutes in the *Classified Conversations of Master Zhu*, one article mentions, "Most of the royal family in the chamberlain added titles like *Hwanghyeong** or *Hwangsuk*** to their official titles when taking government offices." Therefore, by looking at this, you will know that the "hwang" character did not designate something beautiful and large. What do you think about carefully verifying this matter? I worry endlessly that the harm produced by failing to study one letter may lead to greater evil practices. In addition, I ask you look upon this with lenient eyes.

---

* Title for older brother.
** Title for husband's younger brother.

[Letter #66 Toegye Writes Gobong]

Discussing the Title of the King's Parents[1]

    I bow as I offer this reply.
    I read your last letter. Although the "hwang" character seen in titles like *Hwanghyeong, Hwangsuk, Hwangchin*, and *Hwangja* among others is the same as the "hwang" character, which means emperor, the "hwang" character referred to in the "Summary of The Rules of Propriety" was used for generations in average households and it truly meant "beautiful" and "large." Therefore, the character is used in the royal shrines. If the "hwang" character was indeed the character which meant emperor, how could they use it in the royal shrines! The courts of the Yuan Dynasty ordered the acceptance of the usage of the "hyeon" character. However, we cannot use it in this title. Moreover, in the *Classic of Rites*, they referred to all princes with higher degree relationships and similar surnames to the emperor as "baekbu." If we eliminate the use of the "hwang" character and started using "baekbu" in its place, this becomes a general title. This would create more distance between the king and his parents. Wise men of the past said we must establish an entirely different title. Now, on the contrary, regarding this single character, people are fighting tenaciously, claiming this title is different from the name used conventionally in ordinary households. What would be the best thing to do? On top of that, it is not as if the character will be used in ancestral tablets! The king is simply looking for a temporary title to call relatives. How can people stubbornly insist that this one character cannot be added to what is used by everyday people? If you absolutely oppose using that character—what if we use the "dae" character instead? I respectfully inform you of my thoughts beforehand.
    From Hwang.

---

    1. This is a letter from *Toegye's Collections*, which is dated from the Year of Snake (King Seonjo's second year, 1569).

[Letter #67 Toegye writes Gobong]

Revising "The Diagram of the Western Inscription" 1

I reply again to you, noble friend.

I was enormously relieved when I received another letter last night. Similar to the phrase, "plow the field with all my strength," the phrase, "did not delay effort," does not mean Shun takes charge of the difficult tasks on his own accord. This means Gu Sou commands Shun to do the difficult work. Although previous Confucian scholars had doubts about the phrase, "Fixing the storage room and digging wells," Mencius did not inquire regarding its validity. Therefore, it would be harmless to use that as proof here. I will add the suggestions you made regarding, "No place he can escape to between the heavens and earth." What if I changed "although the meaning remains" to "although the meaning has lost nothing"? If the annex is without problems after you look at it, please send it to the Office of Royal Lecturers.

From Hwang.

[Letter #68 Gobong Writes Toegye]

Revising "The Diagram of the Western Inscription" 2

Dear teacher,

I prostrate myself and respectfully inquire about your well-being. How is your health? I look up to you and I am missing you. I have slightly recuperated from a long-term illness, enabling me to work barely as others do. I could not fathom the relief and gratitude I felt after reading your words yesterday. I sent the annex immediately to the Office of Royal Lecturers and told them to transcribe it into the original copy of the *Ten Diagrams of Confucian Philosophy*. Please be advised. I respectfully bow and offer this letter.

Bowing, yours truly,

Junior scholar, Daeseung.

[Letter #69 Gobong Writes Toegye]

Revising "The Diagram of the Western Inscription" 3

Dear teacher,

I was very comforted when reading your response letter. The opening lectures have not been delayed because the historical investigation has not been completed. We have been informed that classes will be suspended from the sixteenth of this month due to construction at the Gangneung. Furthermore, I informed the king that classes today and tomorrow will be cancelled because of the *Gukgi* (National memorial service) and the *Sakje* (memorial service held for ancestors).[1] We are considering starting classes next month on the second or third. Furthermore, all the various clauses you wrote in response to the king are all reasonable. If you have not finished it yet, you can inform the king during your lectures. However, in my opinion, I am still apprehensive about the phrases: "fixing the storage room" and "some remaining." I write about them again and inform you. Please consider after looking at it.

I respectfully bow and offer this letter.
Bowing, yours truly,
Junior scholar, Daeseung.

It seems absolutely correct that in *The Works of Mencius* it gave as evidence of toil, the phrase, "Plow the land with all your strength and respectfully do your duty as children."

In the general summary, regarding the phrase, "The Western Inscription explains how the principle is one but its manifestations are diverse," the commentary says, "Although words are exceedingly brief, the principle does not remain." This is completely contrary to the saying, "The principle remains." Please carefully look over this again. What do you think?

---

1. *Gukgi* refers to memorial services held for kings and queens, and *Sakje* refers to the memorial service held for ancestors, which was performed by the royal household on the first day of the month in the lunar calendar.

[Letter #70 Toegye Writes Gobong]

Do You Know Me!

I write to you, noble friend.[1]

Yesterday, somebody came to me and told me the gist of what you had said to the king during the *Yadae*.[2] When I heard what he had said, I was shocked and broke into a cold sweat; I was at a lost and had trouble sleeping all night. How could you be so thoughtless! I have failed in this manner and while ignobly entangled in various matters, I have not been able to leave government service, although I have tried; the reason I am worried and afraid day and night can be attributed to two words: *vain name*.

Suppose somebody else had exaggerated in his lofty praise of me to the king. You should have tried to uproot and stop him. You should have helped me escape the crime of deceiving the heavens, but on the contrary, you personally have praised me so highly that you have dizzied the king's ears. The burdens of my sins grow and the thoughts of people grow more chaotic. If their rage grows fiercer, where can I hide and escape to avoid that wrath? We have grown close and we have grown to acknowledge one another. What happened to those good intentions? Furthermore, people have already considered peculiar our frequent exchanges and our codependence, and now with this ensuing kind of action, who will believe the words you spoke were impartial?

I tried going out for three days as a test, but could not bear it; I planned to return home and cower. Because of this contretemps, I cannot hold my head up and meet people because of the shame. My mental and emotional sicknesses suddenly grow acute. Therefore, I close and lock my doors. I lie down while waiting for the chastisement and punishment. From now on, I want to halt the sending of messengers back and forth that inquire about our respective well-being.

I would be grateful beyond comparison if you leave me in relative peace.

I respectfully bow.

From Hwang.

---

1. This letter was sent during the Year of the Dragon (the first year of King Seonjo's reign, 1568) and this fact was mentioned in *Toegye's Collections*.

2. *Yadae* refers to the Royal Lecture held at night where the king would summon the vassals. Gobong asserted that Seonjo should treat Toegye well enough to make him his teacher. See the *Annals of Seonjo* 2, the first year of King Seonjo's reign, December 6, the Day of the Dragon.

[Letter #71 Gobong Writes Toegye]

Truly Complicated Inside Story

I reply and offer this letter to you my teacher, Toegye.

I was ashamed and afraid immeasurably after receiving your guidance through the letter. My original intentions were not to ennoble you! At the time, while adhering to the king's commands, it appears as if I spoke of many things; however, I spoke only the facts, nothing more. I simply relayed to the king my views. Regarding this matter, I believe there are truly complicated inside stories that you have not been completely considered. I want to visit you this evening. Please understand this with lenient eyes. I respectfully bow and offer this reply.

December 9, 1568 (the Year of the Dragon)
Bowing, yours truly,
Junior scholar, Daeseung.

[Letter #72 Toegye Writes Gobong]

There is No Need to Come

I reply.

How can people know that there are complicated underlying conditions? Although I want to permit you to stop by, there is really no need to come, as it will not be beneficial for this matter and will only attract the eyes of others.

I respectfully reply.
From Hwang.

[Letter #73 Toegye Writes Gobong]

After Hearing News that the Respected Gwahoe's Father Had Passed Away

I inform you, noble friend.

I respectfully inquire. How is your sickness? Lately, I have not heard from you and I truly miss you. I have just heard that the respected Gwahoe's father had passed; I rushed out, walked with him to the entrance of the village, and sent him off. I walked back shedding tears.[1] People say you never know what is going to happen. I see these kinds of things do occur.

From Hwang.

---

1. The respected Gwahoe, Susin No, expressed his desire to retire as his parents were both very old. The King Seonjo accepted his wish and appointed him governor of the Chungcheong Province, which was near his native village. See the *Revised Annals of Seonjo* 2, the first year of reign, December 1, the Day of the Pig.

[Letter #74 Gobong Writes Toegye]

I Want to Visit

I reply and offer this letter to you, teacher.

I received your letter. I was shocked and saddened immeasurably when I heard that the governor of the Chungcheong Province had rushed home because his father had passed away.

I am sad and lament to the utmost the fact I have not been able to visit you even once lately. As my wife's condition has improved, I wanted to visit you sometime and in the morning. I sent someone to look into the matter but discovered you had left your home. I hesitated and ended up not going. I am at my friend's house, and I am planning to visit you in the evening. Please be advised of this.

I respectfully bow and offer this reply.
Bowing, yours truly,
Junior scholar, Daeseung.

[Letter #75 Toegye Writes Gobong]

The Moral Principle for Leaving Government Service 1

I reply to you again, noble friend.

I received the letter you sent. I sensed your gratefulness. I read it and as you informed me in your letter, you did not mention everything that was on your mind. Sometime tomorrow, I intend on visiting the king and telling him my thoughts, but I fear the result will be the same as in the past. When I assume a course of action, controlling the speed has always been difficult. Although it will always be difficult to leave government service, one scheme might be to act decisively when I am free of a government post. What do you think?

Yesterday, one of the things the trusted vassals informed the king of was the possibility of opening a way to leave government service. However, I lament as that way does not seem suitable for me—someone who is so base and clumsy. As for the rest, I could not hear all the theories regarding the figure of linear signs. I wait to see you soon and end this letter here.

From Hwang.

[Letter #76 Gobong Writes Toegye]

The Moral Principle for Leaving Government Service 2

I write to you again, teacher.

I was extremely grateful and comforted after receiving your letter. However, I have no choice but to inquire, as some of my thoughts remain troubled. Social duty must assuredly decide whether you go or stay, leave slowly or leave quickly. How can you base your decision on whether you are free of a government post or not? If somebody were to conduct himself in such a manner, he would most likely fall into a pit void of any heavenly mandate or social duty. The king has already royally sanctioned your leave after truly believing your earnest request to leave your government post! However, by taking advantage of this opportunity and making plans to escape (while free from government post)—is that the way to repay faithfully the sincere trust the king has placed in you?

This is not what I expected for you.

As I have expressed my thoughts, I have not been able to speak moderately and have dared to be cumbersome and impertinent in informing you. Please understand with lenient eyes.

Before I was able to peruse the theories regarding the figure of linear signs carefully, various events transpired, but I have not heard anything exact. Please be advised of this.

I respectfully bow and offer another letter.
Bowing, yours truly,
Junior scholar, Daeseung.

[Letter #77 Toegye Writes Gobong]

The Moral Principle for Leaving Government Service 3

I reply to you again, noble friend.

After receiving your words of guidance again, I admired your utmost intentions. It goes without saying that you were right when saying I should not base my decision on whether having a government post or not. However, I worry that after I have been assigned a government post, I will not receive orders that allow my exit from office. If I do exit after the king assigns me a government post, I would be guilty of discarding at will the duties of a civil servant and leaving. How can this be taking advantage of my situation of being without an office! While walking out of the city gates, on one hand, I intend on writing a letter, requesting resignation orders. It would be very nice if I received such permission and even if I do not receive permission, there will be a way to leave. I consider this the best plan among various. I am not sure, but will you condemn this to be wrong to the end? I do not want to sneak away. Furthermore, how can you say waiting for orders after walking out the city gate is leaving stealthily? However, if a situation arises where I should come back and stay, I will have no choice but to act according to the "two characters."[1]

Graciously, I respectfully bow.
From Hwang

---

1. Refers to the word *dun-geo* which means leaving stealthily.

[Letter #78 Toegye Writes Gobong]

Afraid Like Stepping On Spring Ice

I write my reply.
After reading your letter, I learned that you were working night duty every day despite the fact you were not feeling well. My worries grow twofold. I spend each day, afraid as if I am stepping on spring ice because I suffer from asthma in cold weather such as this. I met Ijeong and I heard through him that you still do not accept my ideas. However, I cannot act irreproachably because according to circumstance, there is an unavoidable aspect. I cannot explain them fully without meeting you face to face. Therefore, for the moment I reply in this manner.
Hwang bows and greets you.

[Letter #79 Gobong Writes Toegye]

Ijeong Did Not Understand My Intentions

I offer this reply to you, teacher.
I was endlessly grateful and comforted after receiving your enlightening letter. When we met on the day you retired, you told me to refrain temporarily from sending a messenger to inquire about your health. Therefore, I did not dare send somebody the next day to inquire about your well-being. The following day, I wrote a letter to Ijeong saying that I was worried because I could not check on whether you were getting along peacefully since you had forbade sending somebody to inquire about your well-being. Because Ijeong from the beginning was not aware of the full story and misunderstood my letter, he wrote me many words trying to show me the error of my ways; however, I did not write a detailed reply because I was going to meet him soon and tell him everything. How could it be possible that I still to this day do not accept your thoughts? I sigh as I think Ijeong has misunderstood my intentions.
I have been unable to meet you for a long time because I am bound to the duties of the government office; I am saddened, feel-

ing stifled making it difficult to endure. My chronic illness grows progressively worse as the weather grows colder. In time, I intend to scheme, trying to leave office due to my illness. As this is the case, it will not be easy to go and meet you in person though I have dared to trouble you through letters. Please be aware and advised of this. I respectfully bow, offer this letter again, and end here.

Bowing, yours truly,
Junior scholar, Daeseung.

[Letter #80 Toegye Writes Gobong]

From Long Ago, the Difficulties that Exist Between Sovereign and Subject

I reply again.
I learned in detail Ijeong's mistake through your letter. Yesterday, somebody showed me a collection of Jeongam's speech while he worked at the imperial court. Among them, some surprising things arose. People should look to it as an example of what to be cautious of. From long ago, people considered the relationship between sovereign and subject to be difficult—why would this not be the case? I respectfully reply.
From Hwang.

[Letter #81 Gobong Writes Toegye]

Yesterday, After Reading Your Letter

Dear teacher,
I respectfully inquire about your well-being. How have you been getting along with each passing day? My revering and longing heart grows more profound. Braving my illness, I forced myself to go to work, which made my cold grow more severe. However, because I cannot leave my post even if I wanted, I can only be needlessly sad. In the letter you gave to me yesterday, the words, "Turn your head around," were profound in meaning; therefore, I savored

them for a long time. I was comforted and overjoyed. I want to change the last line of the poem written in Chinese style verse. I have written it on the backside. Please observe and consider it. What can I do, as I am sad and regretful that I have not been able to visit you for a long time? I respectfully bow and offer this letter.

Bowing, yours truly,
Junior scholar, Daeseung.

[Letter #82 Toegye Writes Gobong]

Poems Do Not Mind Being Corrected

I bow and reply.
I received your letter. I feel uneasy as I heard you have gone to work despite your illness. Your revised poetic phrase has profound meaning and the tempo is correct. Old sayings remark that poems do not mind being corrected and probably for this reason. I respectfully inform.

From Hwang.

[Letter #83 Gobong Writes Toegye]

My Colleagues Ask Me to Enter a Government Post

Dear teacher,
I respectfully inquire about your well-being. How is your health? My respect and longing for you grow more profound with each passing day. Lately, I have been ill suffering from the symptoms of fatigue and lack of strength; however, I have just now slightly recuperated. Nevertheless, once again, my colleagues submitted a request to the king, asking that I be ordered to return to a government post. I am very worried. While all this was occurring, I met Ijeong yesterday and he relayed your letter. I was extremely grateful, as well as very comforted. I will tell you the rest when I find time and meet you in person. Please excuse me. I respectfully bow and offer this letter.

Bowing, yours truly,
Junior scholar, Daeseung.

[Letter #84 Toegye Writes Gobong]

Conduct Becomes Gradually Difficult

I bow and reply to you, noble friend.

I learned through your letter that people had made requests to the king for you to return to government service. Thinking about it, you will have a difficult time leaving, regardless of how you may try to block those events or worry.

Although it has been nearly forty days since I have received my vacation, I have not received the king's favor, which would have me replaced from my government post; I am terrified and feel miserable. Although the year is about to change,[1] more than several uneasy matters burden me as I am away from my government post in a noncommittal, ambiguous way. I intend on visiting the king tomorrow and making a plea for my permanent resignation. If I do not receive permission from the king to resign and I cannot do the work assigned to me, conducting myself between these two circumstances will become more difficult.

What Ijeong said was true; however, I am not sure what character you can use in substitution. Outside of this, what can I do, as I face many difficult to decide problems? In short, I cannot say everything unless we meet face to face. For the moment, I bow and write this reply.

From Hwang.

---

1. As he mentions the year is about to change, this letter appears to have been written in December, the Year of the Dragon. As mentioned previously, there seems to have been a mistake in sequencing the letters.

[Letter #85 Gobong Writes Toegye]

After Hearing You Were Ill

Dear teacher,

I respectfully inquire about your well-being. How is your health? My reverence and longing for you knows no bounds. I was very worried when I received the letter from Ijeong that said you were ill.

Although it is difficult, I am working hard at my assigned task. However, I left late yesterday and the day before yesterday because of work. I sighed as the day grew dark and I was not able to visit you.

Yesterday, the king sent the *Ten Diagrams of Confucian Philosophy* to the Royal Secretariat and ordered the attachment of the drafts and the making of the folding screen. However, up to that point, the king has not submitted the "Presentation Address." Please be advised and consider this matter. I respectfully bow and offer this letter.

Bowing, yours truly,
Junior scholar, Daeseung.

[Letter #86 Toegye Writes Gobong]

Facing Deep Waters and High Valleys

I bow and reply to you, noble friend.

Thanks for asking about how I was doing. I have had a difficult time taking care of my health, as snowstorms grow fierce and my illness throws fits everyday.

As if facing deep waters and high valleys, I pass the time in caution.

In your letter, I became aware of the fact the *Ten Diagrams of Confucian Philosophy* had been submitted, and I read about this thoroughly in the gazette for the Royal Secretariat. Although I assume there were many negligent parts to it, since the Office of Royal Lecturers pointed out the mistakes, it would be safe to assume they corrected it leaving no blemish. However, I would be truly relieved if everybody lucidly examined and searched for mistakes. I respectfully bow and write this reply.

From Hwang.

[Letter # 87 Gobong Writes Toegye]

Departure on the River, Remote as a Dream[1]

Dear teacher,

Our departure on the river was as remote as a dream; when I heard from the *Byeoljwa* Gim who had returned from Yanggeun, about the way you looked when you departed, I was sad and my longing for you grew twofold. Although I could not check on you after that—how was your health during the journey?

It is difficult to put into words how much I miss you.

Right about now, I am guessing you are getting close to your native village. I am guessing the relish of returning home is lovelier than ever. I am barely getting along and have nothing pertinent to say. Sadness fills me automatically, every time I think I will not be able to serve you from a close distance.

I have expressed my feelings matching the rhymes I read in the "Ode to Plum Blossoms," which you had sent. I would be relieved if you chuckled as you read it. Outside of this, endless thoughts come to mind but I cannot put them all to words. Please observe and understand. I respectfully bow, offer this letter, and end here.

March 15, the Third year of Longqing (The era of Muzong's reign of the Ming Dynasty)

Bowing, yours truly,

Junior scholar, Daeseung.

---

1. On March 4, 1569 (the Year of the Snake) Toegye offered his resignation to the king and left the capital city before lodging at Mongnoe Cottage in Dongho part of the Han River. This day hundreds of important figures in and out of government sent him off. The next day, Toegye rode a boat across the Han River and lodged at Bongeun Temple. Gobong accompanied Toegye to this point before bidding him farewell.

[Letter #88 Toegye Writes Gobong]

Reliving in Dreams the Tender Feelings of Departure

I respectfully bow and reply to you, Myeongeon.

I relive in dreams the tender feelings we exchanged while standing on the boat in the Dongho part of the Han River; that night was truly significant, the way you accompanied me all the way to Bongeun Temple and stayed with me overnight. We were both inebriated and we said our farewells while silently looking at each other (before departing our separate ways). When I received your handwritten letter and poem, I cannot express how relieved and comforted I was. It seemed you were right in front of me again. While starting to pass the Yeogang,[1] the ship suffered enormous difficulties because of the horrific wind and severe rain. However, after reaching land and stepping foot on Chungju, I walked on snow-covered paths and passed over mountain peaks, but I did not acquire any other illnesses. When I arrived in the land of my birthplace, spring was in full blossom and they greeted me as if they had always known me. You could say my feelings were significant.

When I look back and circumspect, I tremble and feel ashamed that I could not repay the king for all his kindness, even though I was indebted to him. On one hand, I meant it as a joke, what I had told everybody while we were gathered together; however, unexpectedly, what I had said went so far as to be considered words worth impeachment. I shuddered when I heard that. If things were in reality as portrayed in those words spoken by people demanding my impeachment, I would have to put an end to this insignificant life and die alone somewhere. How can something like this happen in an era ruled by a good and wise king?

The possibility of meeting in the future grows remote and we can make no promise to meet. I only hope you make an effort in the important matters and in raising and deepening your intentions so that you can satisfy the wishes of the ages. The poem you sent was very good. Although it is not worth much, I have written a response poem in the annex.

I respectfully reply.
April 2, 1569 (the Year of the Snake)
Hwang bows his head.

Although each of the eight poems of the "Ode to the Plum Blossom" respectively held their own feelings, they were written for the sake of a temporary joy. However, unexpectedly, you sent me a poem in response from far away—I was very grateful as I sensed the way you felt about me in the poem. Lately, I wrote two poems after seeing the plum blossom upon my arrival home. Since I do not intend to hide them from you, I send them to you again. Please chuckle as you read them.

---

1. Refers to Yeoju in the Gyeonggi Province.

[Letter #89 Gobong Writes Toegye]

Appointed to One More Position at the Office of the Censor General

I respectfully reply to you, teacher.

I cannot compare anything to the worry that refuses to leave my heart since we said our farewells. However, while in that state, I unexpectedly received your letter on the twelfth, and I read of your journey and heard news you were getting along perspicaciously and peacefully after returning to Dosan. I was truly comforted and my worries were appeased. However, my wits grow dull as I become sad every time I think the day we will meet again is far off, removed. Even today, I am impertinent, barely preserving myself thanks to your concern.

However, starting from the end of last month it had been hard to pass the time in comfort; as my psyche grew fatigued and languid, I felt stifled. Furthermore, I grew uneasy because I was appointed to another position at the Office of the Censor General unexpectedly; I have reached the point where I can barely eat and sleep. I cannot control my depression and anguish because concerns and worries stack to the height of mountains inside of me.

While in this state, you sent me three poems. I felt blissful and fortunate as I relished their meanings. I do not know how to express my gratitude. Although very presumptuous, I have written down my thoughts in the annex. In addition, I seal and send together another two-page annex I have written. Please look over them. I cannot express all the remaining thoughts in my heart with words. Only, I hope your studies and health will grow more robust. I respectfully bow and offer this reply.

April 17, 1569 (the Year of the Snake)
Bowing, yours truly,
Junior scholar, Daeseung.

[Letter #90 Toegye Writes Gobong]

I Cannot Remain Calm as if Nothing Had Happened

I inform you, noble friend:

The symptom of growing remote, which arose when thinking about our farewell and return, did not heal for the longest time. However, how comforted I was to receive your letter! Have you been getting along fine after sending word the last time? Even before you could grow tired of the teaching[1] lifestyle, you were moved to the Office of the Censor General again. As you shoulder the responsibilities, which grow more prodigious, of this generation, I do not know how you are doing.

I was useless even while I was at the imperial court. What could I possibly be involved with now that I am in the remote country? However, if I hear talk regarding my unfinished work, I have a hard time remaining calm. I have a difficult time acting as if nothing has happened—you could say I am senile. I cannot hide these thoughts from you and have written curtly. It would be nice if you did not share them with others. I have many thoughts outside of this, but I leave them to your conjecture. Be solely reserved and prudent, making an effort to raise and deepen virtuous deeds so that you can hopefully satisfy the trust of the ages.

April 21, 1569 (the Year of the Snake)
Hwang bows his head.

---

1. Or *Sukban*, meaning a dining table set by only a trefoil—refers to a teacher's poor and frugal life. A trefoil is a kind of bean. *Miwon* is another name for the Office of the Censor General. At that time, Gobong moved from the dean of the Royal College to the *Daesagan* of the Office of the Censor General.

[Letter #91 Gobong Writes Toegye]

Carefully Transcribed in the Annex, the Outlines of the Arguments Regarding the Munso Shrine

I respectfully reply to your letter, teacher.

While in the midst of missing you more with each passing day and being unable to suppress my emotions, I unexpectedly received from somebody at the *Jikjang* position, who was on his way back to Seoul, your handwritten letter and annex, which had your detailed explanations. I was thankful and relieved beyond expression when I learned of how you were getting along and of your present situation through your own detailed words.

Impertinent, I am barely getting along thanks to the benefits of your concerns. However, yesterday, I was promoted one official rank and have been entrusted with more work at the Royal Secretariat. I am helplessly embarrassed and although this is quite disagreeable to me, I can do nothing but quietly enter the post and fill my spot. I have carefully transcribed the outlines of the arguments regarding the Munso Shrine on the annex, and I am sending you the gazette for the Royal Secretariat. Please look them over. I end the letter here, as the rest is quite cumbersome. I respectfully bow and offer this letter.

Longqing (The era of Muzong's reign of the Ming Dynasty)
April 28, 1569 (the Year of the Snake)
Bowing, yours truly,
Junior scholar, Daeseung.

[Letter #92 Gobong Writes Toegye]

Clamorous Arguments inside the Imperial Court

Dear teacher,
I respectfully inquire about your well-being. How are you getting along? The leisurely atmosphere of your lifestyle is probably tranquil and abundant—I can do nothing but miss you. I am barely sustaining this worthless body thanks to your care. However, these

days, because I have no place to turn as people point fingers at me, I ignore them and let them do as they please. What else can I do?

Furthermore, recently, my heart has been broken because clamorous arguments inside the imperial court have been going back and forth. Fortunately, at the moment, I am consoled because things have somewhat subsided, but I am still boiling with anger inside. I cannot individually, one by one, tell you of all the rest. Please understand. I respectfully bow and offer this letter.

May 24, 1569 (the Year of the Snake)
Bowing, yours truly,
Junior scholar, Daeseung.

[Letter #93 Toegye Writes Gobong]

Requesting the Epitaph of My Deceased Father

I write this to you, noble friend.

Last month, I received two consecutive letters dated April 17 and 28. In addition, I read the numerous poems you had written in response. I was relieved immeasurably while meticulously reading and examining them. Because we always correspond through letters delivered by couriers, I end up writing my letters forthwith. I am very embarrassed and ashamed that I cannot send my responses regularly. I send you an annex, which barely conveys my ideas. I hope you will send a response that contains your teachings.

I make a compassionate plea regarding one of my earnest wishes. Thanks to my deceased older brother, my departed father was posthumously honored as the *Gaseondaebu*. At the time, I had already set a tombstone in front of the grave, but the tombstone in front incurred a blemish and fell apart. I planned to replace it. While making these plans, my family had met a misfortunate situation; in fear and disconcerted, time passed but nothing had been accomplished. After that, because of me, my father was posthumously honored on several more occasions. I had already firmly believed that this was more than I deserved and something with which I would not be able to cope. However, it was of no use to decline and my father was posthumously conferred a government post. Therefore, I have no choice but to erect, once again, a stone landmark on the path to the grave according to my father's posthumous rise in official rank. Accordingly, I have purchased another piece of stone and will work on and erect it in the fall. On the last tombstone, we inscribed his birthplace, family line, and contents of that nature outlined in *Zhu Xi's Family Rituals*. However, there was no epitaph.

As I quietly think about it, although my dead father was very ambitious, he never realized those ambitions and he never left his mark in history. As a son, I would be filled with enormous lament if his life were recorded in this manner and his lifetime achievements, buried. Therefore, seizing this opportunity of placing another tombstone and using your words—a man of virtue for these times—I hope to reveal his hidden lifetime achievements for following generations to see. I respectfully enclose and send a biography of my deceased father, which I have written.

When I look back, I was less than fortunate and not inherently blessed. I was an orphan before reaching my first birthday. Growing up as an orphan, a person gradually grows distant from his previous generation, and as ancestors continue to pass away, soon there is nobody to visit and question. For this reason, although there may have been various concrete facts regarding his words and deeds, I have left out and failed to write about many things; I feel extreme pain because I was not being able to take care of my parents to the end.

When writing my father's biography, I might have been a little too detailed when mentioning the achievements of previous generations, who their children married, and the names of their children. However, since the form for creating a record of the deceased is usually very complicated, I have recorded everything in detail and will wait for you, the writer, to delete and add content as you see fit. I do not want you to include everything I have written.

I know that I am asking a hard favor, as (you are busy) working near the king at the Royal Secretariat. However, my thoughts are sincere and I could not wait for a later date. The work is urgent. I plan to have the writing finished and want to erect the tombstone sometime between September and October. During that span, do you think you will have any time off from night duty or any leisurely days? Since I feared it could not be accomplished if I asked you sometime near the deadline, I have asked you cumbersomely in this manner. Earnestly consider this and help me to realize my utmost wishes. I am overcome with sincere supplication.

June 9, the Third Year of Longqing (The era of Muzong's reign of the Ming Dynasty)

From the *Panjungchubusa*, Yi Hwang.

I will wait and send my response regarding the theory of the Indeterminate and the theory of *Wuge* on a later date.

[Letter #94 Gobong Writes Toegye]

Sending Along Various Writings

I write a thankful letter to you, teacher.

The monsoon season continues for the month. I have not been able to check to see how you have been doing, as you pass the time in leisure. Because I am so far away, I miss you uncontrollably even more. Impertinent, I am barely continuing government service without change thanks to your affectionate grace.

Just as I was feeling somewhat relieved and comforted after hearing news about you through *Cheomjeong* Seo, I met somebody from the *Jikjang* position who gave me your letter—I was shocked after reading your request. After opening the letter and reading it carefully, I realized you had overrated me by asking me to write the epitaph. Unspeakably daunted and ashamed, I wanted to return the letter and graciously decline. However, when I thought about it again, since we have been acquainted, I have received much guidance and help; however, my gratefulness was always buried deep in my heart. I have never had the opportunity to express my gratitude. Therefore, in light of loyalty, I could not refuse such a request. Although I dare to accept such a task, I cannot halt the perspiration caused by my shameful heart.

Within a few days, I had written a rough draft of the epitaph and to a certain extent I had come up with an outline; however, I was extremely worried as the tone of the words were coarse and feeble—they did not flow together. Of course, I will inform you of these matters by making a copy and sending it to you through a courier. Please examine and rectify.

Considering the earnest teachings you wrote in the annex, your strict lashing had me eliminate a bad habit and had me reflect on some weak points I possessed; I was filled with enormous admiration. Certain clauses like, "Displaying your vigor and disregarding and cutting down others by debating at will," refer, in fact, to a chronic disease of mine. I was even more negligent in studying things like, "By being retrospective and maintaining discipline over your body, be cautious of anger, curb desires, correct mistakes, and move to the right side." Although I tried on numerous occasions to demolish (such diseases) in my everyday life, I did not have the strength to do it. Now, after you have scolded me in this manner, how can I not try with all my heart! I hope you understand this.

The situation here is not good and the pervading atmosphere from morning until night is one that suggests a surprising, impending crisis. However, regarding the fortune and misfortune related to life or death, I leave it to the heavens, which is similar to Zhuang-zi who said that since he learned he was powerless, he considered everything a heavenly mandate and was at peace with this.[1] What do you think? I miss you unbearably and am truly moved when I imagine you standing outside the filthy secular world, having left before being blamed for any evil doings. I cannot express my many, many thoughts in writing. I will send the rest in the annex.

Please look over and consider it. I respectfully bow and offer this letter.

June 8 (leap month), the Third Year of Longqing (The era of Muzong's reign of the Ming Dynasty)

Bowing, yours truly,

Junior scholar, Daeseung.

From the start, while attending the royal lecture, Gae Gim[2] slighted you by making an insinuating remark about honoring cabinet members. Subsequently, many people considered him monstrous; he intended to drive the faultless people into a corner by ensnarling them speaking ill of those people who were killed during the Year of the Rabbit.[3] Later, he entered the royal lecture and schemed to make excuses saying, "Because younger people took turns slighting the three ministers, I spoke of it to try to nip it in the bud." These are atrocious words intended to bring an incalculable calamity to the *Sarim* faction (the literati) in the future.

Therefore, I discussed this with my colleagues and after requesting to meet the king personally, I did my best to inform him of the acts of this wicked crony. I pressed him about this problem facing us, and without knowing—emotions running high—my innermost feelings turned to rage and I briskly spoke many words; I was not as selective as I could have been with my words. However, since I was correct in the broad sense, it was not the time to query success or failure, sharpness or dullness.

However, the debate outside clamorously places the blame on *Seungji* Sim[4] and me. Some people want to impeach us. Even among friends, many of them driven by personal interests declared that both of us were in fault. Mr. Sim did not show up to office offering his illness as an excuse, and he was replaced today. Furthermore, I intend to leave on this occasion and lay low as well. Worldly customs are fickle. Looking at the way the world turns, people look after their personal interests only—they know nothing of moral principle! I have made pledges with these people, but it is hard to gain strength from them. I am flabbergasted, growing this lonely in my pursuit of the *dao*.

Lately, since I have polished and examined an extremely sordid study, I have understood the teaching that said *not* to be concerned with neither a premature death nor a long life.[5] My views have progressively grown clearer, as if I am standing with *understanding* fronting me and as if I am sitting in a carriage with *understanding* attached to the yoke.[6] However, it seems as if I am not sufficiently equipped with the study of *waiting* in the cultivation of my personal character. Therefore, it is difficult to eradicate diseases contaminated by habits although I am at the height of exerting an effort in this direction. Cautious and fearful thoughts easily grow lax: this is my only worry. Although this may be the case, I can only be cautious and make the effort—do you really think I would be squelched or become mired in troubles because of all the other things outside of this! Although this is the way my heart feels, I do not know what you think. I hope you will guide, teach, and prevent me from losing my way and wandering aimlessly.

Bowing, yours truly,
Junior scholar, Daeseung.

---

1. See the *Chuang Tzu*, Chapter 4: "Man Among Men."

2. Refers to Gae Gim; his pseudonym was Bangbo; his pen name was Doksongjeong; and his ancestral home was Gwangju. In the second year of Seonjo's reign, he was refuted by Gobong and removed from office because he blamed the scholars (literati) who were killed in the Year of Rabbit.

3. Refers to Gae Gim who slandered the good in the Year of the Sheep including Gwangjo Jo, saying at the Royal Lecture, "Gwangjo Jo made a mistake taking care of affairs because he recommended his followers and ostracized those who opposed him." He also said, "How could it be that so many people of the Year of Sheep were only good, moreover, how can it be that among those people that were good, some people did not make mistakes in their thinking?" See the *Annals of Seonjo* 3, the second year of reign, June, the Day of the Snake.

4. Refers to *Useungji* Uigyeom Sim who took the lead in the impeachment of Gae Gim with *Jwaseungji* Gobong.

5. "Mencius said, 'He who has exhausted all his mental constitution knows his nature. Knowing his nature, he knows Heaven. To preserve one's mental constitution, and nourish one's nature, is the way to serve Heaven. When neither a premature death nor long life causes a man any doublemindedness, but he waits in the cultivation of his personal character *for whatever issue*;—this is the way in which he establishes his *Heaven*-ordained being.'" See *The Works of Mencius*, Book VII: "Tsin Sin," Part I, Chapter I.

6. "Tsze-chang asked how a man should conduct himself, *so as to be everywhere appreciated*. The Master said, 'Let his words be sincere and truthful, and his actions honourable and careful;—such conduct may be practised among the rude tribes of the South or the North. If his words be not sincere and truthful, and his actions not honourable and careful, will he, with such conduct, be appreciated, even in his neighbourhood? When he is standing, let him see those two things, as it were, fronting him. When he is in a carriage, let him see them attached to the yoke. Then may he subsequently carry them into practice.' Tsze-chang wrote these counsels on the end of his sash." See the *Confucian Analects*, Book XV: "Wei Ling Kung," Chapter V.

Previously, I was in the king's presence on consecutive occasions and I benefited from having the time to answer the king's questions. I was overcome with emotions. Since our king's temperament is lofty and lucid, there is nobody else like him in the world; however, what can we do, as there is nobody beside him to help him? Please be advised of this. I had copied the first words spoken by Gae Gim and have sent it to you through Ijeong. I am copying now what he said later and will offer them to you now. I ask you to look over them.

I think there was something very wrong in the interpretation regarding the Indeterminate. Opportunely, I have copied one piece of writing by Mr. Wu of Linchuan who had passed the civil service exam. Please examine and consider it. Furthermore, when we talked by the riverside, regarding my opinion of eradicating faults and making it clear in the light of principle, I confused it with what I had learned when I was young. When I look back and think about it, I think I was very wrong. Please consider with leniency. I apologize. Please look over again the *Wuge* theory when you have some leisure time. I am worried and feel stifled. Without fail, please lucidly look over this again.

I respectfully bow and inform.

Bowing, yours truly,

Junior scholar, Daeseung.

I hope you chuckle as you accept these two round fans I have sent.

[Letter #95 Teogye Writes Gobong]

How Has the World Become This Chaotic?

I bow and write this reply to you, Myeongeon.

Saheon Baekchun Yi[1] came all the way here and delivered your response, several pages of annexes, and one response poem. The content of your letter transcended mere sincerity. Earlier, propelled by a sense of urgency, I was very cautious, as I tediously requested that you write about my deceased father. However, although only a brief time has passed, I learned through your letter that you had already designated the sequence, accomplishing it faster than I had anticipated. I have kept the joy and profound emotions deep inside of me—I am speechless. Hoping to see your writing quickly, I stand on my tiptoes everyday. I can do nothing but wait.

I have no other concerns, as I pass my time hiding in the mountains and valleys; however, more than other occasions, I am having difficulty taking care of my body, which has grown weak because of suffering through the monsoon season. I get tired easily because of this.

From time to time, I hear rumors that confirm the state of the world is as you said. I can only helplessly sigh like the saying in Zhu

Xi's poem, "Sighing alone while solemnly placing a sparse table before me." After starting midlife, I played into the hands of other people as I if were a target located within the shooting range of Yi's arrow.[2] I thought I would never confront this kind of anxiety again, as I have met a good life—how has the world become so chaotic! Although people generally think that it would be enjoyable to hide and live in the mountains and forests, how can those in the mountains and forests live only in peace when events like this continue to transpire!

Regarding what I said last time, like someone who discards his own field to weed the field of another, I was being very presumptuous. However, because I heard many people I knew blaming you, using what I had told you last time, I could not turn a deaf ear and refrain from telling you. I ask you to keep this deep in your heart. I have written the rest in the annex. I end this letter here. I respectfully bow and reply.

Longqing (The era of Muzong's reign of the Ming Dynasty)
June (leap month) 27, 1569 (the Year of the Snake)
From Hwang.

Although the Gae Gim matter seems truly strange, ultimately, there is nothing strange about it. Today, we do not possess any superior talents nor have we completed our studies. Yet, since our names have spread (before we are ready), it has become difficult to try to govern the country. In addition, since a fallen carriage lies before us,[3] we must take it as a grave warning. Therefore, there is nobody who wants to change the system, disarrange the established laws, expel the old vassals, set himself high instead, and plant his cronies while unreasonably saying that he has met a favorable opportunity, that he has received the confidence of the king. There is tremendous difference when comparing these people to those people of days gone by who set the country straight and entrusted themselves with the work of governing the world.

However, Gae Gim is determined to push us into a quagmire by accusing us of faults we did not possess, by forcibly treating us as sinners through fabrications that we are somehow like those (people who were killed during the Year of the Rabbit). He mentions faultless things from the past and accuses us of using this as evidence to betray the times. It is worth noting the oddity that he should suddenly arrive at such schemes without any reason. On top of that, if he had been harboring such bad intentions, why did he visit me, acting friendly and talking all night, appearing to reveal his innermost thoughts—chatting on—urging me emphatically not to leave office? I do not know how to interpret this. That is why I said this was very odd.

Although this may be the case, this kind of group has always existed starting from way back, there is no need to be shocked and amazed because of this man. That is why I said there was nothing here to be considered odd. Although this may be the case, our studies have not approached the levels the ancient ones had reached, but as we are ridiculed and persecuted in this manner, I do not know how we can cope with this problem so that we do not shame our ancestors.

You said you went too far when informing the king of this matter. Although I am not going to ask what you said, I was worried after hearing you had talked to the king. Although I am in a remote place, what is relatively fortunate is that your situation has some resemblances to my experiences. For that reason, I am always concerned about this matter. Although I think the *Seungji* Sim did not retire from office solely for this reason; nevertheless, it turned out for the best. Because following him by leaving office will overly expose your situation, it will be difficult for you to leave. It would be an enormous relief if you handled this matter by looking at the situation and surmising the cause of the problem.

From way back, since there were many occasions you could not gain strength from those you had made pledges with in ordinary times, it is best to be prudent when making friends.

You must not dash in excess to the front but must always step back.

You must not quarrel and you must exert more of an effort to polish yourself on the inside while refusing to be broken.

The most important duty of the present day is to be indulged with this concern.

I am glad to hear you had reached some understanding regarding being unconcerned with neither a premature death nor a long life. However, this is possible when accompanied with the study of the cultivation of personal character and *waiting*. If man proclaims he is not concerned with neither a premature death nor a long life while others are not satisfied with his moral training, he should admit to having a blind spot.

Letter #95

Although there are many things I want to say, I will stop here, as those words would be trifling.

Hwang bows his head. I saw everything Gae Gim had given to the king on several occasions. Thank you.

Since the present king is truly one of a kind, this is a boundless blessing for the royal family and the state and a matter of congratulations that peaceful times will continue until eternity. Regarding everything that is going on these days, since there is not even a trace of "penetration on the left side of the belly,"[4] who has ordered them to behave like this! Prostrating myself and listening to what people are saying, they say the luminous virtue of our king grows brighter daily. I cannot restrain my supplication for the king while residing in the countryside.

Gratefully, I have heard that the wood engraving of the *Ten Diagrams of Confucian Philosophy* has been completed. If the orders to print and distribute this are given, following proper etiquette—will a copy be given to the king? If you happen to submit the *Ten Diagrams* on the day you are at the Royal Secretariat, I do not think you need to inform the king tediously of the minute and unimportant parts among the additional revisions I made. However, regarding the corrections that fall under the classification of those made on the second and third diagrams of the "Diagram of 'The Mind Combines and Governs the Nature and Feelings,'" please take care of the matter after thinking profoundly to avoid any negligence since you have no choice but to inform the king of the reason such corrections were made.

All the sages and wise men were deeply concerned regarding the *Ten Diagrams* and even my insignificant devotion as a foolish vassal is represented in the *Ten Diagrams*. However, I have heard rumors that words maligning the work are widespread; already there appears to be someone who is chattering on about beguiling words inside the *jugwang*.[5] Quietly thinking about this, although the king possesses the foundation to spread luminous virtue, he has not studied precisely enough to reach a stage where he can be pleased with a flourishing *dao*. However, before the king gathers his psyche and unites his heart, if he has the mind to despise and be inhospitable to the *Ten Diagrams* foremost, in the end, there will be no help in assisting the king. However, I can do nothing about this.

What can I do? I can do with everything I have without remains and bravely inform the king of the *Ten Diagrams*. That is all.

In the beginning, I lengthened the height and width of the letters amply, as people mentioned the writing might be too small. After doing that, while making the drawing, the letters had become too big and they were not appropriate to use on the folding screen. Before I could even think about correcting it, the wood engravings were already completed. How can I at this stage risk reproach and say that I will make corrections again? I can only lament.

Since principle and material force combine to make the mind, naturally, there is a divinity of empty and spiritual, knowing and perceiving.

Something tranquil and asserted with all principles is nature, but it is the mind where the stacked nature is loaded.

Although feelings move and stimulate all events, once again, it is the mind that spreads and uses this feeling.

That is why the mind combines and governs nature and feelings.

I have heard that the king had frequently in the past asked about the mind governing nature and feeling, and on the day I left office, he asked me about it again, but I could not give him a satisfactory answer. I think it would be correct if I answer in the manner I just mentioned—what do you think? I say this because I heard you also lamented that my answer was not satisfactory.

---

1. Refers to Yangwon Yi (1526-1592). He was Toegye's pupil and Baekchun was his pseudonym.

2. Yi refers to an expert archer, Hou Yi of the Younqiong tribe who lived during the Chinese Xia period. Yi symbolized the power figure of the time; it meant people could not escape from the shooting scope of the archer's hand (power figure) who would do with the people as he pleased.

3. Refers to Gwangjo Jo who set out to make reforms but failed.

4. Penetrating the left side of the belly means that a man of small character flatters the king while being in a high government position and gains the confidence of the king by using wicked schemes. See the *Book of Changes*, Book I: "The Text," Chapter 36: "Ming I."

5. Although meaning yellow cotton cloth, this refers to a part of the king's crown. This yellow cloth covered the ears and meant not to foolishly listen to faulty words.

[Letter #96 Gobong Writes Toegye]

The Wood Engravings for the Ten Diagrams is Near Completion

I respectfully inquire about your well-being. Autumn is upon us; how are you getting along? I look up to you and yearn for you unceasingly. Impertinent, I am passing time, barely sustaining myself thanks to your affectionate grace. However, I had no alternative but to leave my duties at the *Seungji* position because I had been growing mentally fatigued. I have a little more leisure time now that I have been assigned to a position in a military related post.

I have received your letter dated on the twenty-seventh of the leap month and an annex. After contemplating your meticulous teachings, I was moved to the point of being speechless, whereby engraving (your teachings) deep in my heart. Regarding your teachings, "You must exert more of an effort to polish yourself on the inside while refusing to be broken," I will exert an effort with everything I have! However, lately, as the situation becomes more anarchic and the throngs of people who lack the fundamentals scramble, boisterously quarreling, I do not know how this situation will be resolved.

I can only wait quietly.

What else can I do? However, the luminous king who resides above will follow the right path by adapting to the heavens; therefore, I could not be bothered with other sudden concerns. Teacher, what do you think? Inside my heart, I silently say, "If I do not think like this but put forth selfish wiles and worry—this is probably not the way to self control."

The wood engravings of the *Ten Diagrams* are near completion and in a short time, I hear it will be printed and submitted to the king. Although the diagrams are too large and the letters are anything but small, there is no discomfort in looking at it. However, people were very surprised when they glanced at this because they had never seen writing like this before; therefore, I worry it will not help people comprehend the deeper pleasure by examining it repeatedly, ruminating over it.

Not too long ago, at the royal lectures, the king ordered: "I want to call somebody on a later date and have him teach a class regarding the *Ten Diagrams.*" In response, the royal lecturer made the excuse, "Please wait for a later date as the wood engravings have not been completed due to the revisions being made."

Most people hesitate teaching a class about the *Ten Diagrams* in front of the king because they are not fully knowledgeable about its contents. This is truly lamentable. Your teachings regarding the theory that the mind combines and governs nature and feelings are truly correct. On a later date, if I am sent to the imperial court and come to serve the king, I plan to inform the king of this in detail. However, in the end, I am not sure if the king intends to have the people act according to the *dao*. Therefore, I think quietly waiting for the heavenly mandate to unfold seems like the appropriate thing to do. What do you think?

Daeseung respectfully replies.

Previously, there was an occasion you taught me meticulously regarding my poem. It is difficult to put into words how grateful I was and how much I miss you. The few words you corrected were truly appropriate. Although at first, I wanted to ask you to make corrections, I have something else to tell you. The *Jwadaeeon* official of the Royal Secretariat is temporarily staying in a one-room pavilion and as the room has a great view, the southeast is worth seeing. When I am there everyday and look to the south where you reside, I sigh as the clouds lying across the sky block me from seeing the end of the heavens.

I felt like that again when I received your letter and wrote my response. Even if I could write just one response letter, I could not express all my emotions—they continue to amass inside of me. Therefore, in my poem, I wrote the "sang" character and that my emotions were piling up. Most of the time, although these are thoughts that arise after meeting and having emotions collide, these thoughts were appropriate for the circumstance of the time. Therefore, although the word, "hajeong," is vulgar, I did not avoid using it. I am not sure about the meaning. Because of this, I wrote two quatrains and expressed my emotions—I hope you chuckle as you read them.

July 21, 1569 (the Year of the Snake)
Bowing, yours truly,
Junior scholar, Daeseung "Gobong" Gi.

[Letter #97 Toegye Writes Gobong]

We Must Examine Ourselves

I respectfully bow to you, noble friend, and reply.

Because you included the epitaph in your response dated July 21, my children did not carelessly deliver it to me through a courier. For this reason, I finally received it in early September and through that letter, I learned that you had retired from and left your *Seungji* position and were currently without a government post. However, recently, I soon discovered after reading the list of appointees that they had reinstated you as the dean of the Royal College. I have noticed you have changed government posts and government ranks frequently; how are you getting along these days and how is your health? Saying that I revere and miss you are not empty words. I carefully read, one by one, about the various situations you mentioned in your letter. I have already responded in the annex about each subject; amidst my response, if there is anything that is unreasonable, please respond and enlighten me. How was the imbroglio you mentioned in your last letter resolved? Those people on the other side should demarcate themselves and stop. However, they refuse to stop and seem bent on stirring trouble, which is something I cannot understand. Nevertheless, on that day, the attacks levied against the other side by several people on our side were excessive, as well. Since that is the reason this recent situation has become so impetuous, we cannot entirely blame them. We must examine ourselves.

The luminous king resides above.

The government and the people collectively look up and depend on the king.

Both sides have been free from harm because of these facts even after trouble rose and the situation became chaotic. However, did you see the wagon traveling ahead of you overturn! This wagon overturned because they believed in extremes; they behaved negligently; and, they attacked too impetuously.

I implore you to, once again, reconsider profoundly regarding this matter.

By brashly requesting in writing that you compose the epitaph for my deceased father, I am at the peak of embracing an apologetic heart; however, you did not consider me lowly, and with the utmost of sincerity refined the language and revealed my father's unrevealed ambitions. After receiving the epitaph, reading it repeatedly and reciting it, I could not overcome my extreme tears of emotion. As a child born into a household, if I were to ask someone to write this—although success would be possible if I was earnest about it—the possibility exists that I could never find somebody to write this. There are many cases where it is never written, although many generations pass. However, since I have realized my wish while exchanging letters for just several months, what greater fortune could there be! However, when inspecting the writing, I could not cope with several of the lines. Furthermore, because I have one or two different requests, I have spoken about them in the annex. Please look them over carefully, and I hope you can accommodate my various, diminutive wishes.

In conclusion, I end this letter while hoping you preserve yourself, hoping you act prudently, and hoping you increasingly watch over yourself for the *dao* and the ages.

The third year of Longqing (The era of Muzong's reign of the Ming Dynasty)

The last day of September, 1569 (the Year of the Snake)

Hwang bows.

I have heard rumors that people on the other side despise you the most going so far as to exclaim boisterously, "How can he dare to stay in the imperial court, defying the animosity of many people without volunteering to leave for the country?" I am not sure if you have heard this. I am not sure from which side the people who said this stand—if they are from the side growing in strength or the side that is shriveling—but I will not deliberately ask you about it. However, I think it is wrong for you to leave on your own accord when the king does not intend to distance himself from you nor expel you.

I have another concern. A long time ago, although it was not by accident that the king of the Song Dynasty, Xiaozong, acknowledged and praised Zhu Xi, every time Zhu Xi entered government service then sought to leave absolutely, it was because there were those who worked to alienate Zhu Xi from the king. At that time, even when Xiaozong had acknowledged Nanxuan[1] and they were happy with each other and depended on each other, Zhu Xi, on the contrary, worried that the prime minister at the time, Yu Yunwen, lacked any sincerity and Zhu Xi consistently advised Nanxuan to leave.

Today, because people identify you with the *Learning of the Way*, they want to remove you as they did with me; however, since you have not conducted yourself in the manner of Zhu Xi and Nanxuan, will you regret this immensely in the end? Will you be able to resolve this matter? What do you think? I am also suspicious about the words of Hu Kanghou who said, "Somebody else cannot plan for another person leaving or retiring from office." I offer you my foolish thoughts.

After reading the various words in the letter you sent regarding the *Ten Diagrams*, I was extremely grateful for your wonderful ideas. Although the diagrams might have been large, you were correct when saying they were not a great obstacle in observing. However, because it is too wide, I fear a person will have difficulty placing it on his desk or bookshelf. Therefore, I want to reduce slightly the size of the diagrams, densely packing in the writing and eliminating the space occupied by the third and fourth line, whereby making it the appropriate size. However, I can do nothing if it has already been printed and submitted to the king.

I have respectfully heard that the luminous king shows great interest and intends to have someone lecture about this in his presence. If I could be of the least bit of help in this issue, die, and then be cast into a brook, I would die without regrets. Merely, in times like this, I lament the fact you are not at the Royal Secretariat.

Among the contents, now that I carefully look at the "Diagram of the Great Learning," as I see one or two parts that look weak, I have drawn and attached it to the annex and offer it to you. What do you think? I want to say such corrections must be made in order for (this diagram) to be without blemish. However, since it will be difficult to inform the king to make such revisions if it has already been printed and submitted, I lament that I have reached these circumstances because I was negligent in consulting and revising at the time. Please show these corrections to Hwasuk Bak—what if you discuss the revision matter with him?

---

1. Refers to the Confucianist Zhang Shi in the Song period. His pseudonym was Jingfu and Namxuan was his pen name. He was a contemporary of Zhu Xi and they had a special relationship in learning.

[Letter #98 Gobong Writes Toegye]

Incurring the Wrath of the High-Ranking Official

I reply to you, teacher.

After writing you a letter while autumn was in full season, I was worried because I had not received any letters from you although I was able to hear news about you through rumors. However, unexpectedly, I received your letter on the eighteenth; I was unceasingly moved and comforted after reading your response letter where I learned you were healthy. I also received your meticulous, painstaking guidance. Impertinent, I am barely preserving this insignificant body thanks to your concerns. However, starting from last August, I was very busy and unable to rest because there was a lot of work at the royal household; therefore, my mind and body became pestered and I became very dizzy. It appeared as if I would not make it through another day. Recently, I have closed, locked the doors, and am taking care of myself, as things have become a little more stable.

Meanwhile, as I witnessed the situation here progressively deteriorating, I could not abandon my personal concerns and irrational schemes; however, after receiving your guidance, although I lack any merit whatsoever, I am prompted to action. Furthermore, what you said in the annex accurately peered into my heart. Because I cannot move lightly while harboring greater intentions, I can do nothing but work hard in the meantime. Please understand this with lenient eyes.

Furthermore, I could not respond to each of the provisions you mentioned in your letter because I was not feeling well at the time. I am thinking about waiting for the next courier. I intend to send you the epitaph again after making the corrections you instructed. Although I have many things to say, I end my letter here. Please be advised.

Respectfully bowing, I offer this reply.
October 23, 1569 (the Year of the Snake)
Bowing, yours truly,
Junior scholar, Daeseung.

In the beginning, because the low-ranking officials[1] were not obedient to him, Minister Hong's[2] anger grew. After Hong made an effort and pulled *Daesaheon* Gim[3] to his side, together, they planned to snare the low-ranking officials into a trap. However, they did not succeed with their plans because public opinion attacked them just at that time; therefore, they grew more enraged and met with the high-ranking official,[4] furtively spreading false charges. These false charges spread rampantly. They went so far as to accuse Bangsuk[5] and me of scheming to enter as proctors for the civil service exam. The high-ranking official was very upset about this; he planned to inform the king of this at the royal lecture. Opportunely, this crisis was resolved because several close acquaintances made explanations on my behalf and saved me. Later, Minister Hong repeated those words but thankfully, nothing came of it, as the high-ranking official did not acquiesce.

However, the high-ranking official was extremely upset with the Munso Shrine debate and people considered me the leading figure; therefore, it looked as if the high-ranking official did not favor me, and somebody said it would be good for me to fill a position at a regional government post. Some people suggested that I should not be nominated as a candidate for the *Daesagan* position. I was aware of the situation and planned early on to leave government service, but I have not been able to reach a decision because my colleagues hold me back. I am in agony and feel stifled.

Earlier, while the *Yeonguijeong* official said during a royal lecture that it would not be appropriate for opposing sides to meet face to face, he went on to say that looking back fifty years this event had no precedence. Bangsuk, the *Daesagan* official, was present at the time and enraged the *Yeonguijeong* official even more by saying, "Was there ever a precedence for grabbing the collar and breaking the railing in the past!"[6] The dark and cunning forces continue to grow progressively and the right path grows weaker with each passing day. By entrapping the king into a situation where he passes each day submissively and uneventfully, the king cannot accomplish anything substantial. Saying this breaks my heart but what can I do? If someone continues to question who should take responsibility for these crimes, the culprits will be exposed; therefore, although I cannot be sure, we can safely say some great historian will rise and will look unfavorably on the *Yeonguijeong* official! I lament. Since I cannot tell you the rest, I hope you will quietly seek enlightenment on your own.

Regarding the Munso Shrine tabernacle affair, because King Seongjong had two wives, they have placed three tables on *So's* side. Please be advised of this.

---

1. Refers to the lower class officials of the post.
2. Refers to Dam Hong; his pseudonym was Taeheo, his posthumous name was Jeonghyo, and his place of origin was Namyang. He was the Minister of Personnel. See the *Annals of Seonjo* 21, the second year of reign, June, the Year of the Rat.
3. Refers to Gae Gim.
4. Refers to the State Council. However, at this point it refers to Jungyeong Yi who became the prime minister at that time in concrete terms. Jungyeong Yi's pseudonym was Wongil and his pen name was Donggo. As a chief vassal he was prime minister from the end of the Myeongjong period. He was famous for setting Seonjo on the throne and assisting him. He assisted in setting the scholars free, who met calamity in the Year of the Rabbit and the Snake. However, at that time he opposed Daeseung Gi and disagreed with him.
5. Refers to Uigyeom Sim. Bangsuk was his pseudonym.
6. Seizing the lapel and breaking the banister rail are both events that signify strongly opposing the king on his faults. Xin Pi of Wei China opposed Emperor Wen's plan of moving a 100,000 saga (scholarly houses) to Hunan and strongly remonstrated against Emperor Wen who attempted to enter the inner palace without reply. Just then, Xin Pi seized him by the lapel. See the *Annal of Three Kingdoms* 25, "Annals of Wei," which contains the "Biography of Xin Pi."

While Zhu Yun of Han China was making admonishments, he mustered the anger of Xiao Chengdi; he was dragged down from the jeonsang (pulpit). He stood firm holding on to the banister, continuing to admonish and they say the banister broke. See the *Book of Han* 67, "Biography of Zhu Yun."

[Letter #99 Toegye Writes Gobong]

Unable to Avoid the Cold Sinking Through[1]

I bow and reply to you, noble friend.

During the beginning of this month, I received the letter dated the twenty-third of last month through my son who was on his way home. I learned that you were experiencing some discomfort, took time off, and were taking care of yourself. I am not sure how you are getting along these days as this winter has been particularly cold. I am overcome with admiration day and night. Although I hid deep inside my home, cloistering myself off, I could not avoid the cold sinking through. The phlegm started to gurgle before I became fully ill. Because I cannot seek medical attention or find medication at will, I am more than slightly worried this will become a chronic disease.

Regarding the epitaph, thanks to your hard work, I have realized an impassioned wish; I am extremely grateful. However, I am deeply apologetic that I made things cumbersome for you by attempting to make engraving the words in the stone more convenient. Looking at your response, I cannot tell you in full how grateful I was when I looked at your response and you said you would follow my wishes without placing any blame on me! Since I intend to erect the tombstone next spring, I am respectfully waiting for the day the revised words arrive.

Because I have heard nothing about the events that have been transpiring lately, I can only speak according to what you have mentioned in your annex. Indebted to the luminous king who has settled things down, you are passing the days temporarily in this manner; however, ultimately, this is not a comfortable situation. Therefore, I cannot help but to be concerned about you while leading this squalid kind of lifestyle. Because I am unhealthy and cannot tell you everything one by one, please consider this with leniency. I respectfully bow and reply.

November 16, 1569 (the Year of the Snake)

Hwang bows his head.

---

1. This letter does not appear in *Toegye's Collections*.

[Letter #100 Gobong Writes Toegye]

When Spring Arrives, I Will Discard my Government Post

I respectfully reply to you, teacher.

When Bonghwa[1] left, I could not chase after him, send him off, and express my ardent sincerity because I was slightly ill. Merely, after sending off the last letter, every time I thought about how you were doing, I could not stop my heart from inclining towards you. I have just received your letter and learned that you were not in good health; I was consoled and at the same time worried. My longing affection for you grows extreme. In the future, by nursing yourself and improving, I sincerely hope you will gradually recuperate.

Impertinent, I am preserving this mediocre body thanks to your affectionate care. Not only is this winter particularly cold, but also I am experiencing some paralysis incurred in the line of public duty, which has me forcibly following the obligatory rituals of public ceremonies; however, I am barely able to endure. Although I have not reached the point of being bedridden, I am witless like a doll made of dirt and wood—I lament and worry because I am unable to cast aside all work to take care of the (paralysis). Although I have one or two questions to ask you again regarding your last teachings, flustered, I did not have the time to write and send them to you; I am truly sorry and feel regret. I have not been able to lay a finger on the epitaph. I am waiting for things to quiet down before making the appropriate corrections and returning it to you.

Furthermore, among the events that have been occurring lately, I cannot even begin to express how many worrisome things there are going on; therefore, I think about it until late at night, but my fear grows. When spring arrives, I want to discard my government post and visit the graves of my ancestors. It is not that I am not earnest about discarding my post; I am worried that something unexpected will thwart (my intentions). I am not sure how I will eventually leave. I cannot tell you through this letter the many things that have been occurring. Please understand. I respectfully bow and offer this response.

December 6, 1569 (the Year of the Snake)
Bowing, yours truly,
Junior scholar, Daeseung.

Letter #100

I have enclosed nine pages of the gazette for the Royal Secretariat. Please look them over. When the *Jisa* Song returned to the south, I accompanied him to the riverbank and sent him off. While the *Jisa* talked about the day you returned home, the *Jisa* offered a poem he had written previously. When I asked the *Jisa* to write the poem down and deliver it to you, he wrote the poem down on a small piece of paper. I humbly send it to you now. I hope you appreciate it.

Ilcho Bak[2] has come to Seoul and is staying at my house because he intends to purchase a *shen-yi*[3] (long garment). He continues to stay here because he has not received instructions from you, as to whether it should be stitched or not. What about informing him through letter? I place one frozen fish and a living pheasant in a sack and send them to you. I hope you enjoy them.

---

1. Refers to Toegye's son.

2. Refers to Geunwon Bak. His pen name was Mangiljae and Ilcho was his pseudonym.

3. Referred to the Confucianist's vestment, which was hemmed by a black silk line. Because Zhu Xi recommended it as a Confucianist's vestment in the *Family Rituals*, it spread in popularity along with the philosophy of Zhu Xi throughout Korea. It was a common attire for Confucians of the day. See the *Zhu Xi's Family Rituals* 1, "General Principles of Ritual."

1570
THE LAST YEAR OF LETTERS

[Letter #101 Gobong Writes Toegye]

Whether or Not One Will Be Exalted

Dear teacher, Toegye,
I respectfully inquire about your well-being. How is your health? As I prostrate myself before you and think, I respectfully congratulate you, wishing you great fortune as we enter the new year. Impertinent, I am getting along fine without any major worries thanks to your affectionate care. However, before the start of the new year, I resigned from office due to my cold and while passing the time in leisure, it is difficult to put into words the resentment and worry that kindled inside of me. That is why I am planning to retire completely from government service and return to the south. I think I will be leaving no later than early next month. Most assuredly, it will be difficult to exchange news, as there are mountains and streams blocking us, as well as great distances separating Honam and Yeongnam.

I am truly saddened and heartbroken.

I have revised the epitaph; please look over it and make a decision. I cannot tell you the many things that have been going on through letters.

I grew one year older this year and I simply regret the fact that my studies have not progressed.

What can I do? Please excuse me. I respectfully bow and offer this letter.

January 16 (lunar calendar), 1570 (the Year of the Horse)
Bowing, yours truly,
Junior scholar, Daeseung.

Not too long ago, during the royal lecture, the Prime Minister[1] informed as the evil practice of the scholar's mores the unjustness of scholars to discuss political matters while being indolent regarding self-cultivation. Subsequently, he accused the public officials of the Royal College of treating the students inhospitably by perpetrating the transgression of being negligent in preparing meals. He pointed out, "They submitted the *paeja*² to the students of Confucius, and did not personally inspect the dining facilities."

Consequently, the Royal Secretariat informed the king of this matter and received orders to call and investigate the *Jigwansa*³ and those below him that were accountable in the matter, but I was not summoned a *paecho*⁴ because I was on leave at the time due to illness. Soon after, I was replaced. People on the outside argue that they did this to oust me.⁵ Although it is true, that I never personally visited the dining facilities, I never submitted a *paeja*. Since whether or not one is exalted in the world depends on destiny, how can he (Jungyeong Yi) control destiny? This is absurd.

Hwasuk is also on the receiving end of the Prime Minister's bitter hatred. Not too long ago, while gathering opinions regarding the improperness of sending envoys to China, the Prime Minister made this very apparent while speaking. Because Hwasuk was not comfortable with the situation, he resigned and left his post at the Minister of Personnel.

These are the present circumstances.

I do not know how far we will have to go before this concludes.

I am very afraid and worried. Please be advised.

---

1. Refers to the Prime Minister at the time Jungyeong Yi (1499-1572).

2. This was also called a *paeji*. A superior delegated power to a subordinate in this document.

3. Refers to the *Jiseonggyungwansa*; this was a senior with a 2nd class ranking who took charge of the Royal College. He was also called the *Seonggyungwanjisa* and also held the *Daejehak* position at the Office of the Royal Lecturers.

4. Refers to a wooden plate, which was used when the Seungji summoned a vassal according to a king's order. The summoned vassal's name was written on it and delivered on a red platform with the character, *myeong*, written upon it.

5. At the time, Gobong was the dean of the Royal College.

[Letter #102 Toegye Writes Gobong]

Savoring Words, Destitution Becoming More Enjoyable

Dear noble friend,

Early on, I knew after reading the gazette for the Royal Secretariat that you had resigned from your teaching post.[1] Subsequently, after reading letters written by my grandson and Ijeong Gim, they mentioned that your situation had become more blessed with the advent of the new year; I congratulate you with a joyful heart. They also mentioned that since you planned to finish my father's epitaph by the middle of this month, they would send it to me after receiving it. Because I will be able to receive in a short time the words you worked hard on writing, I am extremely moved—I stand on my tiptoes and anxiously wait.

In your letter, you mentioned it had already been decided that you would be returning south around the last day of the month. If you do this, you would have as Zhuang Zhou said, "Strive for what fishes desire."[2] This is a good event and something upon which you should exert an effort; however, I say this to you because these thoughts have suddenly come to mind. Looking back in time, in similar circumstances, if somebody had become the object of the present prime minister's hatred and the prime minister had gone so far as to attack him publicly in front of the king, would there ever be a case when that person would hesitate in leaving?

In your last letter, you said your friends were trying to prevent you from leaving—these are truly ridiculous words. How can you wait for your friends to come and save you in times like this![3] Because I live in a remote place and have not been able to hear the gist of what has been going on lately, I think the situation grows worse because of the debates surrounding the king conferring a title to his deceased father.[4] However, from ancient times, this kind of crisis has always reached this kind of conclusion; therefore, is there any reason to lament? Should we consider this profoundly odd? The only thing you can do is to leave.

After returning last year, I requested to resign only once but my request was denied. After that, I was very afraid of being a burden by submitting another request to retire; therefore, I laid low and kept by mouth shut, dragging the situation into the present year. Now, just as the term for my government office expires, there is no reason I should be denied once I submit my official request for resignation. If my request is rejected, I will continue to submit my resignation. I swear to you that my intentions will be realized. Since this is justified and reasonable, worrying that I will trouble the king is not my concern. If this hope comes to fruition, I keep telling myself the mountains will become deeper, water will grow clearer, writings will become tastier, and destitution will become enjoyable.

However, as I will move farther away from you, it will be difficult to exchange correspondences frequently. A long time ago, a certain wise man exclaimed, "Who will clarify my doubts and who will warn me of my faults?" I particularly lament, as I find myself in that position.

However, if we both immerse ourselves in the studies everyday,
it will be as if we are together, our desks facing one another.

How can one become flustered or impatient in advance regarding worries about fortune and misfortune when the blue heavens are looking down upon us?

Let us promise to make the effort to raise luminous virtue
until our hairs grow white!

This is my hope. I respectfully offer this letter as a substitute for bidding farewell.
Longqing (The era of Muzong's reign of the Ming Dynasty)
January 24, 1570 (the Year of the Horse)
Hwang bows his head.

I have sent this letter to Seoul and have asked Deoksu Choe[5] to deliver it. Even if you have already left for the south, since I have no other way, I will try to give it to him and have the letter delivered south. However, if you have a servant remaining in Seoul who can make the delivery, I would consider it fortunate if you let me know.

I have not been able to write a response to your letter dated December 6, and since I have not been able to write a response regarding the discussions surrounding the Indeterminate among others, which you sent the last time, I fear I am much too lazy. I have been pouring all my efforts into the epitaph and did not want to talk about other less pertinent topics. I received the frozen fish and the plump pheasant. I am grateful and embarrassed.

1. Or *gobi*; refers to tiger leather because all the teachers of the past sat on tiger leather when they taught. Here, it refers to Gobong leaving his position as the dean of the Royal College.
2. See the *Chuang Tzu*, Chapter XXIV: "Hsu Wu Kuei."
3. Or *Bungnaejibok*. This is mentioned in the "Fu" hexagram of *Book of Changes*. It implies: Although one yang is recovered, it cannot win several yin because of its weakness. Only after several yang are recovered will it be able to perform the meritorious work of saving things. Similarly, if a Superior man wants to be victorious over a man of small character, he must wait for many Superior men to gather. See the *Book of Changes*, Book I: "The Text," Chapter 24: "Fu."
4. After Yingzong of Song China ascended to the throne succeeding Renzong as the son of Prince Pu Anyi, he was determined to call Prince Pu Anyi his deceased father. This caused a variety of opinions in the imperial court. Here, Seonjo conferred a title to his real father, Prince Deokheung.
5. This was the husband of Toegye's niece.

[Letter #103 Toegye Writes Gobong]

If You Cannot Control Your Drinking

My response to you, noble friend.

A few days ago, I wrote a letter and gave it to one of our local scholars who was leaving to take the civil service examination and instructed him to entrust the letter to Deoksu Choe for delivery to you. While that letter was on its way, *Champan* Taeho Ryu came. I received and read your letter.

Furthermore, I also received the epitaph, which you have made much shorter by reducing the number of words. You took into consideration my wishes and reduced more than four hundred words, eliminating my concerns that not all the words would be engraved. I cannot express the deeply felt gratitude etched into my heart. What I requested in my last letter was nothing more than a similar kind of request. How could I have wanted the facts to be buried because too many words had been deleted?

I understand your respectful opinion regarding the titles; however, since I am afraid that there are still some unsuitable words that have been written impertinently, I ask you to slowly examine them again. It is truly a relief that you have edited out the four characters that praised me. Outside of this, there are still some excessive sayings—I am in fear and anxious when thinking about my deceased father because you do not eliminate them. What would be the best thing to do?

Although I heard that you were fixed on returning home, it was not clear whether you were going to or not. However, after reading your letter, I learned it would not be long, that the time was approaching when you would brusquely leave for home. This is very good news and truly appropriate. Although I lament it will be hard to correspond as Honam and Yeongnam are far apart and blocked off, we will find a way to correspond by sending news to Seoul and asking around for favors.

Whether we are exalted in the world or not depends on destiny. The way those people have treated us is only a matter of destiny.

> *Merely, when we confront such a crisis, we must look back and painstakingly self examine everything, one by one.*

These days, I hear people saying that while holding the world in contempt and looking down on others, you are not careful with your words, as well as being negligent in controlling yourself. If this were true, it would be proper for you to make an effort to correct these things. Even if this were not the case, it would be right to incite yourself to action regarding these matters.

Furthermore, I hear that you have lost control of your drinking again and that sometime soon, you will become afflicted with a serious illness. How have you come to earn such a reputation!

I truly hope that from this moment you will sever all extraneous matters. *After closing the door and sweeping the courtyard, polish and regain control of your old studies.* Ponder deeply and make the effort to conduct yourself properly.

> Since one must speak honestly with credence and behave sincerely and respectfully, stand as if these things are standing right before you and when sitting on a wagon, sit together as if leaning against the crossbar—one must never separate oneself from these acts.[1]

These are the great teachings of the sages and the wise men.

> *Do not consider these empty words but absolutely pledge to experience this personally, to manifest this kind of behavior physically.*

Then, do not forsake the prodigious responsibilities that are placed upon you. Many in the world argue that I do not have an eye for seeing people and have consequently made a bad recommendation. However, I reply that I do not have any regrets for the recommendations I have made.[2] That is because not everybody can know the expectations I have of you; however, if you continue to waste your gifted talents and become entangled with debauch habits, suffering because of alcohol and falling prey to amusement and self-indulgence, at last, you will distance yourself greatly from the world of the sages and wise men. The attacks waged against you by the people of the world will have been justified. Then, what choice would I have but to regret my recommendation!

Confucius said to Zhong-gong regarding the worthiness of respect and forgiveness, ". . . to have no murmuring against you in the country, and none in the family."[3] While Zhu Xi was pleased to hear Wang Duanming had received a vacation, Zhu Xi advised him to study and exert more of an effort in keeping his mind forthright. My hope is that you will think profoundly and make the effort to turn yourself around: I would be extremely relieved if you did this. In conclusion, by all means, cherish and take care of yourself. I end my letter here.

Respectfully bowing, I thank you.

The last day of January, the Fourth Year of Longqing (The era of Muzong's reign of the Ming Dynasty)

Hwang bows his head.

Ijeong delivered the *gungha* (made of angelica polymorph) soup. I heard that you accompanied him in seeking the medicine. Thank you.

I heard today that Hwasuk Bak had retired from the Minister of Personnel post. Although this is a great relief for him, I can see the way the world is turning through this affair. However, I am not sure what he has done regarding the *Daejehak* position. According to Hwasuk, only after retiring from both positions will his actions become a true example—but do you think he will be able to do this? I feel a sense of loss and hurt, as I see the imperial court evicting people in this manner.

---

1. See the *Confucian Analects*, Book XV: "Wei Ling Kung," Chapter VI.

2. When Toegye met the king before he left Seoul for his native village, he recommended Gobong. See the *Annals of Seonjo* 3, the second year of reign, March 4, the Day of the Monkey.

3. "Chung-kung asked about perfect virtue. The Master said, '*It is*, when you go abroad, *to behave to every one* as if you were receiving a great guest; to employ the people as if you were assisting at a great sacrifice; not to do to others as you would not wish done to yourself; to have no murmuring against you in the country, and none in the family.'" See the *Confucian Analects*, Book XII: "Yen Yuan," Chapter II.

[Letter #104 Gobong Writes Toegye]

The Defects Incurred Because of Uneasiness at the Core of My Heart

Dear teacher,

I respectfully inquire about your well-being. How are you getting along as we approach the turn to spring? I miss you terribly. I asked *Champan* Ryu to deliver a letter and the epitaph. I am not sure if you have received them. My inclining heart grows more profound.

Near the end of the previous month, I was relieved of my government post through his royal favor. On the fourth of this month, I was at the riverbank outside the capital city where I spent a night and now I have arrived at Jiksan. When I left Seoul, aware of my departure, many friends followed and came to see me off. As I felt very remote, I drank to the point of feeling pain. I continued to moan and suffer as I made the journey and was barely able to settle down.

However, from *above*, as I departed from the king, I could not help but to feel devotion like a dog or horse missing his master, and from *below*, as I parted ways with my friends, I could not help but to feel a sense of loss from the thought of saying farewell. For several days, I felt unbearably uncomfortable. Such defects have occurred because of the uneasiness I felt in the core of my heart. What can I do?

I have something apologetic to mention. I give you a small notebook. In your free time, do you think it would be possible for you to transcribe the large letters in *The Doctrine of the Mean* and return it to me? I want to look at it throughout my life. My supplicating heart reaches extremes, and I hope you will assent after considering my earnestness.

Although it is difficult to hear news on a continuing basis because Yeongnam and Honam are so far apart and the road between is rugged, I hope your abundant virtue will continue to be relayed to me. It would be an enormous relief if this would happen! Unable to express all my feelings in words, I languished as I placed this sheet of paper before me. Please understand. I respectfully bow and offer this reply.

The night of February 6, 1570 (the Year of the Horse)
Bowing, yours truly,
Junior scholar, Daeseung.

I have attached three short poems in the annex. Please respectfully look over them. This letter has not been presented in an orderly fashion, as I have written this under candlelight. I deserve a scolding.

[Letter #105 Toegye Writes Gobong]

What Kind of Dao Says to Act Both Reverently and Impudently

I bow and offer this reply to you, Myeongeon.

On January 26, *Champan* Taeho Ryu came and delivered your letter and the revised version of my father's epitaph. Even though you were preparing to leave for the south, as you have placed aside all cumbersome tasks and fulfilled my wishes by tidying up and revising the epitaph, I am speechless. I overcome with emotions.

Soon after, Ijeong Gim sent somebody and I learned through the letter he sent that you had already left for the south. Furthermore, on the day of your departure, I heard in detail about how he had spent the night with you at Giseong Arbor. In addition, I have received two quatrains which included his response written in rhyme to the "ryu" character among others. While reciting that poem and becoming lost in thought, the sadness of departure was double the sorrow I felt last year when we departed at the Dongho part of the Han River.

I had already sent a letter through Ijeong asking him to deliver it to Honam. Yesterday, the respected sir Cheongji Yi's[1] son, Hamhyeong, brought me a letter and I received the letter you had entrusted to Ijeong Gim. You had sent this letter on the day you arrived at Jiksan. I can only guess how pleasurable it must have been to return home. Looking at this through the eyes of the ancient ones, how was the pleasure of returning home this time?

I carefully looked over the writings you sent. It seems you have not been able to settle the matters troubling your heart, channeling that energy into your drinking, letting it show in your physiognomy. What is going on?

Looking back to ancient times, regarding relationships above and below, you are not the only one who lamented resigning from the king and leaving friends. However, since they acted joyfully without deviation, they passed through (these difficulties) serenely with broad and capacious hearts.

If you continue to act in this manner, even after returning home, you will have difficulty living comfortably in the shabbiest of abodes; you will have difficulty enjoying the simple foods; you will feel stifled because of your gloomy heart; and, the emptiness you feel will make you dissolute. Then, since you will not make progress in your studies and will amass only faults, what guarantees are there that you will not turn out the way those people who tried to expel you have claimed you would end up while ridiculing and clamorously scoffing at you! Why am I giving you the words, "Hold fast to the meaning of the *dao* and stand firm"? I implore you, Myeongeon, to think repeatedly about this profoundly.

In February, I offered my plea and begged the king to allow me to leave my government post because of my old age, but on the contrary, the king summoned me. Apologetically, it was difficult for me to rush to the king and I wrote a letter courteously declining the summons. These days, I have written another gracious decline, and while being very cautious and afraid, I am waiting for orders. I have heard about the latest state of affairs and it will be hard to guarantee that things will pass quietly. I know that this is not the right time to act in this manner; however, if this body, which is saturated with a lifetime of sin and fault, does not take advantage of this opportunity to leave office, I may never be able to leave. Therefore, I have thrown everything aside and swear to make my wishes come true.

Letter #105

On one side, the epitaph had arrived just at the time the handling of the tombstone was completed. I was happy and relieved beyond comparison. However, unexpectedly, while the work of grinding the stone was nearly completed, we discovered a decaying part of the stone. The more we tried to grind the decaying part away, the more decaying parts we discovered. Therefore, we had no choice but to stop engraving the letters. I will wait for fall or winter and look for another stone upon which to engrave. I cannot explain how lost I feel that the heavens have not helped with this important project.

Although you have made some slight revisions to the places where you have overly praised me in the epitaph, it is still hard to show this to other people. However, since it is difficult to request revisions repeatedly, I am very worried. In the beginning, although my vision was poor, I wanted to write it personally. However, if I personally wrote and engraved words that were hard to show people and people saw these words, this would summon their scorn all the more. Although I wanted to pay someone to write it, I was more worried because I could not find anybody suitable.

In the annex, I am not saying you must absolutely make revisions on important parts of the epitaph in this manner; therefore, please consider this with luminous eyes and reply as to whether you will be able to comply with such revisions. If you send the letter to Seoul and entrust it to either Deoksu Choe or Ijeong Gim, they will not lose the letter. As the household of Hamhyeong Yi's wife lives in Suncheon, I have sent this letter through a servant of theirs who was on his way home and I will have Hamhyeong deliver it to you. However, the reason I am asking you to send your reply through Seoul is that if you ask Hamhyeong to deliver it, I worry he will travel a long ways to do it, as he is stubborn and has a tendency to go overboard for others.

I have not been able to express my intentions with a pellucid heart because the thoughts I hold inside are splintered. I only hope you will take advantage of periods of leisure such as these to compose yourself.

Contemplate profoundly upon the great tasks.

Exert an effort to raise luminous virtue to meet the expectations of the time.

Make these plans to have your household resound forever.

Starting from ancient times, what kind of *dao* says to use principle and desire together, to act reverently and impudently simultaneously? What superior man resembles Master Cheng and Zhu Xi on the inside while acting like Xi Kang and Ruan Ji[2] on the outside? I respectfully bow and reply.

Longqing (The era of Muzong's reign of the Ming Dynasty)
March 21, 1570 (the Year of the Horse)
Hwang bows his head.

The notebook where you wanted me to transcribe *The Doctrine of the Mean* has arrived, and I understood your request. However, since my vision is poor and I am tired in addition to lacking strength in my wrist, I have difficulty writing small characters; therefore, it is growing progressively difficult to comply to such requests. I fear I will be unable to accommodate to your wishes.

Do you occasionally meet Gyejin Gim?[3] We grew very close while spending time together a long while ago. I have written him a letter. If Hamhyeong has instructed somebody and it was personally delivered, please do not concern yourself with the matter; however, if the letter has reached you, please deliver it to Gyejin, although it may be troublesome.

---

1. Refers to Sik Yi. His pen name was Sonam, Oeam and Cheongji was his pseudonym.

2. Xi Kang was from Jin China and his pseudonym was Shuye. As a member of the Seven Sages of the Bamboo Grove, he liked the philosophy of Lao-Zhuang and wrote "Nourishing Life." Ruan Ji was also a member of the Seven Sages of the Bamboo Grove and was from Wei in the Three Kingdoms Period. He liked wine and was skilled at playing the *geomungo* (the Korean harp).

3. Refers to Eongeo Gim. His pen name was Chilgye and Pungyeongjeong; Gyejin was his pseudonym.

[Letter #106 Gobong Writes Toegye]

Honam and Yeongnam Are Far Apart

I respectfully reply to you, teacher.
I respectfully prostrate myself and inquire about your well-being. How are you getting along? I miss you unceasingly. Indebted to your affectionate graces, I was able to return home and barely escape calamity. A few days ago, I received from my house in Seoul the letter you wrote dated January 24. It is difficult to express in words how grateful I was after slowly meditating upon the words written in the letter. Last time, I wrote you a letter on my way down—I am not sure if you have received it.

Fortunately, it is of great solace when I think I will be able to learn the things I have heard in the past now that I have broken free from (government service). However, since Honam and Yeongnam are far apart, it has become difficult to correspond frequently. What can we do? How can I not heed your caution to make an effort to raise luminous virtue! Please understand.

I am thinking about having my wife and children come here sometime next month, but if they do, we will lose another way of exchanging correspondences. If you send word to where *Byeoljwa* Deoksu Choe and *Byeoljwa* Ijeong Gim are stationed, I will be able to receive word through people traveling back and forth. Please consider these thoughts as well. I have many things to tell you but could not write them all. I respectfully bow and offer this reply.

March 11, 1570 (the Year of the Horse)
Bowing, yours truly,
Junior scholar, Daeseung.

[Letter #107 Gobong Writes Toegye]

Your Words, the Right Medication for My Disease

I reply to you, teacher.
I prostrate myself and respectfully inquire about your well-being. How are you getting along these days as summer begins? I miss you twofold, more than usual. Thankfully, I am passing the

days, hiding in the country peacefully and avoiding illness thanks to your affectionate graces. After returning to the south, I have not stopped thinking about you for a moment from a distance. It is difficult to express in words how grateful and comforted I was by the letter you had sent earlier. I have already written a thank you letter and have entrusted it with someone traveling to Seoul. I am waiting for it to be delivered; however, I am not sure if you have received it.

On March 16, I received the letter you sent on the last day of January. While receiving your instructions, I was happy and at the same time extremely afraid as I profoundly contemplated (your words). In the beginning of the month, by way of Hamhyeong Yi, I received another one of your letters. Carefully examining the letter repeatedly, I was all the more grateful and frightened when you scolded me to exert an effort in self-cultivation. As the enlightening words you wrote in your seriatim letters were just the right medication for my disease, how could I not dare to ponder them profoundly and make an effort to execute accordingly, whereby eliminating my disease and making an effort to see the effects? In leisure times such as these, if I submit to your keen admonishment from above and manage my studies from below, it would be a relief if I could be filled with the hope *not* to discard my studies. I prostrate myself before you and hope that you will guide me even more. I supplicate earnestly tens of thousands of times that you will shed your magnanimous grace upon me.

However, while saying this, I want to evince my foolish heart. Although I am cautious, as it may sound like I am making excuses, I cannot remain silent and dare to mention a few things. I hope you consider this with leniency.

I read that you had heard I scorn the world and look down on people, but I personally believe that I do not possess those kinds of intentions. However, since I was unable to suppress my vigor when discussing matters and sparked others to speak ill of me, it would be proper to painfully lambaste myself and straighten this askew disposition.

Regarding the criticism that I lack caution when speaking and that I am inflicted with the disease of neglecting to control my body, I have always been aware of these (problems). I have been unable to escape such accusations even though I have always been wary of this and reflected upon this. Because my roots are not planted deeply nor are they thick, I think (these problems) make an appearance every time a situation arises, which has me reach these conditions. My roots are not deeply planted and I think things will slightly improve once I exert more of an effort.

You also mentioned drinking. Lately, I have stopped drinking because I became frequently ill. Furthermore, I realized that doing that helped not only in nurturing my body, but also in nurturing virtue. From this point on, I sternly discipline myself, making an effort not to fall back into drinking, but I am not sure if I will be successful.

You also mention that people say you made a mistake in recommending me to the king. I agreed with that from the beginning; therefore, how can you avoid the disparaging comments and ridicule from others? However, I made assumptions about myself so that I could make an effort in the right proportions to eliminate a fraction of that (ridicule). If I sought to enter a high office after overestimating my abilities and desiring to accomplish great tasks, I would be in danger of making the mistake pointed out in "Foo teen."[1] What do you think?

When leaving Seoul, I was not resolute about a certain point. If I consider the conduct of the ancient ones, it appears as if I am with fault. That is the reason I rattled on regarding various matters in my last letter. I am grateful and embarrassed after reading your biting lessons. Although I am ignoble, I know a little something about righteousness—how could I not have spent a lot of time thinking about the frame of mind, the conduct of the sages! Being sad with melancholic faces is the crude act of an impetuous person.[2] Although I want to tell you that I have transcended this kind of tumult, I do not know what others think when they see me.

When I returned, lying on the floor in my room—accepting that what I had studied in the past was worthless—I savored the taste as I learned and rediscovered the studies once again.

> *It will be possible to hope that I will know the comfort of a dilapidated home, the delectable taste of rugged food.*

I am contemplating building a straw hut on a precipice near my home and spending time there. I am thinking about naming it *Yo* (enjoy). I name it this as an expression of my desire and longing to adhere to your words, "You must learn to enjoy destitution." Although the mountain is not very deep, the view extends a far distance. If I build this house and stay here, this will be the ideal place for me to cultivate myself placidly. If I make an effort in my studies in this place, the beautiful scenery of the surroundings will blossom into enjoyment. Besides this, what else could captivate me and prompt me to speak about this or that? I would be relieved if you commented after watching and observing.

I have heard you need a new tombstone after discovering some hidden blemishes. I am very worried about this from afar. How can I not comply with one or two of the corrections you asked to be made on the epitaph? However, among the corrections, some issues needed to be resolved after carefully discrimination, but just at that time, I was busy greeting people and could not give the matter much thought and several days later, suffering from pinkeye, I had difficult sitting down and tidying up the epitaph. Furthermore, this is something I cannot rashly revise and submit; therefore, hearing that it will be fall or winter before the words can be engraved in the tombstone, I think it will be better to take some more time to make the revisions, and then submit the epitaph. Please look over and be advised of this.

Although I intended on asking my wife and children who are in Seoul to come, I was told my youngest child suffers from the measles, which has made me very dizzy. Hearing the situation in Seoul is extremely troubled, I do not know how this will all culminate. I want to bring my wife and children to this isolated place as soon as possible, but I sigh as circumstances make it difficult.

Because I have many thoughts harbored inside, I cannot express everything in writing. I hope exalted virtue will grow more abundant as you live your life. I hope you will recognize my sincerity by looking luminously upon this. While respectfully bowing, I offer this reply of gratitude.

April 17, 1570 (the Year of the Horse)
Bowing, yours truly,
Junior scholar, Daeseung.

---

1. "Foo teen" was a poem in which the great officers of Qi Dynasty ridiculed Duke Xiang who aspired to great merit indecorously and desired to be a feudal lord without cultivating virtue. See *The Shih King*, Book VIII: "The Odes of Tse," Ode VII: "Foo teen."

2. "The desire of the child is towards his father and mother. When he becomes conscious of the attractions of beauty, his desire is towards

young and beautiful women. When he comes to have a wife and children, his desire is towards them. When he obtains office, his desire is towards his sovereign: if he cannot get the regard of his sovereign, he burns within. But the man of great filial piety, to the end of his life, has his desire towards his parents. In the great Shun I see the case of one whose desire at fifty years was towards them." See *The Works of Mencius*, Book V: "Wan Chang," Part I, Chapter I.

[Letter #108 Gobong Writes Toegye]

Reading "Ganchunfu" During Leisure Hours

I bow and offer this letter to you, teacher.

After the advent of summer, I was not able to check to see how you were passing time in leisure. While missing you terribly, just at that time, I received Ijeong Gim's letter and I learned that you were getting along fine in good health. Although far away from you, I was greatly comforted. However, I heard that you applied to resign from your government post and rest but that the request was denied. I heard that, on the contrary, the king had called you to service on numerous occasions. When I think about the thoughts you must harbor inside, I cannot overcome my heart, which inclines to you since I am sure you are filled with profound worries.

Thanks to your affectionate grace, I have been able to avoid hardship. Although the dean of the Royal College has been added, I do not think I will be able to fill the position in light of moral principle. Furthermore, my wife has not been able to leave because suffering from the measles, my daughter's condition grows acute. I feel stifled because the discomforts of a scattered family press on me.

I wrote a letter during the middle of last month, sent it to Ijeong, and asked him to deliver it to you; however, I am not sure if you have received the letter. In addition, I have written my comments regarding the epitaph on a separate sheet of paper. I do not know what you will think, as I have followed by own ideas and have disregarded your ideas. I would be relieved if you consider this with leniency. I will end the letter here despite having many remaining thoughts. I hope you receive all kinds of blessings as occasions require. Please consider this. I respectfully bow and offer this letter.

Longqing (The era of Muzong's reign of the Ming Dynasty) May 9, 1570 (the Year of the Horse)
Bowing, yours truly,
Junior scholar, Daeseung.

I had the opportunity to read "Ganchunfu"[1] during leisure hours and I was deeply moved. The words were very earnest because at that time, the king did not accept Zhu Xi because of the prime minister's obstruction and disparaging comments. I do not know what you think about this thought. Please consider it.

I relayed your letter immediately to Jeong Gim. I received his reply letter, and I send it to you. I hope you receive it. I have not been able to greet Jeong Gim yet because after returning I have not stepped outside my home due to laziness and fatigue. Please excuse me.

---

1. See *The Complete Works of Zhu Xi* 1.

[Letter #109 Toegye Writes Gobong]

Cleanse an Old Man's Dark and Intolerant Thoughts

I respectfully bow and reply to you, Myeongeon.

I received two seriatim letters during the summer. You sent one letter on April 17 and the next letter on May 9. After receiving your letter, I learned that the leisurely lifestyle agreed with you, that you were getting along fine and living abundantly. It is difficult to suppress my comforted and longing heart even though we are so very far apart. However, recently, as recent events are very convoluted, I could not write a reply for a long time. Were you able to return to the right path of physical harmony and moderation regarding self-caution with the coming of July, in the seventh month when Mars passes the meridian?[1]

I know that you cannot enter the position at the Royal College; however, recently, I have heard that you have been ordered to leave as the envoy to China. Since the appointment of the envoy this time seems different from ordinary times, I think you will have a difficult time turning them down although you may not want to go. I do not know how you will resolve this matter. It might be very uncomfortable for you to return suddenly for another matter considering the people who are in charge of governing were the ones who were responsible for ousting you. If the Board of Personnel paid some attention to the personnel entering and leaving government posts, this kind of nomination would not happen. However, as things have evolved in this manner, I am worried more than usual because there is no fitting way to decline even if you conduct yourself properly.

In my last letter, my various counsels on your behalf were mostly the result of my plethoric concerns. However, in your last letter, you did not consider that a fault but attentively replied one by one. Everything you said helped in the explanation of ideas and was considerate of the *dao*. Therefore, from this moment on, if you will incline your will and remain immutable for a long time, the words of the ancient ones—"I am overjoyed that I can complete unfinished studies during these times of leisure"—will apply to today. I dare to congratulate you in advance.

I have already left, and having just turned seventy, I only have one thing left to do: retirement, which is enough to be considered a fortune bestowed by the heavens. If people had not disregarded my intentions and had me selected and assigned (to posts), this lowly vassal would have realized his wish a long time ago. This was always the case: when one nomination was filed, the Royal Secretariat would immediately confer with the king, which led to my calling every time.

Even last month, I received a royal order for me to gather myself and come. Immediately after that, for the time being, I refrained from writing a letter stating my intentions of leaving because I thought they might consider it an ignoble scheme to buy time. Although I am currently in a fresh and quiet place, I sense some dizziness as people are pulling me from the right and left.

I read and understood that you had built a library on a high and spacious piece of land, which you had obtained, and were filled with joy, devoting yourself to the studies. Furthermore, naming it *Yo* seems like a fitting and perfect name. I sigh as I am unable to visit you, spend several days there, and hear about that joy. While carefully deliberating about the things you possess and the new things you have acquired, if these two match and you possibly discover something new, please do not hesitate to send me (a letter)—I sincerely hope you will be able to cleanse this old man's dark and obstructed thoughts.

I read your various remarks regarding my father's epitaph. Although there were occasions you made corrections and other occasions you did not, I respectfully adhere to your suggestions. As the epitaph has reached this point, I do not have any sad emotions left regarding the unrealized will of the deceased and the sorrow and longing devotion of a son. Waiting for the farming work to finish, I am planning to find a new stone in Yecheon, engrave the words, and erect it. How can I repay your deep and affectionate kindness! Merely, the sincerity carved deep in my heart is as endless as the heavens.

I can guess the hardship you are enduring as your family continues to stay in Seoul for a long time. I am not sure how things are now, as your daughter suffers from the measles. I feel uneasy every time I hear you mention it. My grandson, Ando's son, also died at an early age from the measles while in Seoul. Filled with sorrow, I was speechless. I felt such pity for him.

The situation in Seoul continues to change and it is not stable. Furthermore, I have heard a great debate will arise.[2] I am truly concerned as the outcome is indistinct. What can we do about this? I have many things I want to say to you but this letter has a long way to travel and I am suffering from pinkeye, which has prevented me from telling you everything without remains.

Please cherish yourself for the *dao*.
I respectfully bow and offer this letter of gratitude.
July 12, 1570 (the Year of the Horse)
Hwang bows.

"Ganchunfu" is truly as you described. Because he felt something profound, the superficial, manifested expressions flowed without obstruction in the ("Ganchunfu") and the ideas were profound. He (Zhu Xi) was immeasurably happy even while amidst times of great worry. Whenever I have spare time, I recite the poem while keeping tempo, and when I reach parts like, "How can a thousand years be so remote? My heart alone has reached an understanding!" I end up repeating it three times and am moved every time! When looking at your words, it is fair to say you have already felt what I am feeling now. However, since there are some parts, which are hard to discuss with others, I ask that you do not show this letter to others.

Because a rift has already formed in the faction, it has become difficult to distinguish what is right and wrong. If the king's heart is moved to one side in the least bit—who will be able to block this spirit strong enough to move mountains and change waters? Furthermore, reinstatements and stripping of titles would continue year round without pause, and I have heard they want to receive royal sanctions to do this.[3] It would have never reached this stage if the sages and wise men had settled this matter. I am truly worried and afraid. What can we do?[4]

---

1. Refers to Mars gradually moving down to the west in the 7th lunar month. See *The Shih King*, Book XV: "The Odes of Pin," Ode I: "Tsih yueh."
2. In May of that same year, officials under the Office of the Inspector General and the Office of the Censor General and the Office of the Royal Lecturers repeatedly asked to exonerate the people who were blamed in the Year of the Snake, the Year of the Sheep, and the Year of the Chicken.
3. (Officials) of the Office of the Inspector General and the Office of the Censor General and the Office of the Royal Lecturers repeatedly asked to reinstate the people who were falsely accused, asked to enshrine their tablets, and asked to strip the title of the unqualified *jeonggukgongsin*.
4. In *Toegye's Collections* this article was attached at the end of the letter dated January 24, the Year of the Horse. Here, it is arranged according to *Gobong's Collections*.

[Letter #110 Toegye Writes Gobong]

Arriving at the Principle of Inanimate Objects[1]

I respectfully bow and reply to you, Myeongoen.

I wrote one letter during autumn and while sending it to Seoul, I asked that it be delivered to you, but I am not sure if the person will deliver the letter without losing it. Because Honam and

Yeongnam are far apart and blocked off, it is too remote to send news. I cannot stop my heart from leaning to you, as I am oblivious of the charms of how you must be leisurely collecting your mind.

Although many people may have been shocked after they learned you had submitted several appeals, this is not an anomaly. This kind of event has occurred in the past to some degree. Do you think things are the same as they were in the past? How could you reveal your innermost thoughts so keenly? By doing that, as you severely provoked the people who had been harboring resentment against you, it does not seem likely that the situation will quiet down. Although this is not something about which to worry profoundly, I do not want to see problems rising because of me. That is why I am writing to you in this manner.

Recently, I have submitted a request to retire again, but I am not sure if a beneficial consent will be given. Although my age and sickness are uncommonly severe, I am melancholy day and night because this matter has not yet been resolved. During that time, Ijeong sent me something you had written in a letter to him, "Principle arrives at the Indeterminate." As I read this, I suddenly realized my past views were wrong. I would be relieved if you lucidly looked over some of my realizations I have written on the annex.

A friend from my native village was appointed the magistrate of Muan. While his son was on his way to Muan, he stopped by and greeted me. After asking him and discovering that Muan was not far from where you live, it seemed as if I could send a letter, so I roughly write this letter while briefly talking to him. I send it to you now.

I respectfully inform you.
October 15, the Year of the Horse
Hwang bows his head.

The dispute at the imperial court continues in this manner but since we are the only two who have remained silent, many people will consider this very odd. I do not know what you think about this.

I will respectfully listen to your teachings regarding your assertions about "arriving at the principle of inanimate objects" and "not having not arrived at the ultimate principle of inanimate objects." The last time, the reason I stubbornly asserted a false theory was because of Zhu Xi's words:

Principle has no emotions or will; it does not calculate; and it does not produce or create.

I only knew of this theory and intended on adhering to it and I thought that I could arrive at the ultimate principle of inanimate objects but thought, *how could principle arrive at such an extreme point on its own?*

Therefore, I understood the "arriving at" in "arriving at the principle of inanimate objects," and the "arrived" in "not having not arrived at the principle" to be *my* arrival at the principle. Last time, when we were in Seoul, after being enlightened by your theory regarding the "principle arrives," I went over it again and deliberated upon it carefully, but I could not resolve my suspicions.

Recently, Ijeong Gim gave me a few clauses you had discovered regarding Zhu Xi's comments about the "principle arrives." After receiving and reading them, for the first time I started worrying that my opinion might have been incorrect. Thereupon, I washed away all my old opinions, opened my mind, made an effort to be cautious, and first searched for the reason that principle arrives on its own.

Zhu Xi's theory manifested amidst the supplemented fifth chapter of the commentary[2] in *Questions and Answers on the Great Learning* reveals this meaning; it is as clear as the sun and stars. Although I had always recognized the meaning of those words to be profound, I have never understood it so clearly as this. The theory states:

> The targets of a person's studies are the mind and principle. Although the mind supervises one body, as its substance is one of emptiness, it can manage all the principle of the universe through its divinity, and although principle is dispersed through all creation, its function is delicate and in reality, it never leaves a person's mind. Therefore, from the outset, one cannot compare and argue the inside and outside, fineness and coarseness.

The minute notes say:

> When someone asked, "The function is delicate—is this not the function of the mind?" Zhu Xi replied, "Since principle has an absolute function, how can you only say that this is, once again, the function of the mind? The substance of the mind is endowed with this principle, and this principle applies everywhere and there is not a single inanimate object that does not possess principle. However, its

effect never, in reality, leaves a person's mind. Although principle exists inside inanimate objects, in reality, its function is in the mind."

When you look at the saying, "Although principle exists in the world's creation, its function does not, in reality, leave a person's mind," I am guessing it must wait for a person's mind since principle cannot have a function on its own. If this is the case, it appears that we cannot say that principle arrives on its own; however, it states:

> Since principle has an absolute function, how can you say that this is, once again, only the function of the mind?

Then, the function of principle may not leave a person's mind, but the delicateness of its function consists in principle's manifestation; there is nothing (of principle) which does not arrive nor is exhausted following what a person's mind approaches. Therefore, we must worry only about completely examining the principle of inanimate objects; we do not need to worry if principle arrives on its own.

Therefore, when saying, "arriving at the principle of inanimate objects," I am saying that I have completely arrived at the ultimate principle of inanimate objects. If I have arrived at the point of saying that I have arrived at the principle of inanimate objects—why can I not say that the ultimate principle of inanimate objects arrive simultaneously according to my complete arrival?

Here, if the substance of principle, its true character, is without emotion or will and does not produce or create, we can know the divine function of principle according to the extent that we look at each case and how they arrive simultaneously. Last time, although I only knew that the original substance had no function, I did not know that the mysterious function was manifested and able to move. Therefore, since I regarded principle to be lifeless, how far is this from the true *dao*! Thanks to your earnest teachings, I have discarded my incorrect views and have gained new insight. I have fostered a new understanding. This is truly a relief.

Regarding the interpretation of the phrase, "While being Indeterminate, it is the Supreme Ultimate," I have only recently learned that my views were incorrect. From the past, I was not fond of considering the assertions of various Confucian scholars and pursued my own views, perceiving "ultimate" as "principle," which led me to say incorrectly:

"Assuredly, when mentioning the Indeterminate, this refers only to the point that it is formless. How could this mean that principle does not exist?"

Therefore, consistently I regarded your interpretations to be wrong, and even after receiving the transcribed copy of Lu Caolu's[3] theory early on, I did not open my mind nor did I carefully look over it. After that, upon receiving numerous warnings from you and other friends, I started to examine one by one carefully, the theories of previous Confucian scholars. Among them, Huang Mianji's[4] theory was the most detailed and complete.

He said:

> Future readers will not know that the Ultimate was used as a metaphor and by equating this to principle, they will be unable to understand not only the words, 'principle must exist,' but also Zhu Xi's word, the 'Indeterminate.'

It was as if he knew in advance that I would harbor such suspicions and personally taught me. There is somebody in Seoul named *Sangsa* "Yangjung" Yi.[5] Have you had the chance to meet him? He sent me a letter before and clearly elucidated on these matters. I was very happy to know that there was somebody like this among the upcoming (scholars). I have tried to make at least some minor changes by cautioning myself and being apprehensive of my fault of misunderstanding things after skimming through books, something I have done from long ago. However, I am not sure if I will accomplish this before dying.

---

1. In *Toegye's Collections*, this letter was attached at the back of the discussion on the "Diagram of 'The Mind Combines and Governs the Nature and the Feelings.'" However, here it is arranged previously according to *Gobong's Collections*.

2. Refers to the fifth chapter of *The Great Learning* which Zhu Xi supplemented himself after thinking the text was lost.

3. Refers to a follower of the Cheng-Zhu school, Wu Cheng, in the Yuan period of China.

4. Refers to a follower of the *School of Principle*, Huang Gan, in the Southern Song period of China. He learned from Zhu Xi. He became the son-in-law of Zhu Xi and wrote "The Biography of Zhu Xi."

5. Refers to Yangjung Yi who was Toegye's pupil and his pseudonym was Gongho.

[Letter #111 Gobong Writes Toegye]

Life without a Government Post [1]

Dear teacher,

I respectfully inquire about your well-being. How is your health? I revere and miss you unceasingly. I hope you will take care of yourself during the harshness of the winter's first cold, and I supplicate that only good things befall you. I am meagerly passing day to day thanks to your affectionate assistance. I was able to receive your letter dated July 12 through my wife and children who were returning south. I was grateful and comforted beyond measure after receiving your detailed teachings. However, I was shocked and could only grieve when I heard that your first great grandchild had passed away at an early age. I respectfully imagine that your sorrow and sadness must have been great.

Previously, although I was appointed the envoy to China, I submitted a written request to be dismissed because it would have been hard to force myself to go when considering righteousness. Because I could not conceal all the intentions harbored inside, I wrote a few words, asking the king to kindly reconsider, but the discussion in the outside world was clamorous, and malign and rebuke sprouted everywhere. Trembling in fear, I hid and prostrated myself, reflecting and rebuking myself. Although I planned to write you in early autumn, I suddenly encountered this awkward affair and did not have time to attend to any other affair. On top of that, after my wife and children returned home, as I was severed from news from Seoul, I had no way of sending you a letter. Furthermore, I wanted to send someone from around here to inquire about your well-being but everyday things did not go as planned and half a year passed without being able to send a response. I have personally cut contact with you because I was not thorough and on top of being lazy, I lacked earnestness; I am overcome with shame and remorse. Changing topics, what happened to your request to retire from office? I cannot stop worrying. Fortunately, thanks to my submission of a rather insolent request, I have all but realized my lifelong wish and now I am able to live leisurely, free of any government posts. However, starting from the fall, since many events grew very chaotic, I cannot concentrate solely on reading books; however, what is the point of worrying?

Although I want to ask you about many things, I have not been able to properly prepare and write to you because I have been busy lately. However, I will wait to prepare and ask you in the next letter. As I was pressed to merely inquire about your well-being, I have written this roughly. Please excuse me. I respectfully bow and offer this letter.
November 1, 1570 (the Year of the Horse)
Bowing, yours truly,
Junior scholar, Daeseung.

I have not been able to hear word from Seoul for some time now. I have looked extensively through books: has there ever been a time such as the one we are experiencing now? I do not know the reason why there is such unrest in public opinion. If the sages and wise men had encountered such times, how would they have resolved this matter? Sighing, I have no place to make this appeal. Please be advised.

Discussion of teacher Toegye's Revised "Diagram of 'The Mind Combines and Governs the Nature and the Feelings'"

Byeoljwa Gim delivered the second and third diagram of your revised "Diagram of 'The Mind Combines and Governs the Nature and the Feelings.'" After I looked at them, since I had suspicions and did not know what to say, I wanted to write them down immediately in a letter. I wanted to ask for your guidance. However, busily flustered due to all kinds of work and unable to find someone to deliver it, I was unable to act immediately. Now, I have dared to present you with a gist of my views—I would be relieved if you looked them over.

The *He Tu* and *Luo Shu* diagrams have been past on from olden times. If somebody were to subsequently write about this and attempt to reveal the facts, it would not be wise to create chaos by presenting another assertion. However, in your revised *Diagram*, you exchanged the right and left sides, divided the self and the other, and it appears as if you poured your efforts into explanations while lacking in your exposure and elucidation of righteousness, which only fosters the evil practice of making people guess at will and freely imagine things. What do you intend to do about this? On the contrary, I worry that this will dim righteousness. I worry this will be harmful to younger scholars.

If a man sits in the north, faces south, and spreads this diagram in front of him and looks at it, this man's left and right will become the diagram's left and right. Even if this man considers the diagram to be his mind and looks at it, there would be no damage inflicted upon the moral principle. This is what Zhu Xi referred to when he said, "If I gain control of my mind, I will preserve what I have lost." Furthermore, this is different from when Buddha said, "Preserving your mind with your mind is like two objects grabbing hold and not letting go of one another." Not to mention, since we are already endowed with humanity, righteousness, propriety, and wisdom, why would I not see *me* in *myself*?

However, looking at the new diagram, when I spread the diagram while sitting in the north, a rift occurs between *me* and *myself* since it is made so that a person looks to the north from the south. This has me toil to look for the axe far away when in fact I am holding it in my hand.[2]

Since the positions are reversed, it is more complicated in comparison to the old diagram. I think this is worse than simply leaving without much hassle the old diagram, which is already in sequence and has no defect. This is what I think but I am not sure if I am correct. Please consider this and I truly hope you will not make the revisions.

Although I have spoken incoherently, I hope you look over and accept what I have said. If you make several corrections of the characters and write them down and if you clarify their meanings, future evil practices can be avoided. I would be enormously consoled.

---

1. In *Gobong's Collections,* Gobong's writing about Toegye's revised "Diagram of 'The Mind Combines and Governs the Nature and the Feelings'" was arranged next to Toegye's reply to that letter. Here this letter and Gobong's writing are arranged before Toegye's reply.

2. When hewing wood with an axe in order to make an axe-handle, the pattern of the axe-handle is the one grasped in the hand, yet man does not understand this; he looks askance. See *The Doctrine of the Mean,* Chapter XIII.

[Letter #112 Toegye Writes Gobong]

Responding to Gi Myeongeon's Discussion of the Revised "Diagram of 'The Mind Combines and Governs the Nature and the Feelings'"

If you look at the revised "Diagram of 'The Mind Combines and Governs the Nature and Feelings,'" that you sent, according to the direction of the *He Tu* and *Luo Shu*, the diagram and the person looking at the diagram are sequenced as if facing the south. This is the same direction as my original diagram. However, if I follow your revisions, "PROPRIETY," which needs to be shown clearly, ends up being placed near the top of the diagram in useless space, and "WISDOM," which needs to be placed covertly, ends up arranged in the frequently used lower space.

They have both lost their reasonableness.

If one wants to avoid this mistake and exchanges the top and bottom, the "PROPRIETY," which was originally arranged in the front of the south, would move to the back of the north, and the "WISDOM," which was originally arranged in the back of the north, would move to the opposite side, to the front of the south. This would also be unreasonable for both.

Therefore, after pondering this problem from early on, this is the reason the direction of the *He Tu* and *Luo Shu* is the way it is:

The transformation of the Yin and Yang forms from below, then grows in the east/left.

After reaching maturity in the south/top, it then weakens from the top, then diminishes in the west/right.

It then falls to its weakest state in the north/bottom.

The direction of the *He Tu* and *Luo Shu* imitated this model. The fact there is no content in the lower part behind the northern side, and the fact there is no need to debate the correctness or incorrectness of the additional concepts have nothing to do with the "Diagram of 'The Mind Combines and Governs the Nature and Feelings.'"

In the case of the "Diagram of the Supreme Ultimate," it only makes the discrimination that the left is the Yang and the right is the Yin; there is no concept of position that says the south is the front and the north is the back. Therefore, even though the Five

Elements and the remaining parts may be placed in the lower portion of the diagram, there are no difficulties in how to place the additional concepts. However, this revised "Diagram of 'The Mind Combines and Governs the Nature and Feelings'" is an old diagram which models after the *He Tu* and *Luo Shu* diagram. Nothing else matters, but as I mentioned above, it was particularly difficult to place "PROPRIETY" and "WISDOM." Therefore, I had no choice but to revise the diagram and change the directions in this manner. However, you suggested using the north as the standard for the diagram and using the south as a standard for people looking at the diagram. Nevertheless, when I quietly thought about it, if I did as explained above, "PROPRIETY" and "WISDOM" would go back to their proper spots, "FEELINGS" would be placed below, the additional concepts would find their appropriate places, and everything would be arranged correctly. I do not think it would reach the point you worried about in your letter.

In your letter, you mentioned there are great points of disparity regarding the placing of accurate names and whether this diagram was effective in studying to the point you could "feel it in your bones." However, in my opinion, if you set the standard of the diagram to be south, people will look towards the south, and if you set the standard of the diagram to be north, people will look towards the north. Merely, the direction people will look depends on the direction of the diagram; then, how can there be great points of disparity by misplacing names! Originally, this diagram simply elucidated the principle that the mind combines and governs nature and feelings. From the beginning, it does not bring attention regarding what a person should learn. That being the case, how can you debate what is right and wrong by comparing this diagram to the study felt to the bones!

I have mentioned the division between owner and guest, self and other in the small words, which I attached while making revisions; however, when I think about it now, I fear I may have been too drastic in making divisions. For example, it will be proper to unquestionably correct or delete certain parts like, "The diagram becomes the owner and the observer becomes the guest" or "The diagram is regarded separately as another person's mind." Therefore, as you contend in your letter, if you ask me to delete these phrases because they are misleading, I can do that. However, quoting the words of Zhu Xi:

I gain control of my mind.

If you say that the "Diagram of 'The Mind Combines and Governs the Nature and Feelings'" does not have people reflect and seek the answer but perpetuates the fault of pushing people into the wrong direction, you will be unable to avoid the criticism that you possess the flaw of rejecting unceasingly the views of others before fully comprehended everything they have said. Why do I say this? While making this diagram, although I did not mention how to study, I have been attacked based on that issue; how can you say that you fully understood without remains what I was saying? Not to mention, if it is as you state in your letter: if you sit facing the south and consider the mind inside the diagram to be your mind, spreading the diagram some distance away and sitting away from it, you would end up looking at the mind of the diagram with your own mind. This confusion is no different from Zhu Xi who criticized the Buddhist's "Looking to the mind," by saying, "Bite your lips with your lips and see your eyes with your eyes." In reality, since there are parts that are not like this, please tell intelligent people the reason so that they can make a decision about it.

When somebody is born, gaining both the material forces from the heavens and the earth, he regards it as a part of his body, and by gaining both the principles of the heavens and the earth, he regards them as nature. When the principle and material force gather, they form the mind. Therefore, my one mind is exactly the minds of the heavens and earth, and my one mind is exactly the minds of many people. Consequently, from the beginning, my *inside* and *outside*, the *self* and *other* were not different.

Therefore, starting a long time ago, when the sages and wise men discussed the study of the mind (*School of Mind*), they did not mention the explanation of 'my' mind by gathering and attaching the (minds) of many people. For the most part, they referred to it as 'man's' mind, discussing what the views and principles were, what its substances and functions were, and what to seize and what to discard. Therefore, since their views had pierced through the essence, their explanations had become clear. Consequently, if somebody acts accordingly, the principle of 'my' mind has already become like this, and if he takes this and teaches others, the minds of others will become like this, as well. We can compare this to many people drinking at the river, but each person will drink to his satisfaction without shortage. How can I foolishly divide myself from others, develop logic based stubbornly on myself, and then worry that there will be even the slightest amount of meddling and interest from others?

Are you still willing to insist that the "man's mind" is not correct? If this is the case, when Confucius said, "It is the mind!"[1] would you say it is only right if 'my' is attached to the above the mind? Mencius said, "All men have a mind which cannot bear to see the sufferings of others,"[2] and "Benevolence is man's mind, and righteousness is man's path."[3] In words like this among others, would you say this is correct only after changing 'man' to 'my'? In Zhu Xi's "Renshuotu," it says, "What a man gains becomes his mind." In something like this, would you have to change 'man' to 'my' as mentioned above for this to be correct? From a long time ago, when looking for and finding places where mind is mentioned, there are many such cases. Even if this were the case, would you continue to insist that after I made the correction to 'my' mind, I would be free from the faults of pushing people down the wrong path and I would be right regarding the meaning of the words, "I gain control of my mind"? I am sure this is not the case. Therefore, I will delete the problematic words among the small letters while I make revisions on the diagram. I intend on using this new diagram. Will there be anything that deviates considerably?

Furthermore, I have one more thing to add. If you—someone who is so eminent—can properly place the two words, "PROPRIETY" and "WISDOM" in the proper place in the old diagram, I earnestly wish to use the old diagram. With an unbiased open mind, please discriminate and observe; teach me after you have pondered this matter meticulously and minutely. Lowering my head and bowing, I earnestly supplicate to you.

---

1. "Confucius said, 'Hold it fast, and it remains with you. Let it go, and you lose it. Its outgoing and incoming cannot be defined as to time or place. It is the mind of which this is said!'" See *The Works of Mencius*, Book VI: "Kao Tsze" Part I, Chapter VIII.

2. "Mencius said, 'All men have a mind which cannot bear to see the sufferings of others.'" See *The Works of Mencius*, Book II : "Kung-sun Chau" Part I, Chapter VI.

3. "Mencius said, 'Benevolence is man's mind, and righteousness is man's path. How lamentable is it to neglect the path and not pursue it, to lose this mind and not know to seek it again!'" See *The Works of Mencius*, Book VI : "Kao Tsze" Part I, Chapter XI.

[Letter #113 Gobong Writes Toegye]

Long Time Since Giving Up the Thought of Saving Myself

Dear teacher,

Not too long ago, after writing a letter inquiring about your well-being, a man from Muan unexpectedly delivered your letter dated October 15. After respectfully learning that you were healthy, I was endlessly pleased and comforted. Since I received your detailed teachings, could I be happier? My extreme emotions increased to a higher degree.

I am well aware that my recent past behavior did not suit well with average standards. However, when I think about it quietly, since the loyalty that exists between a king and vassal is rooted in nature, which is the Heavenly Mandate, although I had left because the king did not accept me, it would not have been right for me to feign ignorance. Therefore, I risked being shunned by the world and dared to roughly inform the king of my earnest concerns and nothing more.

> *Since fortune and misfortune depend on the heavens,*
> *it is not right to act overly timid because one is afraid*
> *of the future troubles that may arise.*

Noble officials these days are so afraid of hardship that their actions and mental attitudes become very biased. As a result, I am worried we will be unable to exterminate the evil practices remaining from this trend. Although I am lowly, on the account of consistently worrying about this aspect, it has been a long time since I have ignobly given up on the thought of saving myself after entering my government post. Why would I suddenly scheme otherwise at this point?

During the appeal process, because I thought about it repeatedly and considered (the matter), I was able to quell at least a fraction of my extreme emotions. If I had expressed all the views I held inside, I can only guess, but how angry would the people of the world have gotten! Since the situation has occurred in this manner, please understand and consider this. Even if this was the case, after receiving your detailed instructions, how could I not dare not to straighten my coarse nature and feeling and seek to conform to the *equilibrium*? Merely, I have a weak will and my learning is insignificant; therefore, I am worried I will be unable to repay the kindness you—someone who has recognized me—have bestowed upon me. I pass the days and nights in discomfort, filled with fearful thoughts.

Regarding the interpretation of "arriving at the principle of inanimate objects" and the "Indeterminate" among others, thanks to your kind interest, our exchanges of confusion in ordinary times have finally been resolved into one (view). Could there be a greater happiness? I would not be able to express this joy entirely, even if I were to dance and jump around!

Honam and Yeongnam are so distant and blocked off; since I have no way of visiting you, I lament that I cannot personally uphold your words of caution and ask you about suspicious and ambiguous matters. I was filled with sad thoughts as I spread a sheet of paper before me and cried as I faced the east. We are approaching the last day of December and as the cold grows fiercer, I beg you many times to take care of yourself. I end my letter here. Please understand.

I respectfully bow and offer this reply.
November 15, 1570 (the Year of the Horse)
Bowing, yours truly,
Junior scholar, Daeseung.

I was unspeakably relieved and overjoyed after receiving your detailed teachings regarding "arriving at the principle of inanimate objects" and "principles arrive." Your arguments regarding "the substance that does not act" and "the exceedingly divine function" manifested with greater lucidity and accuracy a very delicate and covert principle. Looking over it repeatedly and savoring it, I was struck with admiration, as it seemed as if you were teaching this right in front of me. However, as I looked over it carefully, there were certain spots where the reasoning did not seem natural. I am not sure what you think about this. Please look over and consider this.

I am very relieved that you accepted the interpretation of the "Indeterminate" to be correct. Mianji's theory is more clear and absolute. Although I did not have the opportunity to meet the *Sangsa* Yi early on, after reading his precise theory, I am happy that there is a scholar who excels among the younger scholars.

The dispute at the imperial court has grown serious, but I am not sure if it is justified when cast in the light of moral principle. Due to the fact our times did not accept me, I begged to be released from service and I received permission; therefore, I do not think it would be right for me to open my mouth and discuss these events. In the future, I intend to only keep my mouth shut and remain silent. Please be aware of this.

After receiving the letter *Byeoljwa* Gim had written, I learned you had been set free from the *Jejo* position by the king's grace. Although I am far away, I was greatly consoled. Although I am not sure how the world is turning these days, listen only to heavenly fate, and by all means, it would not be proper to be worried and frightful before anything else.

Recently, while reading the *Great Compendium on Nature and Pattern*, I by chance had the opportunity to read Huang Mianji's discussion about Chen Taiqiu.[1] Stern and prominent, his words were enough to revive the feeble, and in reality, those words captivated my heart. It would be a relief if you considered this.

---

1. See the *Great Compendium on Nature and Pattern* 62, "Lidai" 4, "Donghan."

[Letter # 114 Toegye Writes Gobong]

My Views Were Incorrect

I bow and write this reply.

After receiving the priceless letter and accompanying annex, which you arduously sent through a person who had to travel a long way, I learned that you were savoring the *dao* in leisure and were living a life filled with blessings. My worried heart was greatly appeased.

My worries and concerns continue without pause. I cannot go back and undo the pain of seeing my young great grandchild buried in the ground, and the wife of my son, Jun, has been suffering from tuberculosis for several years now. Starting from this fall, her symptoms included boils and while she has been ill, within the past few days, her condition has grown critical. Since I do not know what is going to happen, I am at a lost as to what to do as the situation has become so urgent.

This year, I have shown signs of fatigue and have been particularly weak. However, without considering me, younger scholars from everywhere take turns visiting me. I employ all kinds of methods to turn them down and send them off, but sure enough, others come and visit. Among these visitors, there are some people I cannot flatly refuse—I have no choice but to receive them within my means. As this was the case, I grew tired as I continued to sit down, and while reading a book or writing, on some occasions I grow dizzy, unable to distinguish anything around me. You can get some notion of how severe it is by the fact it hinders my day-to-day studies!

Recently, phlegm has been gurgling in my chest and other symptoms overlap adding to the pain of my entire body stiffening. As I was moaning while lying down, your letter had arrived. Unable to write a response after full contemplation, shame overcomes me. However, regarding the revisions of the "Diagram of 'The Mind Combines and Governs the Nature and Feelings'" you considered improper, I was able to write a short argument earlier because Ijeong Gim had copied your letter and sent it to me. I copied (the short argument) in advance, sent it to Ijeong and since I am sure he will not lose the letter, you should be receiving it in no time. Because I wrote down my thoughts in that letter, it is not necessary to mention them again.

I have only changed the position of "PROPRIETY" and "WISDOM" because I was not comfortable with their placements. If I can place these two words in the proper place, then truly I would want the old diagram to remain untouched. However, if it is not possible to place these words properly, keeping in mind the revisions, I think there are some parts you must accept. When I consider it, the evil practices will not reach the levels about which you worry. Ijeong is just now making a smaller scale version of the "Diagram of 'The Mind Combines and Governs the Nature and Feelings'" and as he said he wanted to copy the rest after our debate has been settled; I sent him a response, asking him to bring it to me quickly.

Inside your appeal, by including without any inhibitions that their conducts were like Lin Li and Wang Huai among others, people may think you were too careless, however, I believe there was nothing wrong with doing that.[1] Nevertheless, nobody has spoken about those matters in this world; therefore, many people will not be able to accept it as you have depicted it so blatantly. All those sycophants to power have reached the point where they say they will have their revenge at all costs. For this reason, it will become quite tumultuous and in the end, I do not think they will give up easily. Because this is the flow of the times, there is nothing to consider profoundly odd. It is not worth lamenting.

However, because of this one event, your wish of being able to concentrate on your studies in a leisurely and solemn fashion has been realized. Nevertheless, in my case, starting from early on, I am unable to follow my path by standing steadfast against the world. I have garnered the hatred of the world. Now, even though I am old, I am still entangled with the world. Last month, I sent a letter pleading my resignation but my hope was not realized. I am not sure if this will ever end. I can only sigh and be filled with sorrow.

My views regarding, "the arrival at the principle of inanimate objects" and the "Supreme Ultimate while being Indeterminate" were all wrong. Furthermore, I have already transcribed a copy of the corrections and have entrusted it to Ijeong to be delivered to you. However, I think something must have happened in the course of delivery. I send you another copy. Please look over it.

I have roughly written this letter because I am dizzy with apprehension. While respectfully asking that you cherish yourself all the more through these difficult times, do not grow lazy in accomplishing your studies, and fulfill the hopes of the ages, I respectfully offer this reply.

November 17, 1570 (the Year of the Horse)

Hwang bows his head.

---

1. Refers to the behavior of Lin Li who ridiculed Zhu Xi because of his different views regarding the *Book of Changes* and to the behavior of Wang Huai who denounced the *Learning of the Way* as a heretical study because of his dislike of Zhu Xi.

Index

An, Yu, 142
Annals of the Wuyi Mountain, 40, 45, 92
Annotations of Heart Sutra, 61
Annotations of the Rowing Song Poems, 45

Baekdam, 66
Baekyeong, 84
Baishaji, 113
Bak, Hwasuk, 3, 5, 25, 54, 55, 109, 120, 124, 135, 140, 159, 161, 195, 206, 211
Bak, Ilcho, 201
Bangsuk, 197, 198
Bian Zhuangzi, 101, 102, 124
bieun, 104
Board of Public Works, 4, 5, 71
Board of Rites, 95, 135, 138, 142
Board of War, 87, 88, 90, 91
Bonghwa, 200
Book of Changes, 155, 209, 241
Book of Han, 64, 198
Byeon, Seongon, 40

Cai Jiefu, 77, 78
Chen Taiqiu, 239
Chenho, 92
Cheng Hao, 42, 61
Cheng Yi, 19, 61
Chodang, 107
Choe, Chiwon, 142
Choe, Chung, 142
Choe, Deoksu, 208, 209, 215, 217
Chongxiuji, 92
Choseon, 124, 126

Chuandenglu, 64
Chuman, 10, 11, 21, 25, 31, 52, 53, 55
Classic of Rites, 92, 146, 155, 162
Classified Conversations of Master Zhu, 50, 98, 161
Commentaries of the Rowing Song Poems, 40, 41
Commentary on the Doctrine of the Mean, 96, 99
Complete Works of Zhu Xi, 5, 28, 43, 46, 49, 50, 61, 222
Cook Ding, 34, 37

Daeseung Gi, 3, 5, 198
dao, 6, 14, 16, 17, 22, 23, 25, 26, 27, 32, 37, 40, 41, 43, 45, 47, 48, 52, 53, 55, 61, 63, 67, 68, 69, 72, 73, 80, 85, 90, 91, 98, 99, 101, 104, 105, 106, 108, 110, 112, 113, 119, 120, 141, 146, 150, 184, 189, 192, 194, 213, 214, 215, 223, 224, 228, 239
"Diagram of 'The Mind Combines and Governs the Nature and the Feelings,'" 189, 229, 231, 232, 233, 234, 235, 240
"Diagram of the Great Learning," 195
Diagram of the Mandate of Heaven Explained, 11
Dong Mou, 77
Donglai, 23, 145

Emperor Yao, 97
Eorokseok, 121

243

"Fengxiangyemeizhen," 92
Five Classics, 98
"Foo teen," 219, 220
Four Beginnings-Seven Feelings, 4, 6, 7
Four Books, 98, 159
Four-Seven, 18, 21, 31, 56, 59
Four-Seven Thesis, 6, 22, 26, 31, 43, 50, 102, 105, 108, 110, 111, 118, 124
Fu Pi, 40, 42

"Ganchunfu," 221, 222, 224
Gangneung, 151, 164
"General Summary," 102, 105, 108, 110
Gewutong, 113
Gim, Buin, 83, 84
Gim, Chwiryeo, 82
Gim, Gae, 183, 185, 187, 189, 198
Gim, Gyejin, 51, 53, 216
Gim, Ijeong, 82, 83, 84, 85, 87, 89, 91, 126, 128, 129, 170, 171, 172, 173, 174, 185, 207, 211, 213, 214, 215, 217, 221, 226, 227, 240, 241
Gim, Inhu, 30
Gim, Jongjik, 134
Gongui, 135
"Gonjigiron," 126
Great Compendium on Nature and Pattern, 239
Gu, Bongryeong, 66
Gu, Gyeongseo, 64, 66, 69
Gukgi, 164

Han Tuozhou, 73
Hanmuquanshu, 92
Haseo, 26, 30, 35, 40, 46, 52, 53
He Shujing, 115
He Xiong, 92
"Heavy Rain," 143
Hengqu, 99, 155, 157
Heo, Taehwi, 104
Heo, Yeop, 107

History of Goryeo, 133, 134
Hou Yi, 187, 190
Hu Anguo, 19
Hu Kanghou, 12, 19, 23, 195
Hu Qian, 30
Huian, 23, 33, 38, 44
Huian Poetry Collection, 45
humanity, 111, 232
Hunmongjeolgu, 49
Hyojik, 160

imperial court, 74, 86, 111, 171, 178, 179, 180, 192, 194
inanimate objects, 45, 74, 225, 226, 227, 228, 238, 241
indeterminate, 182, 186, 208, 226, 228, 229, 238, 241

Jamjae, 82
jeobo, 21
Jeompil, 133, 134
jeonchoe, 21, 30
Jeong, Jajung, 9, 12, 18, 20, 21, 22, 31, 53, 54, 55, 59, 60, 62, 65, 69, 73, 76, 91, 95, 96, 100, 101, 102, 104, 108, 110, 111, 118, 122, 123, 127, 140, 145, 159
Jeong, Jiun, 11, 16, 17, 21
Jeong, Yuil, 9, 78
Jo, Jeongam, 159, 160, 171
Jocheon Ceremony, 89, 91

Kaotingshuyuanji, 92
Kunzhiji, 96, 112, 114, 126

Lady Hadong, 135
Lao-Zhuang, 30, 35, 216
Learning of the Way, 6, 28, 47, 73, 102, 195, 241
Lianzhushige, 49
Library, 87, 88
Ligian, 29
Liu Xiahui, 141, 143
Liu Zhihou, 64

Liu Zongyuan, 64
Lu Bogong, 71
Lu Caolu, 229
Lu Dynasty, 141, 143
Lu Zuquan, 30
Luo Zhengan, 96, 97

Maoqing, 92
Master Cheng, 6, 16, 19, 34, 96, 97, 108, 115, 116, 117, 127, 216
Master Zhang, 97
material force, 4, 6, 18, 97, 98, 105, 111, 112, 113, 190, 235
Mencius, 6, 37, 78, 115, 117, 130, 132, 135, 163, 236
Mianji, 229, 238, 239
Mindfulness, 113, 114
Minister of Personnel, 198, 206, 211
Mun, Myeonggae, 121
Munso Shrine, 179, 197, 198
Myeongjong, 3, 78, 126, 129, 135, 136, 143, 151, 198
myeonsillye, 7, 9, 10, 14, 25

Nam, Sibo, 141, 143, 144
Nanxuan, 23, 30, 145, 194, 195
No, Gwahoe, 97, 99, 101, 104, 112, 113, 167

"Ode to the Plum Blossom," 177
Office of Diplomatic Documentation, 5, 7, 37
Office of the Censor General, 65, 107, 124, 177, 178, 225
Office of the Inspector General, 65, 123, 124, 225
Office of the Recorders of Political Affairs, 61
Office of the Recorders of the Royal Command, 61, 74, 75, 77, 102
Office of the Royal Command, 71, 102

Office of the Royal Lecturers, 5, 35, 107, 129, 206, 225

Pang Juan, 39, 42
"Poem Written While Staying Overnight at Fangguang and Hearing of the Death of the Elder Shourong," 61
"Postscript Explanation," 102, 105, 108, 110
principle, 4, 6, 18, 50, 97, 98, 111, 112, 113, 116, 153, 190, 226, 227, 235
propriety, 111, 232, 233, 234, 236, 240

Qi Dynasty, 130, 220
Qui Xi, 92

"Renshuotu," 236
"Reply to Chinese Envoys," 133
River Yi, 45
Royal College, 35, 91, 130, 178, 193, 205, 206, 221, 222
Royal Secretariat, 21, 66, 74, 75, 174, 179, 181, 189, 192, 195, 201, 206, 207, 223
Ryu, Gyeongsim, 28, 30, 32, 35, 37, 49, 209, 212, 213

Saengyang Inn, 129
Sak memorial service, 151
Sannam, 84
Sarim faction, 160, 183
School of Mind, 113, 142, 235
School of Principle, 101, 104, 229
Seol, Chong, 142
seondal, 3
Seonjo, 135, 153, 162, 165, 166, 167, 185, 198, 209
Shen Sheng, 155, 157
Shuye, 25, 30, 216
State Council, 107, 108, 111, 118, 125, 126, 143, 198

Sun Bin, 39, 42
Supplement to the Complete Works of Zhu Xi, 60, 61
Supreme Ultimate, 36, 228, 233, 240, 241

Tang Jie, 133
Ten Diagrams of Confucian Philosophy, 152, 153, 155, 161, 163, 174, 189
The Classic of Filial Piety, 155
"The Diagram of the Western Inscription," 163, 164
The Doctrine of the Mean, 20, 50, 104, 105, 107, 121, 212, 216, 232
The Elementary Learning, 146, 156
The Great Learning, 121, 146, 229
The Great Treatise, 105
"The Letter Sent to Wang Guiling," 4
The Supplement to the Great Compendium on Nature and Pattern, 92
The Works of Mencius, 37, 78, 107, 116, 117, 131, 164, 185, 221
Tian Dan, 42
Tsze-hsia, 19
"Two Passages of a Poem Advising Self Caution Written after Seeing the Theme on the Wall of Mr. Hu of Meixi's Tavern," 28, 38, 44

U, Tak, 133

"Valleys of Mount Nanshan," 47

Wang Caichen, 46, 50
Wang Duanming, 211
Wang Moji, 46
Wang Yangming, 135, 143
Wang Yuanze, 36, 50
"Wangchunqiyuanshi," 46
wisdom, 111, 232, 233, 234, 236, 240

Wuge theory, 182, 186
Wuxuan, 92, 96
Wuyi Jingshe Academy, 30, 45, 46
"Wuyi Rowing Songs," 28, 40, 42

Xi Kang, 30, 216
Xiang Yu, 42
Xiaozong, 194

Yadae, 165, 166
Yang Guishan, 115, 117, 142, 156, 157
Yang Zizhi, 46, 47, 50
Yi Hwang, 28, 141
Yi, Baekchun, 186, 190
Yi, Cheongji, 216
Yi, Eonjeok, 133, 143
Yi, Gangi, 112, 113, 116
Yi, Hyeonbo, 73
Yi, Iljae, 36, 97, 112, 113, 120
Yi, Iseong, 89
Yi, Junggu, 140, 143
Yi, Jungyeong, 198, 206
Yi, Ryang, 78
Yi, Sukheon, 140, 143
Yi, Nongam, 70, 71
Yonghakseogui, 121
"Youhuaifu," 91
Yuan Dynasty, 39, 162
Yusannok, 159

Zen Buddhism, 46, 112
Zhang Fengshan, 77, 78
Zhang Shi, 30, 195
Zhong-gong, 211
Zhou Dunyi, 42, 61
Zhu Xi, 6, 16, 20, 28, 29, 30, 33, 34, 36, 39, 40, 41, 45, 47, 49, 61, 63, 71, 72, 73, 76, 96, 97, 98, 104, 107, 114, 115, 116, 117, 127, 142, 145, 150, 157, 186-187, 194, 195, 201, 211, 216, 222, 224, 226, 227, 229, 232, 234, 235, 236, 241

Zhu Xi's Family Rituals, 181, 201
Zhuang Zhou, 207
Zhuangzi, 74, 183
Zhuge Liang, 159, 160

Zhu Zhen, 19
Zi Si, 6
Zuo's Commentary on the Spring and Autumn Annals, 157